The Soviet Threat

edited by
Grayson Kirk
Nils Wessell

Published in cooperation with
The Academy of Political Science

The Soviet Threat
Myths and Realities

 PRAEGER PUBLISHERS
Praeger Special Studies

New York   London   Sydney   Toronto

PRAEGER PUBLISHERS, PRAEGER SPECIAL STUDIES
383 Madison Avenue, New York, N.Y., 10017, U.S.A.

Published in the United States of America in 1978
by Praeger Publishers,
A Division of Holt, Rinehart and Winston, CBS Inc.

89 038 987654321

Printed in the United States of America
Library of Congress Catalog Card Number: 78-56914

Materials in this book previously appeared in the
Proceedings of the Academy of Political Science
Vol. 33, No. 1

Contents

Preface

No problem in foreign policy is more important to the United States than its relations with the Soviet Union. The major question in this area is whether the Soviet Union is a threat to the United States or whether it lacks both the will and the capacity to challenge America. To find answers to this question, an analysis of the military and naval strength of the two great powers is important. If a test of strength comes, it may develop not between the two major powers but in one of the countries to which they are allied. Eastern Europe and especially Yugoslavia may therefore hold the key to peace or conflict in the next decade.

Most difficult of all to study is intent or will to initiate a conflict. What are the points of conflict in various parts of the world that may escalate into violent disputes? What social changes are taking place within the Soviet Union that will make conflict more or less likely? These are some of the questions discussed in this volume.

The authors have had long experience in analyzing relations with the Soviet Union. The views that they express are their own and not necessarily those of any organization with which they are affiliated or of the editors. The Academy of Political Science serves as a forum for the dissemination of informed opinion on public policy questions, but it makes no recommendations on policy issues.

The Academy wishes to express its thanks to Grayson Kirk and Nils H. Wessell, who directed the project and edited this book. It is also grateful to William Farr and Frederick Wegener for their excellent work in preparing the manuscripts for publication.

ROBERT H. CONNERY
President of the Academy

Contributors

RICHARD E. BISSELL, Managing Editor of *Orbis*, is Visiting Professor of Political Science, Temple University. He is the author of *Apartheid and International Organizations*.

BARRY E. CARTER is a San Francisco attorney in private practice with Morrison & Foerster. He was on the staff of the National Security Council from 1970 to 1972.

BOGDAN D. DENITCH, Professor of Sociology at Queens College and the Graduate School of the City University of New York, is Senior Fellow, Research Institute for International Change at Columbia University. He is the author of *The Legitimation of a Revolution: The Yugoslav Case*.

JOHN ERICKSON is Director, Defence Studies, University of Edinburgh, Scotland. He is the author of *The Soviet High Command, 1918–1941*.

JOHN P. HARDT is Associate Director for Senior Specialists and Senior Specialist for Soviet Economics, Congressional Research Service, and a member of the Faculty of Economics and the Institute of Sino-Soviet Studies, George Washington University.

PETER H. JUVILER is Professor of Political Science, Barnard College. He is the author of *Revolutionary Law and Order: Politics and Social Change in the USSR*.

GRAYSON KIRK is Bryce Professor Emeritus of the History of International Relations and President Emeritus, Columbia University. He is also former President, Council on Foreign Relations.

ANDRZEJ KORBONSKI is Professor of Political Science and Chairman of the Department of Political Science, University of California, Los Angeles.

EDWARD C. LUCK is Deputy Director of Policy Studies, United Nations Association of the USA.

G. E. MILLER, Vice Admiral, U.S. Navy (retired), is former Commander, U.S. Second and Sixth Fleets.

PAUL H. NITZE has served as Secretary of the Navy, Deputy Secretary of Defense, and representative of the Secretary of Defense to the United States Delegation to the Strategic Arms Limitation Talks with the Soviet Union.

JONATHAN D. POLLACK is a Rockefeller Foundation Fellow, Program for Science and International Affairs, Harvard University. He is coeditor of and a contributor to the forthcoming *Asia's Major Powers: Toward the 1980s*.

DIMITRI K. SIMES is Director, Soviet Studies, The Center for Strategic and International Studies, Georgetown University, Washington, D.C. He is the author of *Détente and Conflict: Soviet Foreign Policy, 1972–1977.*

O.M. SMOLANSKY is Professor of International Relations and Chairman, Department of International Relations, Lehigh University.

MAXWELL D. TAYLOR, General, U.S. Army (retired), is former Army Chief of Staff and former Chairman, Joint Chiefs of Staff.

NILS H. WESSELL is Assistant Professor of Government, Lafayette College, and Research Associate, Foreign Policy Research Institute. He is editor of *Soviet Law and Government,* a quarterly translation journal.

SIR DUNCAN WILSON, G.C.M.G., former Ambassador of the United Kingdom to Yugoslavia and the USSR, is Master of Corpus Christi College, Cambridge, England. He is author of the forthcoming *Tito's Yugoslavia.*

HANNAH J. ZAWADZKA is Assistant Professor of Political Science, Barnard College.

Overview

GRAYSON KIRK
NILS H. WESSELL

As recently as 1972, American relations with the Soviet Union appeared to have entered a new phase of broader cooperation. Ushering in what was forecast to be a new "era of negotiations," détente between the superpowers held out the promise of eventually controlling the strategic arms race, encouraging mutual restraint in areas of regional conflict, promoting increased trade and economic cooperation, and developing joint efforts aimed at solving global problems of hunger, disease, and environmental pollution. Symbolizing the possibility of a new era in international relations, President Nixon, not yet tainted by the Watergate affair, journeyed to Moscow to sign the first SALT agreements and begin the process of negotiation that led to new bilateral accords promoting cooperation in trade, technology, health sciences, space, and the environment. The warmth of the president's reception in Moscow despite his immediately preceding decision to bomb Hanoi and mine Haiphong harbor reinforced the impression that Soviet-American relations were somehow emerging for the first time from the dark ages. That the president's reception in Moscow may have been conditioned by his historic visit to Peking a few weeks earlier, and by Soviet apprehension over its significance, only added to the sense that the international system might be undergoing a major transformation.

By the time of the 1976 presidential election, the transformation in Soviet-American relations had begun to seem more momentary than momentous. The succession of Communist military triumphs in Southeast Asia, the outbreak of yet another round of war in the Middle East, and Soviet-Cuban intervention throughout much of Africa undermined public expectations that détente was about to create a new era of global stability. In the same period, the Soviet Union accelerated a decade-long program of military modernization at home and in Eastern Europe. Soviet strategic weapons programs burgeoned despite the SALT accords. Soviet naval forces, enhanced in their capabilities, were deployed to new areas of the world's oceans.

Nor was the United States an entirely passive bystander. Dramatic qualitative improvements were made in United States strategic forces, both land and sea-based. New conventional weapons systems, some employing sophisticated precision guidance, were developed and deployed. Thus, the military competition between the superpowers continued unabated in areas not covered by the narrow quantitative ceilings imposed on their strategic arsenals by SALT.

Even in areas outside those of military rivalry, détente was undermined. Large Soviet purchases on the American grain market, accompanied by secrecy and sharp trading practices, encouraged an inflationary food price spiral and turned the economic benefits of détente into a mixed blessing for the United States. The Arab oil embargo and a fourfold rise in the price of OPEC oil, perceived to have been encouraged by Moscow, made joint development of Siberian energy reserves seem fraught with unacceptable risk. In Europe the Communist Party of Portugal and its radical left-wing allies in the Portuguese armed forces failed narrowly to transform that NATO ally into the first example of triumphant Eurocommunism. For its part, the United States Congress prompted Soviet withdrawal from the already-negotiated Soviet-American trade agreement by linking reduced tariffs to the easing of Soviet emigration restrictions and by imposing severe limits on government-backed financing of joint development projects.

Now, six years after the first Nixon-Brezhnev summit, the United States and the Soviet Union are once again approaching a turning point in their relations. The Carter administration, not entirely of one mind, has offered the Soviet Union both increased cooperation and heightened competition. The administration, perhaps reflecting the ambivalent mood of the public, began by confronting the Soviet Union with a series of basic policy choices. By proclaiming the need for drastic reductions in nuclear weapons, it put the Soviet leadership on the defensive in the field of arms control. Worse, from the standpoint of the Soviet leadership, President Carter personally injected fundamental moral values into the superpower dialogue for the first time in recent memory. Despite official reassurances that the American commitment to human rights was universal and not directed specifically against the Soviet Union, Brezhnev and his colleagues came to believe that the rules of the game had changed substantially since the Moscow summit of 1972. The impression of a harder American line toward the Soviet Union was further reinforced by President Carter's statement that the United States intended to compete "aggressively" with the Soviet Union for influence in the Horn of Africa, where Soviet-Cuban intervention became a source of deep concern to Washington.

At the same time, the administration's first year in office witnessed some signs of a more cooperative approach. The president backed away from sharp public confrontations over human rights violations in the Soviet Union, and quiet progress on some aspects of the SALT negotiations replaced earlier public diplomacy. The lack of clarity in American policy was reflected in the Horn of Africa as the administration sought a negotiated settlement of the Ethiopia-Somalia conflict and the voluntary retirement of the Cuban interventionary force and Soviet advisory team.

The conflicting currents in American foreign policy toward the Soviet Union find their reflection in this volume. Although its contributors usually stop short of recommending policies, their analyses of the myths and realities of the Soviet threat reflect the ambivalent sentiments prevailing today among policymakers, analysts, and the public concerning American relations with the Soviet Union. Unlike many books on the controversial subject of détente, this volume deliberately refrains from the support of any single basic viewpoint on the multifaceted question of the Soviet threat. The editors sought out distinguished contributors whose views on the Soviet Union are known to be broadly contrasting. It is the editors' belief that each author has contributed to the ongoing national debate over the nature and implications of Soviet policy and the international Communist movement.

The Global Military Balance

PAUL H. NITZE

There are various ways of assessing the present military balance between the United States and the Soviet Union and its probable evolution in the future. The objective of this essay is to explore some of them.

A common approach is to write off the question as inherently meaningless. Both the United States and the Soviet Union have tens of thousands of nuclear weapons, including weapons with a blast yield equivalent to that of many millions of tons of TNT. In addition, these weapons can produce intense heat and, thus, widespread fires. They can also produce extremely unattractive types of radiation. Some of these take the form of "early" fallout, which can, within twenty-four hours, contaminate thousands of square miles downwind from the explosion. Others can contaminate the atmosphere over a longer time. Thus, it is argued, an all-out nuclear war would be wholly disastrous to the Soviet Union as well as to the United States and perhaps even to the rest of the world. Under those circumstances, what difference does it make if one side has more or fewer nuclear weapons?

Many commentators extend this line of argument to say that any war between the Soviet Union and the United States is bound to escalate to all-out nuclear war. Therefore, in any war between them, not only the United States but also the Soviet Union would be essentially destroyed. While Henry Kissinger was secretary of state, he supported this point of view. If one accepts it, the logical inference would be that the state of the conventional military balance and of the tactical nuclear balance in the European theater, the military balance in the Middle East theater, and the balance in the Far East theater, alone or together, would make no significant difference, since any conflict in those theaters involving the United States and the Soviet Union would be bound to escalate to all-out nuclear war between them. Furthermore, by extension of the same argument, the Soviet Union would not dare to interfere with American ground forces overseas, no matter where deployed, or with any American ships, naval or civilian, or with American airplanes flying over the open oceans or over friendly lands.

If these chains of logic are in fact sound, it makes little sense to evaluate the strategic nuclear balance, the theater military balances, or the balance of American and Soviet capabilities to maintain and exploit the intercontinental seas and the intercontinental air space. The operational consequence for those accepting this approach is that most expenditures for military defense are essentially wasteful to the bodies economic and politic, and that ways and means of getting out of defense expenditures, including arms control and disarmament agreements, even if patently unequal in their provisions and essentially unverifiable, should be supported vigorously.

But are the various steps in these chains of logic valid? Few of the people who advance these arguments appear wholly persuaded that they are. Kissinger bolstered his basic position by arguing that, in any case, there was no danger that the strategic nuclear balance would become unfavorable to the United States. His point was that the United States still retained the advantage in numbers of deployed warheads even though the Soviet Union was building more and much bigger intercontinental ballistic missiles (ICBMs) and more submarine-launched ballistic missile (SLBM) launchers with longer-range missiles than the United States. Each month, the Kissinger argument continued, the United States was also deploying more multiple independently targetable re-entry vehicles (MIRVs) than the Soviet Union and enjoyed a substantial superiority in the payload of the heavy bomber fleet. Kissinger contended that the United States would continue to have such bomber payload superiority for a long time, since the Soviet Union had tested no modern generation of heavy bombers and its new Backfire bomber was intended for theater missions, not intercontinental use.

Paul Warnke, director of the U.S. Arms Control and Disarmament Agency, argued in his confirmation hearings that the strategic nuclear balance was so important that neither side could conceivably allow the other to achieve a meaningful superiority. He asserted, however, that the United States was so much stronger than the Soviet Union in the strategic nuclear field that it had years in which it could cut back on new strategic development and deployment programs and test whether the Soviet strategic buildup represented an effort to achieve meaningful superiority rather than mere parity.

How does the Soviet Union look at this range of issues? A dozen or so of Washington's specialists in Soviet strategic thought and literature, participating in a discussion group in 1977, concurred in the following propositions. First, the Soviet leaders think that a nuclear war with the United States would result in a holocaust. Second, the Soviet leaders do not want a nuclear war with the United States. Third, the Soviet leaders increasingly regard a nuclear war as unthinkable. Fourth, the Soviet leaders believe the Soviet Union must be, if at all possible, in a position both to win and to survive a nuclear war with the United States if such a war, nevertheless, were to occur.

The seminar took a measure of comfort from these four propositions. One can agree with the propositions but not be comforted thereby if one understands the meaning of the terms as used by Soviet strategic thinkers. By the word *holocaust* they mean much physical destruction, but not enough to make it impossible, in the event of nuclear war, for the Soviet Union to win, to survive, and to dominate the world, including any nonparticipants such as China. When Soviet authorities say they do not want a nuclear war, that statement does not conflict with their determination to continue to do everything they prudently can to foster the fulfillment of the Communist dream of a world that is progressing from socialism to communism under the continuing leadership of the Communist Party of the Soviet Union and under the protection of a growing Soviet military predominance.

One must also take precise account of what Soviet spokesmen mean when they say that nuclear war has become increasingly "unthinkable." They have made it explicit that what they mean is that during the last five to ten years, in the era of détente, the correlation of forces and, most importantly, the nuclear balance have moved significantly to the Soviet Union's advantage. Consequently, this development has made it far less likely that nuclear war could become a thinkable response by the United States to a crisis situation, presumably brought on by Soviet actions in support of their expansionist policies.

Operationally, the most important proposition is the fourth—that the Soviet Union, if at all possible, must be in a position to win and survive a nuclear war if one should occur. This is the operative proposition with respect to much of the Soviet Union's military program, including immense efforts to provide itself with hardened, profuse, and even redundant command, control, and communications facilities and a strong civil defense posture. Soviet adherence to this fourth proposition is the prime reason for continued expansion of the Soviet military budget year by year to a level now substantially exceeding that of the United States, both in absolute magnitude and as a percentage of the gross national product. It is now generally agreed that the Soviet defense effort, in relation to other aspects of its economy, is at least twice that of the United States and may be more than three times as much.

Two significant questions arise. The first is whether arms control negotiations, particularly the SALT negotiations, can make these considerations irrelevant. The second is whether this enormous Soviet effort is in any case without practical consequences and therefore represents a waste of time and resources, as those who put forward the overkill argument contend.

The attempt to answer the first of these questions has prompted much of the work that has been done in assessing the current state of the strategic balance and in projecting that balance into the future on various assumptions concerning the terms that might be agreed to in a new SALT agreement and concerning various possible United States weapons development and deployment programs. It is argued, and perhaps correctly, that SALT agreements can potentially contribute to United States security by imposing significant agreed limits on Soviet nuclear deployments, just as they can increase Soviet security by significant agreed limits on American nuclear deployments. The contribution such limits can make to the security of the United States, however, cannot possibly do the whole job. The essential deterrent function must still be carried by those American strategic forces permitted under the agreements and actually developed and deployed by the United States.

Before deciding whether a given SALT agreement should be accepted by the United States, one should attempt to analyze whether the contribution to American security of the verifiable limitations on Soviet deployments, coupled with the military potential of the American weapons programs that the United States can be expected to develop and deploy under the terms of the agreement, are adequate to provide the United States with high quality deterrence and crisis stability. In other words, will the balance always ensure that the Soviet Union would not be tempted to execute a preemptive strike in a crisis and deny it any prospect of winning and surviving a war if it were to do so?

In order to answer that question, one must first decide how and by what criteria to measure the strategic military balance as it has existed and as it may evolve. Such a decision must take into account various possible SALT agreements and various American nuclear weapons deployment programs consistent with the terms of those agreements.

There are three distinct approaches, progressively more sophisticated, by which various indexes, such as the number of strategic nuclear delivery vehicles, the number of warheads, megatonnage, equivalent megatonnage, equivalent weapons, or throw-weight, can be used to measure the balance of relative capabilities and the quality of crisis stability. These approaches focus on: (1) the pertinent strategic military resources possessed by each side before, or in the absence of, a strike by either side; (2) the pertinent resources remaining to the United States and to the Soviet Union after an initial strike by the Soviet Union primarily directed at reducing the American retaliatory potential; and (3) the pertinent resources remaining to each side after an exchange in which the Soviet Union first attacks American forces and the United States responds by reducing to the greatest useful extent Soviet strategic forces not used in the initial attack.

The first approach employs static indicators. It does not assess how these capabilities might interact in an actual nuclear exchange. It tends not to distinguish between those capabilities useful in a counterforce role, i.e., against the enemy's hardened military targets, and those useful in a countervalue role, i.e., holding the other side's population and industry hostage. Because the second approach is the first step in a dynamic analysis, it is more sophisticated. It reflects the counterforce capabilities of weapons used in the initial counterforce strike but does not differentiate between the counterforce and the countervalue capabilities of the forces remaining to each side after that first step. The third approach carries the dynamic analysis a step further. It most clearly brings out the stability or potential instability of the relationship by making it possible to assess the relative countervalue capabilities remaining to each side after a two-sided counterforce exchange in which all counterforce targets have been addressed to the extent it is useful to do so.

The use of these three methods is illustrated in figures 1 through 3. They assume that the United States has received strategic warning and has therefore placed on alert all its forces that it could. They also assume that the United States has proceeded with all strategic force programs approved as of mid-1977 by the executive branch, including the subsequently canceled B-1 program. Furthermore, they assume the Soviet Union would accept a SALT II agreement essentially identical to the so-called deferral proposal put forward in March 1977 by Secretary of State Cyrus R. Vance. Under the deferral proposal, the United States and the Soviet Union would have been limited to an equal number (2,400) of strategic delivery vehicles and an equal number (1,320) of strategic missiles carrying MIRV warheads. Limitations on both the American cruise missile and the Soviet Backfire bomber would have been deferred for future negotiation. This proposal was promptly rejected by the Soviet Union. The curves shown in figures 1 through 3 are conservative and, if anything, under-play the growing imbalance in strategic forces that will be available to the two sides, assuming a continuation of presently authorized American programs and presently estimated Soviet programs. The cancellation of the B-1 program and the provisions of a SALT II treaty as reportedly now being negotiated for by the United States would not significantly alter the trends portrayed in these figures.

In considering these trends in the strategic force balance, it is also necessary to resolve the question of whether the Soviet civil defense program is of sufficient potential to be taken seriously. The evidence is quite persuasive

FIGURE 1

Ratio of Deployed Forces (Static or Preattack Levels)

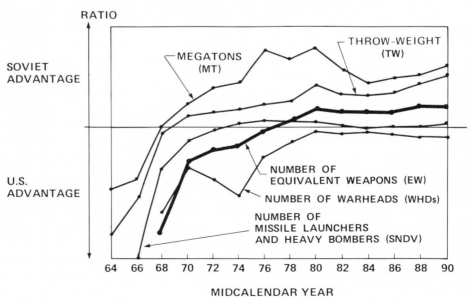

MIDCALENDAR YEAR

FIGURE 2

Capabilities After Soviet Union Initial Counterforce Strike with Strategic
Warning—Against Fully Generated United States Forces

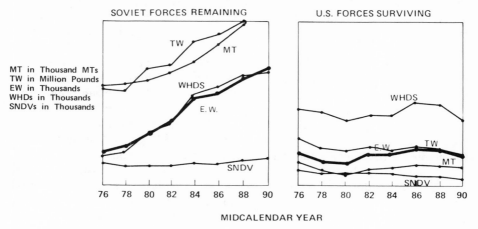

MIDCALENDAR YEAR

FIGURE 3

Strategic Balance After Counterforce Exchange
Against Fully Generated Forces

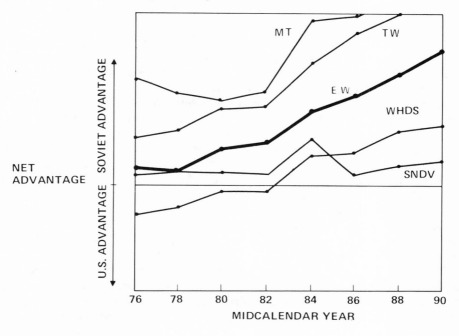

MIDCALENDAR YEAR

that it must be. The Soviet Union is building a large number of blast shelters in cities and near major industrial establishments. These can provide protection against overpressures of 30 to 150 pounds per square inch. These shelters are intended to give protection to that essential fraction of the urban industrial population that the Soviet Union does not plan to evacuate in time of crisis. Soviet plans call for the remainder of the urban industrial population to be dispersed relatively evenly over a wide area and to be sheltered against fallout to a degree that would leave only a small percentage of them vulnerable to an American retaliatory attack, even one designed to maximize fallout.

Some argue that the Soviet Union could not evacuate its urban population without thereby warning the United States. However, the calculations underlying the figures allow for such a warning; they assume that the United States has used such a warning to place the highest possible portion of its strategic forces on alert. Others argue that no plan, including the Soviet civil defense plan, can be perfectly executed and that there will always be a substantial factor of error. This is undoubtedly true; such a "foul-up" factor is a regular part of operations in wartime. It would be imprudent, however, to count on it as determinative. The Soviet Union has put enormous effort into training cadres and into providing some prior training for the whole populace. Under the circumstances of a war alert, with individual survival at stake, the Soviet civil population's responsiveness to orders would probably be relatively high. In sum, one could argue that the Soviet civil defense program would not be perfect in execution but that overall it would be sufficiently effective to be taken seriously.

Even if this assessment of Soviet attitudes toward strategic nuclear war and the trend of Soviet strategic capabilities is true, one might question whether the threat to United States security is serious. Answering this question involves the purpose of American strategic nuclear forces. They are primarily to provide deterrence. In order to do that, however, they must also enable the United States to fight a nuclear war if deterrence were to fail.

A distinction must be made between deterrence and military strategy. Deterrence is a political concept—the ability to dissuade an opponent from doing certain things. Its effectiveness rests on military capabilities in being and on indications of a willingness, under certain circumstances, to use those military capabilities. Military strategy deals with how one would actually use those military capabilities in the event of a failure of deterrence. The threat of pure destruction may make some sense when related to the concept of deterrence. It makes no sense when related to military strategy. In military strategy, the object is to defeat the enemy's military forces and to retain sufficient reserves so as to be in a position to terminate the war on favorable, or at least not one-sidedly disadvantageous, terms.

The threat of pure destruction, even in support of the political concept of deterrence, may be ineffective because it is difficult to convey the conviction that one would carry out a self-defeating and irrational military strategy if deterrence should fail. The Soviet view that the most reliable deterrent is to have the capability to win a nuclear war and survive is persuasive. The United States must not permit the Soviet Union ever to believe that it has that capability.

If the Soviet Union should have reason to believe that it had attained that capability and if the United States should be compelled by the logic of circumstances to acknowledge, either explicitly or tacitly, that the Soviet Union had it, then the United States would be at a severe disadvantage in coping with the Soviet Union. The pressure of constraint would be weighted disproportionately against the United States. In every important clash of interests, in every important contest of purpose, the United States would be the one pressed by the necessity to make concessions and to propitiate. The end of that road would be a progressive weakening of this country's position even without war. If the Soviet Union should believe that it had that capability without the United States's concurrence in that belief, thus creating a discrepancy between the perceptions of the strategic relationship on the respective sides, then the danger of slipping into nuclear hostilities would be seriously heightened.

Either of the indicated eventualities would be dire for the United States. What is imperative is to deny to the Soviet Union any reason to believe that it has the capability to win and survive a nuclear war. That purpose must be a cardinal consideration in American military policy in the years ahead, and can be achieved.

The above analysis indicates that the United States can today probably deny the Soviet Union the capability to win and survive a nuclear war. But the situation has changed over the last ten to fifteen years. As General Daniel Graham has put it, ten years ago only a madman in the Kremlin would have recommended a course of action that did not leave a wholly reliable escape hatch, if the resulting situation were to evolve in a way that might escalate to nuclear war. Today, quite sensible men in the Kremlin may well be arguing that it is the United States, not the Soviet Union, that should be making certain that it has a reliable escape hatch in such a situation.

The Soviets, for example, are clearly aware of the fact that the conventional military balance in Europe has not been favorable to the West at any time since the end of World War II. Part of the disadvantage is inherent in geographic factors, but the variables also pertain to the size and quality of military deployments. In earlier phases the European members of NATO, accustomed to relying on the deterrent shield of American strategic nuclear power, did not develop large and well-trained military forces. The Soviet efforts were distinctly better. For a time, however, American-theater nuclear weapons greatly exceeded those of the Soviet Union. That imbalance more than offset the West's disadvantage in conventional capabilities and made an attack on NATO a remote contingency. Later, NATO conventional capabilities improved, particularly its tactical air strength and antitank weaponry. Five years ago, an attack westward by Warsaw Pact forces would have required significant preparatory reinforcements and forward deployments that would have taken a number of days to complete and would surely have been observed. NATO forces would thereby have had time to make a transition from national to NATO chains of command, to deploy forward, to disperse vulnerable weapons, and in general to put them-selves in position for effective resistance.

The situation has altered in important particulars. Soviet tactical air capabili-ties have substantially improved. The firepower and mobility of the Soviet divisions have notably increased. Logistic support has been strengthened. More importantly, there are grounds to believe that the Warsaw Pact forces could now strike with less prior warning. In addition, the relative quality of the NATO-theater tactical nuclear shield is now less convincing and is likely to become even less so as the Soviets expand their deployments of Backfire bombers and SS-20 missiles. At present the United States's only available compensating nuclear measure is to assign some of its strategic nuclear systems, in particular a number of its Poseidon missiles, to the direct support of NATO forces.

The Middle East theater must also be considered. There the geographic factors would be inherently unfavorable to the United States in the event of a direct conflict with the Soviet Union, which is closer. Airplanes operating from Soviet bases can cover all of the Middle East, the eastern Mediterranean, and the entrances to the Red Sea and the Persian Gulf. It would not take long for Soviet forces to reach the Suez Canal via Azerbaidzhan. Those aspects are constants. In addition, several variables, which appear to have shifted un-favorably to the United States's interests, must also be taken into account.

Ten years ago Greece and Turkey were firmly in the NATO camp. The Soviet Union then could not have counted on getting overflight rights from Yugoslavia. The United States Sixth Fleet represented the predominant power that could be projected in the area. The threat of direct Soviet military action in the theater was insubstantial. Today, however, Greece and Turkey, divided by territorial quarrels, are uncertain factors in NATO. It is not clear that the Soviet Union would, in a crisis, be denied overflight rights by either Yugoslavia or Turkey. The Soviet fleet in the eastern Mediterranean, supported from air bases on Soviet soil and standing to benefit from the potential introduction of a number of parachute divisions into the area on short notice, probably represents the dominant force there today.

In the Far East, Soviet forces have increased manyfold in the last ten years while United States forces have substantially declined. Because the Sino-Soviet split continues to dominate the strategic situation in the area, however, the direct Soviet-American military balance in the Far East theater appears to be less important than the political relationships among the United States, China, and the Soviet Union.

During the quarter-century after the end of World War II, the worldwide military balance was dominated by the Soviet Union and the United States. On the one hand, the superior conventional military power of the Soviet Union potentially dominated the lines of demarcation on the Eurasian landmass. This derived from the size, organization, and interior position of the Soviet Union, and its ability to concentrate superior force at any point on or near its borders. On the other hand, the United States had a superior capability to project power out from its continental position to any point on the edges of the Eurasian landmass as was required to support its foreign policy. An important aspect of this ability to project United States power forward was the structure of alliances, treaties of navigation and friendship, base arrangements, and forward-deployed military units that were developed over the years. The components of this projectible power were the United States's superior blue water navy, a unique amphibious warfare capability, and long-range air capabilities.

Those components still probably outweigh the Soviet Union's counterpart in projectible power. The Soviet Union is putting together step by step its own widespread interlocking system of alliances, treaties of friendship and navigation, base rights, overflight and landing rights, and an increasing naval and naval air capability to do more than coastal defense. In Africa, this system has been developing rapidly. It has included, among others, Guinea, Guinea-Bissau, Angola, Mali, Mozambique, Ethiopia, and Libya. In the Middle East it includes South Yemen, Iraq, and to some extent Syria. In Southeast Asia it includes, at least to a degree, Vietnam and Laos. It now appears that the Soviets are negotiating for base rights as far away as the Fiji Islands in the Pacific and Guyana on the north coast of South America. The Soviet Union has had military base rights in Cuba for many years.

To divine the underlying meaning of these developments requires a sober assessment of Soviet intentions. Many observers have long been impressed with the dogged persistence with which the Soviet Communist leaders have pursued their goals but have been at a loss to understand why they were putting such intense effort into their strategic nuclear program and, in particular, into their civil defense program.

The persistence with which the Soviet leaders have pursued their broad objectives has indeed been impressive. Instead of following a single strategy, they have pressed one or another as their continuing review of the situation indicated which would offer the greatest opportunities and the least risks. Among those strategies one clearly concerns itself with eventually achieving hegemony over the Middle East. This had been an objective of the czars even before the Communists took power. The Middle East lies at the crossroads of Europe, Asia, and Africa, and today whoever controls it and the oil resources of the Persian Gulf controls Europe and Japan.

If one were examining this problem from the Kremlin, how might one analyze its military aspects? In the first place, the military capabilities of the countries in the area, considered singly or all together, are no match for Soviet forces. Massive support from outside the area would be necessary to give the Middle East countries any chance. Who outside the area could give such support? Europe and Japan could not, but the United States could.

The most convenient way for the United States to support an operation in the Middle East would be to use its forces in Europe and its base structure there as a staging area for reinforcement. From the perspective of Moscow, that could be made difficult by building up Warsaw Pact capabilities to a point where the European countries would not dare let bases on their territory be used in such a contingency. Another way the United States could bring its power to bear would be through the Indian Ocean up through the Red Sea and Persian Gulf. This could be made dangerous or impossible by Soviet facilities in East Africa and along the Indian Ocean, or by dominating the entrances to the Red Sea and the Persian Gulf. Another route for United States access to the Middle East might be through the eastern Atlantic and the Mediterranean. This could be made difficult through Soviet facilities along the coast of West Africa, dominating the Straits of Gibraltar, or on the northern coast of Africa in such countries as Libya or Algeria.

But if one were in the Kremlin one would be concerned that if Soviet policy were successful in accomplishing all this, the United States, seeing its truly vital interests at stake, might go on a strategic alert as President Nixon ordered in 1973. The best Soviet answer to that possibility would be a superior strategic nuclear posture designed to deter the United States from doing so. But the United States still might do so out of desperation and not back down; the situation could then escalate to an actual nuclear war. Moscow must therefore try to put the Soviet Union in a position to win and survive such a war. Such a chain of reasoning could well explain the Soviet Union's intense concentration on improving its strategic nuclear war fighting capabilities, including its hardened command and control structure and its civil defense posture.

In conclusion, one further point might be made. More and more people in the world recognize the nature of Soviet intentions. Most do not want to be dominated from the Kremlin. Although many are afraid and some favor accommodation, the general political atmosphere seems to be shifting against the Soviet Union despite its growing military power and the intensity of its political and propaganda campaigns. The situation is obviously full of danger, but, if the United States remains willing to care, to prepare, and prudently to act, the presently disquieting trend of events can yet be reversed.

The Strategic Debate
in the United States

BARRY E. CARTER

The awesome destructiveness and abundance of strategic nuclear weapons today ensure their importance in world events. The United States spends some $20 billion each year on its strategic forces and places great weight on seeking constructive agreements in the ongoing Strategic Arms Limitation Talks (SALT).

Relatively clear boundaries are established on the American decision-making process by the "physical facts" of the strategic weapons the United States and the Soviet Union have deployed, or are now developing and deploying. There remains, however, a considerable area within these parameters for debate. The variety and complexity of strategic weapons and the fact that none have been used in a war since 1945 indicate that there are significant differences of opinion about the consequences of their use or threatened use.

In the United States, unlike in other countries, much of the debate is public and intense. This debate is characterized by widely varying interpretations of the Soviet-American strategic balance. Arguments revolve around the significance of particular physical facts, the interests and motives of each country, and the special interests of the participants in the discussion.

The public dialogue in the United States has often benefited the national interests of the United States and the rest of the world. Not only has it determined at times American expenditures for strategic weapons and SALT negotiating positions, but it has also been the primary vehicle for educating American citizens and the rest of the world in the implications of a nuclear age. The debate on occasion, however, has exhibited serious defects in emphasis or analysis. Improving this ongoing dialogue should and can be done.

The numbers and basic characteristics of the two countries' strategic forces are an important starting point. In the SALT I agreements in 1972 both countries accepted very low limits on their antiballistic missiles (ABMs) and some limits on the number of their strategic offensive missiles. The impending SALT II agreements are likely to impose even more restrictions on offensive weapons.

The eight-year treaty would include a ceiling of about 2,200 on the total number of each country's strategic missiles and bombers, with some separate numerical ceilings on weapons armed with multiple independently targetable reentry vehicles (MIRVs).[1] These sublimits will probably include ceilings of 1,320 for land- and sea-based missiles and bombers equipped with cruise missiles, 800 for land-based missiles alone, and 308 for the "heavy" Soviet land-based missiles. An accompanying three-year protocol will probably impose some restrictions on the range of cruise missiles and on the testing and deployment of mobile missiles.

Both before and during the SALT negotiations, however, the two countries have developed their strategic forces differently for a variety of reasons, and they are likely to continue along separate paths in the future. This complicates any comparison of the two forces. Overall, as detailed in table 1, the

TABLE 1

Operational Strategic Forces: Mid-1977 Estimates

	U.S.	USSR
Land-based missiles (ICBMs)	1,054	1,450
Sea-based missiles (SLBMs)	656	880
Missiles Subtotal	1,710	2,330
Heavy Bombers[1]	418	210
Total strategic delivery vehicles	2,128	2,540
Force loadings[2]	8,500	4,000

Source: *Report of Secretary of Defense Donald H. Rumsfeld to the Congress on the FY 1978 Budget, FY 1979 Authorization Request and FY 1978-1982 Defense Program,* January 17, 1977, p. 58.

[1] Includes the B-52 and FB-111 for the United States and the Bear, Bison, and Backfire bombers for the Soviet Union. There is some debate among American analysts over the range and capabilities of the Backfire.

[2] Includes the independently targetable weapons associated with operational missiles and heavy bombers.

Soviets have more offensive strategic missiles than the United States, and these tend to be larger. On the other hand, the United States has more strategic bombers, and its forces have many qualitative advantages. For example, its submarines are quieter, its missiles are more accurate, and many more of its missiles now carry MIRVs. In independently targetable strategic weapons, both bombs and missile warheads, the United States has an advantage of approximately 8,500 to the Soviet Union's 4,000. The United States is also several years ahead in the development of long-range cruise missiles.

[1] A MIRV is essentially a bomb, carried in clusters of two or more on a single missile. While none of the MIRVs have the same explosive power as a single warhead, their use increases the number of targets that a single missile can attack.

Not only are both countries' strategic forces large but, in spite of the 1972 SALT I agreements and the likely SALT II agreements, there continue to be rapid and expensive increases in both countries' destructive power. Real growth in Soviet defense expenditures has averaged about 3 to 5 percent annually since the mid-1960s, and Soviet strategic forces have participated in this build-up. Not only are the Soviets deploying a wide array of new strategic weapons, but they are also making energetic efforts to narrow the United States's techno-logical advantages.

It should not be forgotten, however, that the United States has been actively modernizing its existing forces and developing and deploying new systems. Especially significant are the addition of MIRVs to its ICBMs, the impending deployment of the Ohio-class submarine, and the rapid development of the cruise missile.

Given the large inventory of existing strategic forces and the long lead time required to develop and deploy new strategic systems, Soviet-American strategic deployments for the next five to ten years can be projected with some confidence. For example, Secretary of Defense Harold Brown has calculated four static measures for the present balance and then estimated them for the two countries' likely forces ten years from now. As indicated in table 2, each country will continue to lead in at least one static indicator.

Interpreting the Physical Facts

Where does all this leave the security of each country now and in the foresee-able future? Answering this question requires more than counting weapons and comparing their characteristics. It requires developing and applying analytical tests. On one hand, as a result of intense research and thought that flourished in the United States in the mid-1950s and has continued, questions today about the strategic balance and strategic policy can be addressed with some sophistica-tion. On the other hand, considerable disagreement still exists among experts about the significance of particular physical facts and the definition of relevant criteria. As Henry Kissinger once said when confronted by some of the more arcane technical debates, "strategic policy attracts the Talmudic scholars and Jesuit priests of foreign affairs."

With those caveats, it is still clear that each country has and will continue to possess what must be considered the threshold requirement for strategic sufficiency and stability—an "assured destruction" capability. This concept, popularized by Robert McNamara while he was secretary of defense, means the "ability, even after absorbing a well-coordinated surprise first strike, to inflict unacceptable damage on the attacker." McNamara defined this explicitly in 1968: "In the case of the Soviet Union, I would judge that a capability on our part to destroy, say, one-fifth to one-fourth of her population and one-half of her industrial capacity would serve as an effective deterrent." Today, assuming zero or low Soviet ABM defenses (a reasonable assumption, given the 1972

TABLE 2

Static Measures of Strategic Balance (United States as % of Soviet)

	1977	No Moderni- zation[2]	B-52/CM[3]	B-52/CM + Representative CM Carrier Force[4]
		Projections for 1986		
Number of warheads (i.e., force loadings)	240	104	126	187
Megatons (i.e., explosive power)	35	26	25	34
Throw weight (under SALT limits)	75	48	48	77
Hard target kill potential[1]	160	28	67	168

Source: U.S., Congress, House, Armed Services Committee on H.R. 8390, *Supplemental Author- ization FY 1978*, 95th Cong., 1st sess., August 2, 1977, p. 14, statement by Secretary of Defense Harold Brown.

[1] The capability to destroy hardened targets, such as missile silos, command centers, air-defense sites, and submarine bases.

[2] Assumes a United States force without the cruise missile, B-1, and M-X.

[3] Includes a United States force of long-range cruise missiles mounted on B-52s.

[4] This force would have some new cruise missile carriers in addition to the B-52.

ABM treaty), the delivered warheads of 220 Minuteman III ICBMs could kill about 21 percent of the Soviet population from immediate effects alone and destroy about 72 percent of the Soviet industrial capacity. The delivered war-heads from 170 Poseidon missiles, which are fewer than the total carried by twelve submarines, could cause a similar amount of damage. As indicated above, the total United States strategic forces are considerably larger.

Even beyond the threshold requirement of assured destruction, there is general agreement among analysts that there is now a state of strategic nuclear equilibrium between the two countries. Neither country's strategic forces have any significant advantage that is not offset by advantages enjoyed by the other country's forces.

While major changes in either country's forces require at least several years, there can be a gradual shift in the strategic balance if one country is more aggressive over time in modernizing its existing forces and in developing and deploying new weapons. Given the possibility of change, what should be the objective of the United States? To seek a capability to launch an all-out attack that would destroy the Soviet forces before they had a chance to retaliate would be dangerous and wasteful. Such an attempt would almost certainly provoke a Soviet buildup. It would have almost no chance of succeeding and would add many billions of dollars to the defense budget.

Secretary of Defense Harold Brown recently adopted the more realistic and stable concept of "essential equivalence" as the means for maintaining strategic nuclear equilibrium. While he defined this concept in some detail, he initially listed four general conditions: "first, that the Soviets do not see their strategic nuclear forces as usable instruments for political leverage, diplomatic coercion, or military superiority; second, that nuclear stability, especially in a crisis, is maintained; third, that any advantages in force characteristics enjoyed by the Soviets are offset by other U.S. advantages; and fourth, that the U.S. posture is not in fact, and is not seen as, inferior in performance to the forces of the Soviet Union."[2] Brown's definition of "essential equivalence" varies in some respects from the definition that then Secretary of Defense James Schlesinger offered in 1972 for the concept. In addition, some commentators have suggested other variations on this concept and have even argued for substantially different objectives. In short, the analysis of "how much is enough" becomes more elaborate and more contentious.

The Debate

The "physical facts" of American and Soviet strategic forces establish in these more sophisticated discussions about the strategic balance certain boundaries on what can reasonably be said. There remains, however, a broad area for interpretation and disagreement. A rich mix of issues including each country's motives, the political perceptions of other countries, and domestic political needs becomes increasingly important.

Debates on these points proceed in private *within* both the civilian and military leadership of many countries. The Soviet leadership obviously weighs the strategic balance when deciding on new defense expenditures, new SALT positions, or certain foreign policy initiatives. In fact, the Soviets seem to place even more weight on the strategic balance and the progress of the SALT negotiations than the United States in assessing the general state of Soviet-American relations. Major Western European countries and Japan also pay some attention to the strategic balance in determining the strength and credibility of American commitments. Third world countries are also influenced in varying degrees.

Similar debates proceed in private *between* the countries. The most in-depth discussions occur between the United States and its major allies—England, France, other NATO countries, and Japan. There is also an extensive exchange of information between the United States and the Soviet Union in the SALT negotiations, though the Soviets generally refrain from providing detailed information about their strategic forces.

The *public* discussion of the strategic balance, however, is essentially a domestic American dialogue. In spite of the Soviet leadership's great concern about the issues, only very general information is provided to Soviet citizens about important developments in the SALT negotiations. Soviet commentators, moreover, castigate rather than analyze major new American strategic weapons or policies.

Public Soviet information about their strategic forces is strikingly sparse.

---

[2] Harold Brown, speech delivered at the 34th Annual Dinner of the National Industrial Association, Washington, D.C., September 15, 1977.

Published economic data provide only a single annual figure for Soviet defense expenditures. That figure does not include some types of defense expenditures, does not accurately reflect trends in defense spending, and fails to distinguish between expenditures for strategic forces and other forces. Articles by Soviet authors on strategic policy are vague and often propagandistic. Indeed, the Soviets publish essentially nothing about the numbers, characteristics, or location of their strategic weapons. Not even the names or designations of the various missiles and bombers are given.

The public discussion in Western Europe, led by such groups as the International Institute for Strategic Studies, is well informed and involves many people. This discussion, however, draws heavily on American sources and usually defers to the debate in the United States, rather than raising new questions or issues. As one observer concluded, the Europeans "apparently assume that the promulgation of deterrence theories and doctrines is an American prerogative and lack the confidence to define a doctrine of their own."[3] Similarly, while the public debate in Japan often involves different issues, there appears to be a deference to American sources and ideas.

The public dialogue in the United States is uniquely detailed, important, and intense. Although some national security issues—notably those involving the foreign intelligence community—have remained generally hidden from the arena of American public debate until recently, strategic budgets and policy have not. Strategic issues evolved from and are still inextricably linked to other military issues that have traditionally been the focus of much public attention, as illustrated by the debates before World War II over the usefulness of air power and in the 1950s over aircraft carriers versus land-based bombers.

Any initial tendency to limit public discussion of the strategic balance was quickly neutralized by the "missile gap" debate in the 1960 presidential race and by Secretary of Defense McNamara's decision in the early 1960s to make public vast amounts of information about both countries' forces. McNamara was not only seeking congressional and public support for the administration's proposed expenditures on strategic forces, but he also felt strongly that deterrence would operate best if each country had an objective appreciation of the other's forces. Both considerations help keep strategic issues in the public spotlight today. Further public interest is generated by the efforts in SALT to limit strategic weapons. When successful, these efforts require congressional approval or at least the consent of the Senate.

The domestic debates in the United States have been useful. They have stimulated much serious thought about the dangers, uses, and costs of strategic weapons. They have educated the American public, including its leaders, about the nuclear age and have increased public awareness in other countries. It is difficult to imagine, for example, how this country would have supported the

---

[3] Lynn Etheridge Davis, "Limited Nuclear Options: Deterrence and the New American Doctrine," *Adelphi Papers*, no. 121 (London: International Institute for Strategic Studies, 1976), p. 14.

1972 treaty sharply limiting American and Soviet deployments of ABMs without the efforts in the 1960s to explain the concept of "mutual assured destruction" and the very serious public challenges between 1967 and 1972 to the proposed ABM system. These prior discussions provided a level of public understanding on which President Nixon, Henry Kissinger, and others could base sophisticated explanations of the new treaty.

Key Actors in the American Debates

Useful as these public discussions have been, they have been seriously flawed at times in ways that could be corrected. Identifying the problems and avoiding them in the future require analysis of the key actors and the dynamics of the public debates.

While a cast of thousands participates in these debates, certain actors are more important because of the entities they represent, their individual abilities, and the particular issue of the moment. With their access to information and media coverage, actors from the executive branch and Congress have a decided advantage over individuals outside government. And, while the actors and dynamics often vary dramatically from issue to issue, there are certain consistent constellations of key actors for each of three sets of issues—general strategic policies, SALT, and new weapons procurement.[4]

In the executive branch, the military are constantly and visibly involved in the public discussions. The military start with the institutional advantage of much inside information and generally high public esteem, though it was dampened somewhat by the Vietnam war. Moreover, since the early 1960s the military have made full use of these advantages on important issues by carefully avoiding interservice squabblings that could dissipate their influence. In addition, military leaders, especially from the navy, have become increasingly sophisticated in promoting their interests by using their close association with many senators and congressmen, their links to defense industries, and selective estimates of the Soviet threat.

As a result, the military services have a major voice in the design and development of new weapons systems, and their approval is very important to the political acceptability of SALT agreements. They have less impact on the formulation of strategic theories, largely because they have avoided this area. They recognize that interservice rivalries here could harm unity elsewhere.

The military's influence is often eclipsed in these matters by the secretary of defense. The secretary has much the same inside information as the military, at least the same access to the media, and usually the general support of the

[4] More detailed and illuminating analyses of the key actors, particularly regarding their roles in the internal decision-making process in the United States government, can be found in John Steinbruner and Barry Carter, "Organizational and Political Dimensions of the Strategic Posture: The Problems of Reform," *Daedalus* 104 (Summer 1975), pp. 131-54, and Graham T. Allison and Frederic A. Morris, "Armaments and Arms Control: Exploring the Determinants of Military Weapons, ibid., pp. 99-130.

president. Moreover, as a civilian and as one who sometimes disagrees with the military, the secretary lacks the military's obvious self-interest.

The secretary can be especially powerful in espousing strategic theories. This takes a sustained public effort that the White House and other actors are either unwilling to conduct or unable to accomplish. For example, McNamara popularized mutual assured destruction, and Schlesinger gave limited attack options their big boost. The secretary of defense also plays a direct role in weapons development and procurement. McNamara was the key decision-maker in stopping the B-70 bomber in the 1960s, and Laird was the major proponent of the Safeguard ABM and the initial development of the cruise missile.[5]

Although less obvious, the secretary often plays a dominant role in public discussion and private decision-making on SALT. McNamara helped prepare the way for SALT with his active role at the Glassboro conference between President Johnson and Premier Kosygin. Laird both slowed the negotiations and shaped the subjects at issue with his concerns about the Soviet Union's intentions to launch a first strike with its large ICBMs. Schlesinger would have made it politically very costly for President Ford and Secretary of State Kissinger to sign a SALT agreement in 1975 or 1976.

The president, his national security adviser, and special advisers can usually be the decisive actors when they want to be, but the White House has many concerns and only limited energies and political capital. Consequently, the White House selectively intervenes on issues that are especially important to the president when action can be dramatic and short-lived, such as SALT agreements and the expensive procurement phase for new weapons. Thus, although Secretary of Defense Laird, the military, and other actors influenced the public debate on the 1972 SALT agreements, Nixon and Kissinger had the most influence over the public interpretation of the agreements' value. Similarly, President Carter has made himself the dominant figure in the SALT II process and in the decision not to produce the B-1 bomber.

Other actors in the executive branch play roles that vary from issue to issue, but their roles are generally more limited than those of the military, the secretary of defense, and the White House. No one else has much influence over formulating strategic theories.

As for SALT negotiations, the secretary of state can play an important role, as Dean Rusk and Henry Kissinger did and as Cyrus Vance is doing now. The secretary of state is often perceived by the public as relatively independent of the military and other "special" interests, although his "toughness" in representing the interests of the United States has sometimes been questioned. Another actor on the SALT stage is the director of the U.S. Arms Control and

---

[5] In the executive branch's internal decision-making on weapons development, though, the military services are the primary actors. See Allison and Morris, p. 123. This internal process encompassses a much longer time and many more small decisions for a particular weapons system than the public debate. Civilian secretaries of defense and their staffs come and go during the long development process.

Disarmament Agency (ACDA). Particularly when he is also the chief SALT negotiator (as Gerard Smith was in 1969-72 and as Paul Warnke is now), the director has considerable public visibility. He is usually a strong complement to White House efforts to explain the negotiations and to gain public support for any agreements.

In regard to new strategic weapons, the only other major actor within the executive branch besides the Pentagon and the White House has been the Central Intelligence Agency (CIA), whose estimates of Soviet forces sometimes deflate the Pentagon's estimates. The new requirement for ACDA to prepare "arms control impact statements" on new weapons systems might provide ACDA with some leverage in the future.

With their access to information and the media as well as their internal alliances, actors in the executive branch probably have the most influence on public discussions. However, individuals and groups in Congress often play an important role. Their effectiveness stems in part from the actual votes, or threats of votes, to halt or modify a particular weapons program or to block a SALT agreement. The congressional role as a forum for airing competing viewpoints and for extracting information from the executive branch is equally important.

Congressional influence, which varies from issue to issue, may be greatest with respect to new weapons programs. Because of the perceived importance of strategic weapons, Congress hesitates more before challenging the executive branch on these weapons than on conventional arms and deployments. Nevertheless, the House and Senate Armed Services Committees release abundant information. Along with the whole Senate, they often become the center stage for debates on strategic weapons programs, such as the ABM and improvements in hard-target kill capability. Committee actions regularly lead the administration to make small changes in the pacing of programs, weapons design, and the size of deployments. While preventing or significantly altering a strategic program is unusual for Congress, the close Senate votes on the Safeguard ABM in 1969 and 1970 probably spurred the executive branch to agree with the Soviets to limit ABMs to very low levels.

Congressional actors also significantly affect the negotiated provisions and public explanations of SALT agreements. While the executive branch negotiated the 1972 SALT accords without seriously consulting Congress, the resulting congressional debate dramatically affected public perception of the agreements and ensured that the views of congressional actors, such as Senator Jackson, would be taken into account in future negotiations. The fight in the spring of 1977 over Warnke's nomination to be head of ACDA and the chief United States negotiator for SALT further reinforced the role of Congress. The White House not only needs to obtain the necessary two-thirds consent for a SALT treaty but also wants to avoid a bruising public debate that could turn a political asset into a liability.

Congress has a role, but a smaller one, to play in formulating strategic theories. A committee might stop or delay a piece of hardware, such as a new warhead, that logically goes with a new strategy. Congress can also provide many forums in its committees for public debate. For example, some senators and subcommittees carefully scrutinized Schlesinger's policy of introducing options for limited strategic attacks. Nevertheless, just as in the executive branch, it is hard to divert or blunt the persistent avowal of a strategic policy by a secretary of defense.

Many participants in the public debate on the strategic balance exist outside the executive branch or the halls of Congress. These "other" actors include defense contractors, academics, former government officials, hopeful candidates for office, and concerned citizens. It is often from these actors, especially the academics and think-tank experts, that the initial ideas for new policies and exotic new weapons flow. These actors also often appear at congressional hearings as prominent witnesses who advocate something other than what the administration seeks. Nevertheless, because of their greater difficulty in obtaining current information and in getting media coverage, these actors generally have only an ad hoc influence on the public debate in the United States.

All the actors listed above are seeking to influence a public that, within limits, can be influenced. American public opinion on questions about the strategic balance is ambivalent on many counts. One detailed study in 1976 found that, even before the recent problems with détente, there was growing public concern that the Soviet Union was seeking to exploit détente against American interests. The public, moreover, was determined to keep United States military forces strong; those interviewed agreed by a 52 to 41 percent margin with the view that "the U.S. should maintain its dominant position as the world's most powerful nation at all costs." On the other hand, there was at the same time a 59 to 14 percent margin supporting an extension of the SALT agreements to control nuclear warheads.[6]

Flaws in the Public Debate

One may question whether these public debates have been as balanced and productive as they could be. The preceding analysis suggests several flaws. First, the strategic balance, significant as it is, has assumed excessive public importance. Whether it is a result of the Buck Rogers technology of strategic forces or the misleading concreteness of specific numbers, such as warheads and missiles, questions regarding the strategic balance assume a disproportionate importance in the public's perception of Soviet-American relations. The relations between these two superpowers should be viewed in the richer mosaic of issues between the two countries, including the balance of conventional forces, trade and investment, cooperation to limit nuclear proliferation, human rights, and competing interests in the third world.

Second, the public debates have tended to focus on one or two strategic

[6] *U.S. Foreign Policy: Principles for Defining the National Interest* (New York: Public Agenda Foundation, 1976), pp. 74-75.

issues at a time, overemphasizing some and ignoring others. This is compounded by an uneven flow of information into the public arena. All this is symptomatic of a situation where a few actors—the secretary of defense, the military, and the White House—can define the outlines of the debate and greatly influence substantive thought. For example, McNamara's espousal of mutual assured destruction educated the public in many ways, but left a popular misperception that American strategic forces were only capable of conducting a massive second strike in retaliation for a Soviet first strike. In fact, the United States's forces have been able since at least the mid-1960s to carry out a variety of other attack options. This misperception gave considerable momentum in 1972 to Schlesinger's call for a new strategic policy allowing for limited strike options and requiring a new generation of larger, more accurate missiles and warheads. In fact, the new strategy required only changes in American target plans and not necessarily new hardware. The new hardware should have been evaluated more thoroughly on its own merits, not merely justified by a so-called new strategy.

Continuing "biases" exist in the public debate. Probably the most prominent example is the concern over "large" Soviet ICBMs. Ever since Laird suggested that the Soviet Union's large SS-9 missile was a first-strike weapon, many American commentators have dwelled on the SS-9 and other large Soviet missiles such as the SS-18. Today the concern is not that the Soviets might attempt an all-out strike against American strategic forces and cities, which would be suicidal. Rather, some people fear that the Soviets might threaten to attack the land-based Minuteman missiles in order to gain some political or military advantage. Reflecting these concerns, the United States regularly proposed in SALT some sublimits on the large Soviet missiles. These proposals have been pushed to the extent possibly of slowing the pace of negotiations or of weakening or dropping other American positions. As a result, the impending SALT II agreements will apparently have sublimits of 1,200 on the number of missiles that can carry MIRVs, of 800 on the number of land-based missiles with MIRVs and of 308 on the number of "heavy" ICBMS. Some critics, however, find these limits inadequate and argue that the supposed vulnerability of the Minuteman is a legitimate reason for opposing or at least seeking "clarifications" in the new agreements.

The critics' well-publicized concern probably overstates the danger to American interests. It is uncertain whether the Soviets will in fact be able in the next ten years, within the SALT II constraints, to destroy the Minuteman force. There are many complications in carrying out such a strike. An actual attack involves firing hundreds of missiles in a short period of time and detonating thousands of warheads, some of which would be bunched close together.[7] Even if such an attack were a credible threat, it is unclear why this would give the Soviet Union a significant political or military advantage. There would still be

---

[7] See John D. Steinbruner and Thomas M. Garwin, "Strategic Vulnerability: The Balance Between Prudence and Paranoia," *International Security* 1 (Summer 1976) :138.

many other American forces, particularly the missile submarines and bombers, to offset this threat.[8]

Even if Minuteman survivability should be a critical concern, the related criticism of the SALT II agreements seems misdirected. The SALT sublimits will push back the time when the Soviet threat could become credible. These sublimits, moreover, are more restrictive than those in the original Vladivostok understanding that President Ford and Secretary of State Kissinger negotiated in November 1974. While they are not as thoroughgoing as the limits in President Carter's comprehensive proposal of March 1977, Carter's plan was a starting point for negotiations and not an expected final result.

Another current problem in the public debate is the budding brouhaha over the proposed large, mobile ICBM—the M-X. Part of the perceived need for this new missile stems from one justification for earlier generations of strategic weapons. This was the need for some redundancy in United States forces as a hedge against unexpected Soviet threats or breakdowns in American systems. This rationale became codified in the "Triad" concept, which initially envisioned only an unspecified degree of redundancy. However, some commentators now interpret the concept to require that each leg of the Triad—ICBMs, SLBMs, and bombers—be "designed to sustain a Soviet attack and retain the capacity to retaliate with sufficient force."[9] Given this interpretation and the possible future vulnerability of existing American ICBMs M-X proponents argue that there must be a new ICBM system. It would seem, however, that before committing itself to spend an estimated $30 billion or more on the M-X, the United States should reexamine rigidified concepts, particularly since the Triad concept does not take into account the introduction of possible land and sea-based versions of a new weapon system—the cruise missile.

Yet another current debate focuses on the extent and implications of the Soviet civil defense program. Concern was actively fueled in 1975 and 1976 by statements emanating from the Pentagon and from outside experts with good sources of "inside" information. The statements raised serious questions about Soviet plans and suggested that the United States might have to increase its strategic programs. More recently, though, a joint congressional committee issued an investigative report, and the Carter administration released more factual information. As a result, the evidence regarding the Soviet program appears fragmentary and conflicting, and the strategic implications are uncertain and not immediately threatening. It took well over a year, however, for balance to appear in the public discussions.

While a continuing flow of information into the public arena is vital, the present system encourages too much public discussion in one area. Although there should be a discussion of the general issues underlying the SALT negotiations and extensive public examination of any SALT agreements, in recent

---

[8] See Sidney D. Drell and Frank von Hippel, "Limited Nuclear War," *Scientific American* 235 (November 1976), p. 27; Barry Carter, "Nuclear Strategy and Nuclear Weapons," ibid., 230 (May 1974), p. 20.

[9] See Bernard Weinraub, "Defense Chief Backs Start on a System of Mobile Missiles," *New York Times,* October 6, 1977.

years there has been excessive disclosure of American negotiating positions. There have always been "leaks" of negotiating positions, but the disclosures have never been as extensive or patently authorized as recently, and never has public discussion been so encouraged. This seems to reflect the Senate's enhanced determination to speak with an independent voice in ratifying the eventual agreements and President Carter's initial tendency to negotiate with the Soviets through the media.

Negotiations are a delicate process. Timing is important, and both sides need to give and take. The extensive public disclosures and discussion of ongoing American SALT positions seem detrimental in two ways. First, some positions that have little domestic support but that might be useful vehicles to wrest major concessions from the Soviets come under public attack in the United States.

Even in the absence of public pressures, the United States government tends to modify positions quickly. Possibly this tendency stems from a general willingness in this country to seek compromise. In any case, the domestic criticism in the United States makes the Soviets even more inclined to be obdurate, and therefore they are more likely to obtain American concessions. Confidentiality was very helpful, for example, when the United States continued to press for some limits on offensive forces in 1970 and 1971 despite the Soviets' preference for only an ABM treaty. There was some public impatience with American negotiating persistence, but "leaks" were minimized and public debate was not encouraged. The United States held out successfully and obtained some offensive limitations to supplement the ABM treaty.

Public discussion of initial American SALT positions can, on the other hand, sometimes unduly limit the United States's inclination to fall back when necessary. For example, President Carter's major new proposal in March 1977 was a good, tough opening position for new SALT negotiations. The rapid disclosure of the terms and the considerable debate about them, however, probably gave greater significance to this opening position than advisable.[10] Some critics of the eventual SALT II agreements will point to the initial United States position and argue that there was a sellout.

Public United States debate on the strategic balance, then, has been seriously flawed on occasion because a few principal actors control the flow of information and the terms of the debate. In addition, there has been excessive disclosure of detailed SALT negotiating positions in recent months.

Improving the Public Discussions of the Strategic Balance

Can anything be done to avoid or minimize such problems as those discussed above? Widespread public discussions about the complex and often arcane issues concerning the strategic balance will by their very nature often

[10] See discussion by Jan M. Lodal, "Carter and the Arms Talks," *New York Times*, April 12, 1977.

include misinformation as well as objective analysis, hyperbole as well.as careful statement, and misunderstanding as well as understanding. Nevertheless,
the quality of these discussions can be improved.

*Debate over the strategic balance should more often take place in the con-
text of Soviet-American relations as a whole.* These relations are multifaceted. Preoccupation with the strategic balance, particularly when there is
now a state of strategic nuclear equilibrium between the two countries, tends to
deprive the other aspects of relations of the private and public attention that
they deserve. Because the principal actors in the executive branch exert the
major influence in defining the terms of the debate, they should bear the responsibility to broaden the public discussions.

*There should be a presumption in favor of extensive, comprehensive dis-
closure of facts about both countries' strategic forces.* Over the past fifteen
years or so, detailed disclosure has educated the American public and the rest of
the world. Problems arise more often from the kind of one-sided disclosure that
recently generated the Soviet civil defense "scare" than from excessive
disclosure.

One must recognize exceptions to this presumption in favor of disclosure.
Some sensitive information, such as war plans and technological details, should
continue to be kept secret. Determining the exact nature of those exceptions is
beyond the scope of this essay. It would seem that the category of secret
information should probably be no larger than it is today, and possibly it
should be smaller. To avoid the special problems explained above, however,
public disclosure and discussion of SALT negotiating positions should be more
limited.

*Efforts should be made to strengthen actors within the executive branch other
than the military, the secretary of defense, and the White House.* The domi-
nance of the Pentagon and the White House on strategic issues often hinders
balanced debate within the executive branch and a balanced presentation to
the public. The military almost consistently favor more weapons and are wary
of arms control agreements. The secretary of defense, reflecting his institutional
position, will often side with the military and only occasionally differ sharply.
The White House has many other concerns and often makes its decisions on
strategic issues on the strength of internal executive branch pressures, where the
military and secretary of defense are very powerful.

Other executive branch actors should be reinforced. The CIA should be
encouraged to prepare and publish independent assessments of the Soviet
threat. CIA assessments would likely be less influenced than the Pentagon's by a
concern to justify new weapons programs. Similarly, the State Department
should speak out more frequently on Soviet intentions. Finally, the ACDA
requires greater support for its views on the value of arms control agreements
and on the arms control implications of the Pentagon's proposed new weapons
systems.

Actors outside the executive branch should be strengthened. Players within
the executive branch are susceptible to White House pressures and will often

be overwhelmed by the expertise and bureaucratic clout of the Pentagon actors. Independent, well-informed "outsiders" must be developed.

The increasing practice of individuals and committees in Congress to obtain important information and advocate their own views is healthy. In recent years, however, balance has been lacking since the key congressional actors, such as Senators Henry Jackson and Sam Nunn, often share many of the Pentagon's values. Those with different values should encourage spokesmen and certain committees, such as the Senate Foreign Relations Committee, to become more active.

Outside Congress, the development of well-financed, independent centers of expertise is critical. While defense industries and government-supported think tanks sometimes provide useful ideas, their independence is limited. More high-quality centers of analysis like the Brookings Institution are needed. The Ford Foundation's recent multimillion dollar grant to Harvard University's Program of Science and International Affairs, which has an active interest in strategic issues, is an excellent step.

It is hoped that strong players in Congress and elsewhere outside the executive branch will ensure that the full implications of new strategic theories are scrutinized and that new weapons systems, such as the M-X, will not proceed simply because of rigid, outdated policies. Such independent-minded outsiders might prevent a secretary of defense from unnecessarily skewing SALT positions and can press successfully for release of comprehensive information about new strategic developments. By seeking and obtaining as much information as possible, by analyzing it independently, and by publicizing their conclusions, these actors will improve the quality of the already valuable public debate on the strategic balance.

Sino-Soviet Relations

JONATHAN D. POLLACK

Few foreign policy issues have been as consistently troublesome for Soviet leaders as their relations with China. Whether as an increasingly independent ally during the 1950s, as a vocal critic of Soviet policies at home and within the socialist camp throughout the 1960s, or as a major military and political adversary in the 1970s, China's leadership has rarely proven responsive to the preferences of policymakers in Moscow. Chinese and Soviet officials and writers agree (though for decidedly different reasons) that a mutually beneficial relationship existed only in the earliest years of Communist rule, when Peking's military and economic vulnerabilities were most acute. Even in those days, the newly established alliance encountered significant strains. Thus, no matter what the prevailing political circumstances, Soviet leaders have always found the China issue difficult to manage, let alone to control.

This difficulty has been again evident since the death of Mao Tse-tung in September 1976. More than any other Chinese politician, Mao epitomized China's long obsession with the Soviet Union. His death seemingly removed a singular impediment to the improvement of relations. His personal preoccupation with Soviet hegemonic ambitions and subversive designs recalled the views expressed by two other recent leaders—John Foster Dulles and J. Edgar Hoover. Their views strongly influenced American foreign policy and domestic politics for at least a generation. One can only speculate as to how long it might take to exorcise similar ghosts from the Chinese political process, particularly if Mao's views were shared by other leaders.

If the time since Mao's death provides any insight, Sino-Soviet differences can no longer be attributed simply to the fixations and suspicions of an aged political leader. While Mao played a pivotal role in the ultimate disintegration of the Moscow-Peking alliance, his successors have yet to judge his actions deleterious to Chinese interests. Contrary to widespread expectations, tensions have not diminished between the two powers. Soviet statements immediately after Mao's death were decidedly low-key and contained tentative, if somewhat vague, overtures to Peking. These included declaratory pledges to seek normalized relations, if not outright accommodation. All went entirely unheeded. Chinese statements promptly and pointedly underscored past pledges to "carry the struggle against Soviet revisionism through to the end." Border negotiations in Peking during late 1976 and early 1977 failed to yield any more positive results than previous sessions undertaken periodically since 1969. No Chinese leader has been willing, at least publicly, to assert or imply a less hostile view of Soviet power and policy. Indeed, recent expressions of official policy and comments to foreign visitors convey an even more insistent denial that long-standing differences may soon be conciliated.

Treating Sino-Soviet relations in highly personalized terms, therefore, seems increasingly inappropriate. While this dimension cannot be overlooked, an undue emphasis on personalities obscures more than it reveals. The long and troubled association between Soviet and Chinese Communists antedates the founding of the People's Republic of China by nearly thirty years. The decade of the 1950s—the period of greatest Soviet influence on Chinese political, economic, and institutional development—left a legacy of bitterness and suspicion whose scars remain. Furthermore, the Soviet Union's progressive emergence during the 1960s and 1970s as a genuine military and economic superpower has troubled many Chinese decision-makers. These factors seem certain to endure well beyond the lifetime of a leader such as Mao, no matter how singular his role might have been. Thus judgment seems all the more valid in view of the increasingly visible challenge to Mao's political legacy in other realms.

Their overtures rejected, the Soviet media and government spokesmen have resumed their verbal attacks, further conceding that China's hostility has not diminished since Mao's death. Moscow and Peking, with momentary lapses, are again engaged in a regular pattern of recrimination and accusation. Even if such polemics ease with the passage of time, neither state can ignore the issues of the past. Their mutual contempt is strongly fixed in the memories and commitments—psychic, political, and organizational—of leaders and bureaucracies in both states.

In such circumstances, what are the probable directions in Sino-Soviet relations over the next decade? Are there no prospects for an amelioration of differences? Are particular issues more amenable to change than others, notwithstanding protestations that no easing of tensions is possible? Should a normalization or quasi-normalization of relations ensue, what are the potential implications for Chinese and Soviet relations with other major powers? Alternatively, will the future approximate the past? If Sino-Soviet relations a decade hence resemble those at present, will they produce even more pronounced political and military realignments in world politics?

This essay will briefly address these questions, focusing primarily on the evolution of Chinese policies. The more detailed attention to the China factor is based on two considerations. First, China's leaders clearly played the more decisive role in breaking the alliance bonds of the 1950s. This is not meant to suggest that policymakers in Peking are necessarily more responsible for Sino-Soviet friction. Any such implication would vastly oversimplify an extraordinarily complex history. Yet, since the Chinese have usually been more active in airing grievances and resisting efforts to overcome them, greater attention to China's role seems justified. Perhaps most importantly, China is clearly in a process of political transition unsettling for both domestic and foreign policy. No matter how one assesses the prospects for Sino-Soviet politics, it is likely that China will more decisively define the future relationship. This essay, however, will assess Sino-Soviet political and military competition and its likely direction in the immediate future rather than attempt specific predictions.

Chinese Views of the Soviet Union

Chinese views of Soviet power and policy have never been uniform. Attention to Soviet policy in one area does not always presuppose a link to other forms of Soviet activity. Thus, any suggestion of possible change or accommodation between China and the Soviet Union must first recognize the variety of forms that the conflict continues to assume.

Among these considerations, three seem the most likely to influence future Sino-Soviet relations. First and foremost is the perception of the Soviet Union as an expansionist global power. Increasingly over the last decade, Chinese spokesmen have considered the Soviet Union the most dynamic power in international politics and hence the most threatening to the security of states in every region of the world. Directly related to this assessment is a belief in the decline and retrenchment of American power. Soviet ambitions have been progressively depicted as insatiable over the past ten years. From the first, their depiction has been closely linked to the evolution of China's broader political and diplomatic strategies. Thus, to describe Soviet intentions as benign would undermine the principal doctrinal underpinning of Peking's growing accommodation with numerous states previously considered anathema by China.

Not all Chinese leaders, however, shared these views. Significant elements within the Chinese leadership have in the past opposed the policy of confrontation with Moscow. Mao's death and the passing of others associated with an avowedly anti-Soviet stance will sharply reduce the constraints on effecting political change. Indeed, major challenges to Mao's overall strategy surfaced on several occasions after the chairman openly diverged from Moscow. In the late 1960s, for example, Lin Piao, minister of defense and Mao's then designated successor, described China's relations with the superpowers as a "dual adversary" relationship. Lin and others apparently considered an increasingly anti-Soviet orientation as unnecessarily provocative, especially in view of the domestic turmoil that continued to plague the nation. He may also have felt that United States policy toward China, even as American involvement in Indochina began to wane, remained predominantly hostile and threatening.

Is it possible that some of China's leaders still view policy in these terms, believing that Chinese security over the past decade has been undermined? While this possibility cannot be dismissed, little evidence substantiates it. Notwithstanding the stagnation in Sino-American relations since the major breakthroughs of the early 1970s, no voices have been raised suggesting that the United States still represents a greater, or even equal, threat to Chinese security.

To be sure, a more even-handed posture vis-à-vis Washington and Moscow would seemingly broaden China's capacity for diplomatic maneuver, conferring greater leverage over both superpowers. Yet two singular facts should not be overlooked. The enhancement of Chinese influence and prestige on a worldwide scale has occurred during the precise period when Chinese policy has been virulently anti-Soviet. Equally important, the depiction of the Soviet Union as China's principal adversary represents more than political hyperbole. The buildup of Soviet capabilities in Asia since the mid-1960s has been a principal element in the overall enhancement of Soviet military power in recent years. Indeed, far from exaggerating the "threat from the North," Chinese analyses continue to assert that primary Soviet ambitions lie elsewhere, most notably in Europe, where the possibilities for encroachment are allegedly far more promising. However one may evaluate such views, a preoccupation with Soviet power has clearly emerged as a decisive element in Chinese diplomatic and military calculations. Should anyone in Peking seek accommodation or normalization in the foreseeable future, the constraint of this pervasive political and military strategy remains. These circumstances do not make change impossible, only more difficult. Serious overtures would surely constitute a contentious issue within the Chinese political process and within the Soviet Union as well.

A broader Chinese critique of Soviet conduct in world politics also limits the prospects for improved relations. Since the early 1960s, Chinese spokesmen have vociferously challenged Soviet claims to preeminence in the Communist world. The terms of this debate have shifted over the past decade and a half. Khrushchev's effort to justify in doctrinal terms his attempts at reconciliation with the West was a principal focus of China's earliest polemics. During the middle and late 1960s, the major Chinese grievance concerned allegations of an emerging great power condominium, aimed at less developed states in general and China in particular. In its more recent guise, the emphasis on a superpower duopoly has been increasingly linked to the broader North-South debate, with the Soviet Union depicted as a major defender of the status quo. Allegations of Soviet exploitation of the third world appear regularly in Chinese commentaries, along with glowing accounts of the efforts of various developing states to combat "the hegemonism of the superpowers," particularly that of the Soviet Union.

All such discussions derive from expressed Chinese beliefs about a global upheaval that has profoundly altered the structure of the postwar international system. According to Chinese analyses, the most significant changes include the dissolution of the socialist camp and the progressive disintegration of the Western bloc. International politics now divides neatly into "three worlds": the United States and the Soviet Union as "the biggest international exploiters and oppressors"; the other developed states "in varying degrees controlled, threatened, or bullied by the one superpower or the other"; and the numerous developing states that "constitute a revolutionary motive force propelling the wheel of world history and the main force combatting colonialism, imperialism, and particularly the superpowers."[1] Not surprisingly, China is identified as a developing country belonging to the third world. Yet this claim cannot be deemed a momentary, tactical justification for China's broader foreign policy strategies. The assumptions inherent in recent Chinese statements—and even some of the specific assertions—have been partially discernible in Chinese analyses since shortly after the end of World War II. Their appearance became far more regular with the decline and dissolution of the European colonial system. Moreover, with China's claim since 1968 of Soviet degeneration into a "social-imperialist country," these views have become more systematic and explicit.

Such categories are no doubt an imperfect guide to Chinese policy, especially given Peking's own accommodation with the United States. Yet the doctrinal and political significance of those beliefs should not be casually dismissed. They clearly embody a core element of what China's leaders consider their "disagreement over principles" with the Soviet Union. To be sure, Peking has drawn a careful distinction between such disputes and the search for normal state-to-state relations. But the former necessarily affect the latter, particularly since Chinese officials continue to insist that such controversies should be aired openly. It is the publicity regularly accorded such views that Soviet officials frequently find so objectionable. Since these beliefs have evolved rather consistently over a long period, any conceivable movement away from them is also likely to take time. Moreover, Chinese policymakers no doubt recognize the considerable political benefits of employing this doctrine. In the absence of an alternative formula, such a conception seems certain to remain a powerful influence in China's foreign policy.

The likelihood of considerable continuity is also apparent at a third level in Chinese perceptions of the Soviet Union—the analysis of the Soviet domestic economy, society, and policy. This was the first sphere of Soviet activity criticized by Mao during the late 1950s. The essential argument is that the world's first socialist state experienced a "retrogression to capitalism" under Khrushchev that has persisted for two full decades. Chinese writers treat the Soviet Union as a decadent system experiencing the periodic and unresolvable contradictions inherent in an advanced capitalist economy. Moreover, internal imperatives are linked to external policy. Frequent analyses in recent years of the Soviet "permanent war economy," with overall investment priorities overwhelmingly skewed toward military needs, constitute substantial and powerful critiques of Soviet internal development.

The virulence of such attacks may be explained by the fact that commentaries on Soviet politics and economics have long been used as an indirect but

---

[1] Teng Hsiao-p'ing, "Chairman of Delegation of People's Republic of China Teng Hsiao-p'ing's Speech at Special Session of U.N. General Assembly," *Peking Review*, supplement to no. 15 (April 12, 1974), p. 2.

vital means of political debate within China. Depicting Liu Shao-ch'i, the most prominent victim of the Cultural Revolution, as "China's Khrushchev" is an example of this tendency. The issue of how a socialist state should be governed and managed is a continuing question for decision-makers, with the Soviet Union constituting what the Chinese term a "teacher by negative example."

These analyses also reveal an ongoing concern about residual Soviet influence over political, organizational, and economic activity within China. Vast numbers of young, educated Chinese were trained under Soviet tutelage during the 1950s; their memories of Soviet advisory and technical assistance may in some cases be far more favorable than those of many Chinese leaders. Chinese claims to self-reliance notwithstanding, the Soviet contribution to China's industrial, economic, and military modernization was enormous. Despite Mao's determined efforts, some of China's leaders may yet remain enamored of Soviet technology and approaches to development. Thus, with Mao's death and the political demise of a circle of dogmatic associates, the prospect of creeping revisionism within China has become more plausible. Greatly increased attention to the task of modernizing China, especially the emphasis again devoted to education and to science and technology, is simply the most visible form this political reassessment has already assumed.

Yet there is no certainty that any such political change will necessarily result in a more positive attitude toward the Soviet Union. While Soviet writers yearn for a return to the 1950s, when "healthy internationalist forces" held sway in the Chinese Communist Party (CCP), the present leaders continue to look elsewhere for broadened political, military, and economic relations. China now has alternative sources of supply for its pressing technological and economic needs. Moreover, dependence on sources in Western Europe, Japan, and the United States does not involve the risk of political concessions inherent in China's previous status as the junior, needy member of the Sino-Soviet alliance.

China and the Soviet Union are now rivals, not partners. The fact that certain conditions existed in the 1950s in no way ensures that they can now be reconstituted. These facts must surely be recognized by those Chinese advocating a more balanced, considered view of the Soviet role during the 1950s. China's new leaders may rapidly distance themselves from the policies associated with Mao. But the political beliefs they espouse and the doctrinal revisions these may entail are unlikely to concede much in terms of the polemics of the past two decades.

Soviet Views of China

Also relevant to this discussion is the extent to which Soviet views might contribute to a redirection in the overall relationship. Are Soviet officials similarly mortgaged to the past? A brief summary provides little grounds for expecting substantial accommodation. To be sure, several recent statements have cited pledges from Leonid I. Brezhnev at the Twenty-fifth Congress of the Communist Party of the Soviet Union and the October 1976 party plenum that "the Soviet Union is striving to improve relations with China as our consistent cause. . . . In our opinion, there are no issues . . . that could not be resolved in the spirit of good-neighborliness." Such pledges, however, have always been based on the belief that the Soviet Union bears no responsibility for the conflict and that accommodation must therefore be based on unilateral concessions from Peking. As a result, these declarations lack any substantive meaning and have yielded no practical results.

Far more prevalent in Soviet assessments is a vision of China equally as alarmist as that which Peking applies to Moscow. Soviet views, however, are not a simple mirror image of Chinese perspectives. Chinese statements retain an essential optimism that the Soviet Union is simply the most recent "paper tiger" on the world stage, and (provided others do not fear it) doomed to ultimate failure and decline. Equivalent optimism is not shared in Soviet writings, which speak forebodingly of a country whose leaders irrationally continue to welcome the prospect of nuclear war. China's determination to pursue a "nationalistic, great power, militarist course," these sources contend, is intended both "to undermine international détente and exacerbate the situation in the world as much as possible," thereby serving "the forces of anticommunism and reaction." Moreover, these tenets are not deemed a short-term proposition but rather a "long-term programmatic aim." Those in the West who take comfort in China's anti-Soviet stance, they further argue, fail to recognize that Chinese power will ultimately be turned against others as well. As a major Soviet commentary recently warned:

It should not be forgotten that China is now the only country in the world whose official circles publicly act as undisguised apologists for world carnage. Moreover, the policy of preparing for war is recorded in black and white in the new Constitution . . . a unique manifesto of overt militarism. Those who are bewitched by Peking's anti-Soviet incantations ought to evaluate its policy more soberly . . . .

It would be an unforgivable error to adopt a passive position with respect to Peking's reckless policy and to wait until the danger has increased to disastrous dimensions. All those who hold peace dear and who want to engage tranquilly in creative labor must aim their efforts together at exposing and suppressing the the[se] extremely dangerous schemes and actions. . . .[2]

Such assessments make clear that the Soviet Union's China problem is a long-term one, not a passing concern that will be easily resolved. As the above quotation implies, the measures required to deal with the China issue could be military as well as political. Whether the above quotation constitutes a serious appeal for reviving what the Chinese in the late 1960s termed "an anti-China holy alliance" remains unclear. At a minimum, however, Soviet analyses view China as both a political and a military challenge requiring urgent attention.

Indeed, it may well be that the Soviet officials are most troubled by the

[2] I. Aleksandrov, "Peking: A Course Toward Wrecking International Detente Under the Guise of Anti-Sovietism," *Pravda*, May 14, 1977, trans. in Foreign Broadcast Information Service, *Daily Report—Soviet Union*, May 16, 1977, pp. C4, 6.

political threat posed by China among the more independently minded Communist states, in international organizations, vis-à-vis the West, and in the third world. After achieving in the early 1970s the long-sought political recognition ratifying the postwar division of Europe, Soviet leaders view China (in concert with other "wreckers of détente") as determined to undermine such accomplishments. No matter what the chosen arena, China is certain actively to oppose Soviet objectives. With China having finally achieved its own diplomatic breakthrough in the early 1970s, culminating in near-universal recognition, Peking's international role and voice can no longer be deemed negligible. Thus, Soviet writers argue, a "wait and see" Soviet attitude seems certain to do more harm than good.

If any grounds for long-term optimism exist, they appear rooted in a perception of domestic turbulence in China that to a considerable extent matches Chinese views of Soviet internal difficulties. According to this view, the burdens of an allegedly militarized society and economy will ultimately prove so overwhelming that the long-suffering "Chinese people" may yet demand change. The implied instrument of such change are elements within the Chinese Communist Party (CCP) supposedly opposed to the grand design underlying Chinese strategy. The presumption of an alternative path to China's industrialization and modernization remains evident in Soviet discussions. No matter how distant this prospect might presently appear, it seems the long-term hope implicit in Soviet commentaries. Moreover, it enables Soviet policymakers to remain comfortable in the belief that it is China, not the Soviet Union, that must discard its dogmatic beliefs and policies. To the extent that this perspective pervades Soviet analyses, leaders in the Soviet Union seem highly unlikely to search seriously for new, more creative approaches to the China issue.

The present perspectives adopted by leaders in both states, therefore, leave little ground for encouragement. In neither country do policymakers seem able or willing to define Sino-Soviet relations on any basis other than more of the same. Moreover, it is not only such negative beliefs and hostile declaratory policies that must be overcome. During the past decade the Sino-Soviet conflict has been extended into the military sphere. What do trends in this realm suggest about the future?

The Strategic Equation

Nothing more vividly conveys the seriousness with which Chinese and Soviet elites perceive their mutual rivalry than the military strength they deploy against each other. While most attention has focused on the confrontation of ground and air forces, particularly around China's northeastern borders, both nuclear and naval capabilities also contribute to the overall military balance. In this context three questions are critical. How extensive are current deployments, and how important are these forces in Chinese and Soviet defense planning?

What trends are discernible in the development of Chinese nuclear doctrine and capabilities, and to what extent might these forces offset the Soviet nuclear threat in the 1980s? Finally, how might China's emergence as a nuclear power affect the future of strategic arms control?

Notwithstanding continued public insistence that Chinese military policy remains based on a doctrine of a people's war, it is clear that China's senior commanders are prepared for a very different form of conflict. The transfer of front-line divisions to disputed border areas during the early 1970s indicates that Chinese commanders do not intend to yield key industrial and urban concentrations without significant resistance. Approximately two-thirds of China's infantry divisions are presently deployed in the Shenyang and Peking Military Regions, i.e., the locales opposite the regions where Soviet forces are concentrated. While the deficiencies of these forces in mobility, firepower, and antitank capabilities are well established, the willingness of Chinese commanders to commit large numbers of their best troops to such operations is indisputable.

In addition, nearly half of China's 5,000 fighter-aircraft are committed to air defense operations against Soviet forces.[3] While these aircraft are based almost exclusively on Soviet technology transferred to China in the late 1950s and early 1960s, these deployment patterns provide incontestable evidence of the centrality of the Soviet conventional threat to Chinese defense planning. Additional regular and irregular forces would also be mobilized in the event of a full-scale war. Moreover, discussions in the Chinese press over the past year have made it clear that China's readiness to withstand a Soviet ground-air attack is now a central preoccupation among those responsible for national security. No more concrete evidence could possibly attest to the shift in Chinese perceptions of external threat over the past decade than the deployment of these forces.

The disposition of Soviet forces is also revealing. Approximately forty-five divisions, seven of them armored, are stationed in Soviet military districts in central and East Asia, quadruple their strength of a decade ago. In Eastern Europe, all Soviet units are at full or near-full strength, but only one-third of the forces deployed against China are presently maintained at full ("Category One") combat readiness. Nevertheless, their mobility and offensive striking power are awesome. Backed by substantial tactical nuclear capabilities and nearly a thousand combat aircraft (including squadrons of SU-19s, MIG-23s, and MIG-25s), Soviet conventional forces clearly pose a substantial threat to China's northern provinces.[4]

Soviet strategic deployments against China, while not as substantial, are

[3] U.S., Congress, House, Subcommittee on Future Foreign Policy, Research and Development of the Committee on International Relations, *United States—Soviet Union—China: The Great Power Triangle*, 94th Cong., 1976, p. 184.

[4] *The Military Balance, 1977-1978* (London: International Institute for Strategic Studies, 1976), pp. 9-10; Russell Spurr, "Ivan's Arms Around Manchuria," *Far Eastern Economic Review* 98 (January 28, 1977), p. 26.

hardly insignificant. Approximately 200 SS-4 and SS-5 intermediate range missiles with one-megaton warheads are deployed in Siberia; an additional 200 SS-9 intercontinental range missiles purportedly equipped with twenty-five-megaton warheads are located in hardened silos somewhat farther to the west. Significant numbers of Soviet long-range aircraft, including initial deployments of the Backfire bomber, have been noted in the Soviet Far East along with reports of the SS-X-20 mobile IRBM. More than three dozen ballistic missile-firing submarines are also stationed in nearby Pacific waters.[5] Although some of these forces are not intended for use against China, the Soviet Union has the capacity to plan and execute a wide array of nuclear options—tactical, countercity, and counterforce—should a major war occur.

Even so, the Soviet military effort in Asia has limits. The ground force buildup was basically completed by the end of 1972. Similarly, the preponderance of Soviet air power has now been in place for nearly a half-decade. Qualitative improvements, while significant, have been gradual. The military buildup of the past decade leaves Soviet forces at a clear advantage. It is on the basis of this heavily armed truce that the Chinese decision-makers have argued that a Sino-Soviet war will be deterred, so long as principal Soviet interests remain concentrated on Europe rather than Asia.

These conclusions hold with even greater force for the growth of Soviet naval capabilities. The upgrading of the Soviet Pacific Fleet (in nonstrategic systems) has not been intended principally for contingencies involving China. Soviet forces pose a far more immediate challenge to the mission of the United States Seventh Fleet in maintaining control over the sea lanes to Japan. Indeed, compared to the Northern and Black Sea Fleets, the Soviet Union's naval forces in the Pacific retain a distinctly lower priority. Only in recent years has the Pacific Fleet begun to demonstrate a significant oceangoing capability.

The Chinese navy remains almost exclusively a coastal defense force. Although its capabilities have expanded significantly in the last half-dozen years, various technological limitations in support systems, antisubmarine warfare capabilities, firepower, and the like, continue to confine its missions. Although recent discussions have alluded to a Soviet naval presence in Chinese waters, the navy's principal concerns lie elsewhere—for example, in asserting sovereignty over various sea islands in the South China Sea and control over ocean resources. Thus, naval deployments are not presently a major area of Sino-Soviet military competition. Short of the development of a Chinese blue water capability, a prospect that remains distant, China and the Soviet Union seem unlikely to extend their rivalry to the sea.

How significant and how costly, then, might the China threat be for Soviet defense planning? The available information on this question is far from satisfactory. Former Secretary of Defense Donald H. Rumsfeld has estimated the

---

[5] *The Military Balance, 1977-1978*; Spurr; and R.D.M. Furlong, "China's Evolving National Security Requirements," *International Defense Review* 9 (August 1976): 558.

average costs of the China-oriented forces as "about 11 percent of the total Russian military budget between 1964 and 1976." His estimate, however, excluded any expenditures for strategic forces.[6] An equally controversial issue concerns the portion of the reported growth in Soviet military deployments attributable to the China factor.Without question, military needs along the China border have claimed a significant share of recent increases in the Soviet ground force strength and tactical air capabilities. In other respects (most notably, spending for the strategic forces), however, China is presently a far less important consideration.

Many of these assessments are shrouded in ambiguity. For example, not all Soviet missiles in the Far East are deployed against Chinese targets. Similarly, the vast and highly sophisticated air defense system in Soviet Asia is only partially concerned with a hypothetical Chinese attack, since large numbers of American bombers would use these routes in a large-scale strategic assault against the Soviet Union. The controversy in the United States over Soviet interest in civil defense measures, however, has largely neglected Soviet fears of an irrational Chinese attack as a possible explanation for continued interest in this issue.

While the need to maintain substantial forces on two fronts causes undoubted complications for Soviet planners, in other respects it may present an opportunity. To the extent that Chinese defense planning continues to focus almost exclusively on the Soviet Union, Moscow can assert that the China factor both explains and justifies an expanded Soviet defense effort. Politburo adviser Georgi Arbatov has alluded to this consideration: "How can one mechanically compare the USSR with the United States? America is separated from the rest of the world by two oceans and has neighbors . . . which are friendly, and militarily nonhostile countries. But the USSR armed forces must defend immense lengths of land frontiers bordering not just on friendly states."[7] If the Chinese expand their defense effort, as recent hints suggest they may, one may ask whether Soviet policymakers will feel impelled to match those improvements. Far more than at present, leaders in Moscow may then have to confront fundamental choices about the continued capacity of the Soviet armed forces and defense industries to match major adversaries on two fronts.

Moreover, such competition may increasingly involve more than Soviet air and ground forces. A potential problem is the further development of China's nuclear deterrent. Its role in the strategic nuclear balance has thus far been negligible. Although China first tested a nuclear device in 1964 and a thermonuclear device less than three years later, the deployment of missiles and bombers has been far slower than originally anticipated. Present delivery systems consist of approximately thirty to forty IRBMs, thirty to forty MRBMs, and eighty TU-16 intermediate bombers. Other aircraft—even older IL-28

[6] U.S., Department of Defense, *Annual Defense Department Report—FY 1978* (Washington, D.C.: GPO, 1977), p. 26.

[7] G. Arbatov, "The Great Lie of the Opponents of Detente," *Pravda*, February 5, 1977, trans. in Foreign Broadcast Information Service, *Daily Report—Soviet Union*, February 7, 1977, p. B3.

medium bombers and F-9 fighter bombers—may to a limited extent supplement these forces.[8] Indeed, these aggregate force levels have remained virtually constant since 1973. Still undeployed, though reportedly under development, are either a sea-launched ballistic missile or a limited-range, multistage ICBM purportedly test-fired as early as 1970. Very small numbers of the latter system, however, may now be operational. The potential vulnerability of present systems—particularly the liquid-fuel, soft-site missiles deployed principally across China's northernmost provinces—remains an enormous problem. Chinese planners have sought to reduce this problem by efforts at dispersal, camouflage, and mobility, and by deploying missiles in small clusters. A few may be deployed in silos, and some are known to be hidden in mountainous locations, such as Tibet. All such measures are designed to reduce the confidence of any first-strike calculations of Soviet military planners. When combined with widespread measures aimed at industrial and military dispersal, China's existing nuclear forces seem to be capable of deterring any preemptive nuclear attack.

It is far from certain whether all Chinese military planners remain agreed on the sufficiency or reliability of such capabilities. For the present, however, the rudimentary nature of China's nuclear forces has necessarily confined Peking's nuclear doctrine to a posture of finite deterrence. Despite occasional discussions of the role of tactical nuclear weapons, Chinese discussions of nuclear strategy, both in internal and external communications, have stressed the need to constrain severely the circumstances under which such weaponry might be employed. A continued denigration of nuclear weapons as an instrument of warfare remains evident in Chinese analyses. Moreover, the strategic weapons program represents only one of China's pressing security needs, with no certainty that it any longer takes precedence over various "middle range" defense options.

The erratic nature of deployment patterns during the 1970s, the uncertainties of the resource allocation process, and the limited nature of Chinese discussions of nuclear strategy and doctrine complicate any straight-line projections of the extent and nature of Chinese nuclear deployments. The Chinese program may well remain a modest one, geared principally to securing a far less vulnerable deterrent. For the present, this seems the most likely outcome. But if an accelerated development should occur (for example, the acquisition of a full-range ICBM), China's nuclear program may also be viewed as threatening states other than the Soviet Union.

For the foreseeable future, the Soviet Union is the only nuclear power that must actively prepare for nuclear contingencies involving more than a single state. At present, however, the China factor remains a subsidiary element in these calculations. The point at which Chinese forces might occupy a more central role in Soviet nuclear planning remains conjectural. In the absence of a genuine breakthrough in the Chinese program—for example, acquisition

---

[8] *The Military Balance, 1977-1978*, p. 53.

of cruise missile technology—Peking's overall strategic effort will remain too modest and vulnerable to necessitate a substantial redirection in Soviet allocations. Thus it appears that most, if not all, Soviet missiles targeted against China derive from older systems of lesser range.

However modest they might be, Chinese nuclear forces play a role in strategic and arms control calculations. The "China factor" in the Strategic Arms Limitation Talks (SALT) has until now been manifested by Peking's unwillingness to participate in any nuclear arms control forum under the aegis of the superpowers. Chinese spokesmen continue volubly to criticize present conceptions of arms control, which are based heavily on the SALT negotiations. Independent of Chinese objections, the quantitative and qualitative disparities between Peking's nuclear forces and those of both superpowers make Chinese participation at SALT wholly unnecessary. To the extent that these disparities continue to prevail, China can plausibly maintain its isolation from these negotiations.

China, however, has already been introduced *in absentia* to the negotiating process. In the SALT II deliberations prior to the Vladivostok meeting, Soviet officials initially "insisted that the American total [of delivery vehicles] include nuclear-capable aircraft in and around Europe as well as British, French, and Chinese nuclear forces."[9] While Soviet arguments subsequently eased, such a negotiating tactic will become increasingly plausible over time. Even if China's capability remains entirely regional, such a contention will carry weight so long as Peking's forces are oriented exclusively toward the Soviet Union. Should Chinese military planners ultimately decide to deploy even a minimal force of full-range ICBMs, the decision will further complicate what is already an exceedingly complex negotiating process. Thus, China's role in strategic arms control will increase over time, whether or not it participates in actual negotiations.

Toward the 1980s

Over the past fifteen years, the Sino-Soviet rivalry has become a virtual fixture in contemporary world politics. The polemics of the early 1960s, never taken wholly seriously in the West, were in retrospect evidence of the gravity of the disputes. However, it was only with the open militarization of the conflict in the late 1960s that its intensity and durability were fully grasped. While the probability of large-scale military conflict now seems diminished, the prospects for a major reduction in tensions remain slight.

Neither state, to be sure, is wholly impervious to external influence. Changes in American relations with both powers have clearly affected their opportunities for diplomatic maneuver and helped set limits on either state's ability to use military force against the other. Explicit expressions of American neutrality and disapproval of a prospective border war in 1969 helped restrain whatever

[9] Leslie H. Gelb, "How U.S. Made Ready for Talk at Vladivostok," *New York Times*, December 3, 1974.

inclination some Soviet officials might have had to launch a preemptive strike against China. But the dispute continues to fester. Neither elite feels impelled to seek accommodation with its rival as a result of United States policy. Domestic constraints in both systems, therefore, seem more pivotal in impeding meaningful change than any unsettled international circumstances.

Even more basically, an issue so central to Chinese politics for the past three decades—indeed, for China's entire revolutionary experience—is unlikely to undergo sudden or decisive change for tactically expedient reasons. The Sino-Soviet relationship must be judged on the terms that the principals themselves have defined for it. Many of these considerations will probably remain as strongly felt in a decade as they do now. Thus, to focus exclusively on the military and strategic element of the rivalry obscures the broader basis of the conflict. Historical constraints will also inhibit whatever modest efforts might be made to bridge the chasm separating both leaderships.

The expectation of substantial continuities, however, does not necessarily imply that the future will wholly resemble the past. History abounds with examples of long-term adversaries who suddenly find their political interests converging, often in unanticipated ways. The quasi-normalization of Sino-American relations is an obvious example of this phenomenon. When and how might past hostilities be eased, and with what political consequences? Would normalization of relations necessarily require resolution of the broader spectrum of Sino-Soviet differences? And how would such change be likely to affect the political realignments evident in international politics during the past decade?

Answers to these questions depend principally on the circumstances under which a hypothetical Sino-Soviet accommodation might transpire. The first possibility, and the most conjectural, concerns the long-term political and economic evolution of China. The rapidity with which major new directions have already been charted in post-Mao China suggests that pledges of fealty to previous policies can quickly become empty slogans. China's economic transformation need not require justification based on threats from abroad. Some Chinese leaders may already prefer that the goal of comprehensive modernization, now enshrined in the new CCP constitution, be justified on a basis other than the imperatives of the international situation. And some may ultimately believe that this enormous task will be more rapidly and efficiently accomplished if the scope of Sino-Soviet economic, technological, and managerial interaction is significantly widened. Of course, such changes would require a corresponding adjustment of political doctrine.

Thus the consequences of a lessened obsession with the Soviet Union might well be felt more in China's domestic politics than in its foreign policy. Whether this possibility would markedly affect the broader Sino-Soviet relationship depends on two additional questions. First, would changes in Chinese internal politics and development strategies be perceived by the Soviet leaders as requiring a shift in their China policy? And would an avowedly revisionist political system be more susceptible to resurgent Soviet influence?

Answers to these questions are far from certain. Moreover, they concern issues that may not emerge fully for decades to come. The more appropriate focus is on Sino-Soviet politics during the next ten years. Does a political constituency potentially supportive of such internal changes now exist within the Chinese leadership? For the present, the answer appears to be no. Current policies remain based on the felt need to enhance Chinese economic and military power in order better to confront a potent and threatening external adversary. This belief is conveyed in different ways by disparate political interests. A change in this overall policy may well require leaders whose rememberance of and involvement in the conflict is less direct and personal. This prospect, therefore, extends beyond the 1980s. Are there more limited actions that might be anticipated in the near future, ones that do not require dramatic readjustment across the spectrum of known differences?

This question speaks directly to a second possibility, a mutual recognition of the benefits of reduced military tensions. As noted earlier, Peking and Moscow have separately indicated their readiness to normalize state-to-state relations. Leaders in both states have cited various formulas for peaceful coexistence, which could apply irrespective of more basic political and ideological incompatibilities. Thus the possibility of such an agreement cannot be ruled out. Surely some Chinese must question the wisdom of indefinitely prolonging the polemics of the past fifteen years. Soviet officials, for their part, have frequently indicated their willingness to reciprocate any such restraint.

Yet how meaningful would any such declaration actually be? It seems virtually inconceivable that a genuinely substantive agreement could be reached without concrete arms control measures preceding its enactment. Soviet negotiators in the border talks have indicated their willingness to sign treaties on the nonuse of force and related agreements intended to reduce the risks of war. Chinese participants, however, refuse to accept such proposals. They argue that a guarantee would be credible only if coordinated with visible restraints in the deployment of forces, including a mutual pullback of forces from disputed territories. They further contend that Soviet officials no longer even acknowledge that specific territories are subject to dispute or negotiated settlement. As Soviet spokesmen argue, however, any such acknowledgement or pullback of forces would imply a degree of validity for Chinese territorial claims—a concession that the Soviet Union is not now prepared to make.

Thus the perennial dilemmas inherent in the search for meaningful arms control also pertain in the Sino-Soviet case. An alternative possibility is the implementation of tacit measures of arms limitation. Restraints on the introduction of specific types of weaponry and force configurations in order to prevent serious or sustained offensive operations might have some appeal, whether undertaken by unilateral action or by mutual consent.

For the present, however, the prospects for such restraints appear bleak. As discussed above, Soviet deployments in Asia suggest active preparations for a range of conflict situations, both nuclear and nonnuclear. These include a clear capacity to launch blitzkrieg warfare against China's northeastern provinces—

hardly the type of deployment designed to convey nonthreatening intentions to Chinese military commanders. The further upgrading of offensive and defensive capabilities in recent years and continued construction work on the Baikal-Amur Railway suggest planning for the long term, not some momentary or incremental accretion to Soviet military strength. All of these actions, moreover, have been undertaken against an enemy wholly lacking the capacity to engage in a serious offensive assault. They further reveal the depth of Soviet fears about supposed Chinese irrationality and obliviousness to the risks and costs of war.

Any assessment of Chinese willingness to consider tacit arms control measures must acknowledge one essential fact: Chinese deployments during a decade of acute military tension have conveyed their readiness for such measures. Even in the vital Shenyang and Peking Military Regions, the Chinese military posture has remained defensive. In other vulnerable areas, such as the Ili Valley in Sinkiang Uighur, China seems even less prepared to blunt a Soviet assault. At present, therefore, Chinese main ground force units are not deployed to meet enemy forces in a forward defense mode.

To be sure, the restraints in China's military deployments may reflect necessity rather than choice. Even though Chinese commanders may prefer a more assertive posture, they remain wholly incapable of implementing one. With China's "gang of four" now accused of impeding China's preparedness for war and with the most visible concern in two decades for military modernization, the task of upgrading Chinese defense capabilities is a principal item on the political and economic agenda. The issue of Chinese preparedness for a possible Soviet ground-air assault has been identified as among the most pressing of these needs. It is wholly implausible that China's principal decision-makers, including a striking number of senior military officials, will indefinitely defer the upgrading of such deficiencies. Soviet policymakers having failed to reciprocate past Chinese restraint, the prospects for tacit measures' succeeding in the foreseeable future must be regarded as exceedingly slim. Here as elsewhere, the constraints of the past seem certain to make the quest for meaningful accommodation difficult, not only between Peking and Moscow, but also within both capitals.

If the political will and requisite conditions to reduce tensions seem conspicuously lacking in both states, what are the possibilities of forcing accommodation on Soviet and Chinese elites? That is, are there any foreseeable circumstances that would compel elements in both leaderships, however reluctantly, to bridge the enormous differences now separating them?

The most plausible prospect—quite possibly the only plausible prospect—would be the reactivation of American military behavior in East Asia in a manner that directly threatened both Chinese and Soviet security interests. One issue that might have this potential would be a resumption of warfare on the Korean peninsula. In view of the explicit commitments of China, the Soviet Union, and the United States to the opposed Korean states, a major conflict could rapidly result in external military involvement. Renewed warfare would in no sense assure Sino-Soviet cooperation. However, it would severely undermine a central premise governing Chinese foreign policy during the 1970s—the belief that the United States no longer poses a military threat to Peking. Heightened Chinese-American frictions over Korea would necessarily distract Chinese attention from the Soviet Union, thereby complicating foreign policy calculations in Peking. This possibility alone surely accounts for Chinese wariness about renewed warfare in Korea.

The absence of an American threat, then, has enabled Chinese policymakers to concentrate on the Soviet challenge. No matter what the strains and limits of China's "United States connection," it will not be cast aside lightly. Even a marked deterioration in Sino-American relations would not directly affect the future of Sino-Soviet ties. Chinese and Soviet elites continue to share a long-term obsession about containing one another's power and influence. The creativity and even statesmanship required to overcome this pervasive constraint seems notably lacking in both capitals. Indeed, the forms of their present conflict make even short-term, tactical adjustments difficult to arrange. Given such circumstances, this long and bitter rivalry seems unlikely to diminish soon or suddenly.

This essay was written under a fellowship from the Conflict in International Relations Program of the Rockefeller Foundation, whose support the author gratefully acknowledges.

An Evaluation of the Soviet Navy

G.E. MILLER

Much has been published in recent years on the expanding Soviet naval threat, which has been diversely viewed according to the source and motivation of the writer. Although the intelligence community reviews the subject in depth, charges are often made that parochial interests dictate the conclusions reached and that the impact of the threat assessment on the budget for an individual organization largely determines the nature of the threat perceived by that organization. Retired intelligence officers sound the alarm and the press publishes their statements, but again their motives are questioned. Are they sincere, informed, and really concerned about the facts, or are their conclusions the result of parochial interests and a desire to remain in the limelight, to be a part of the action?

Various think tanks analyze the data, attempting to reach conclusions. Most defense studies conducted by such organizations start with some version of the threat as a basis for their research, but what versions of the threat do they accept or decide upon? It is sometimes contended that since many think tanks are profit-making corporations, they are inclined to accept the version of the threat that will be most significant in shaping the answer that they hope the study will produce. As one wag has put it, "How can you produce an objective study without knowing the objective?" The version of the threat that is used in the basic assumptions of the study will have considerable impact on the results.

There are also various institutes, committees, and professional arms codifiers that publish detailed technical data, followed by their conclusions as to what the data represent in terms of a total threat. Their numbers are usually accurate, but the significance of their conclusions depends on the qualifications of the individuals making them.

Arms manufacturers and other elements of the business community frequently become involved in developing versions of the Soviet naval threat. It is sometimes charged that the version they advance is one that happens to match an operational combat capability they have developed. Again their motives are questioned, and the threat is suspect.

Nor is the Congress immune from this syndrome. Often the version of the

Soviet threat accepted by individual members is determined to some degree by the impact that version will have on the region and the constituency they represent. If there is no defense related industry in their particular area of interest, the charge is made that the version of the threat they consider valid is the one that requires the least financial expenditures for defense.

Academics analyzing intelligence data are frequently hampered by a lack of information resulting from security constraints. But it is often contended that the views they accept and the conclusions they reach are influenced more by their philosophies than by a lack of information. So their versions are suspect.

In yet another area, the press is often accused of looking for the bad news first and being overeager to publish what will attract attention. Newsmen make forays into the field to see for themselves. As a result of this short exposure, the actual version they transmit may depend on the nature of the people with whom they associated as well as the views of their publishers.

The military commander on active duty, charged with being prepared to counter the threat, listens, analyzes, applies his military judgment, and arrives at a conclusion. He develops his own version of the threat, but he is also constrained, often by the civil authority to whom he must be responsive. His version may be influenced by his future career interests. Also, it must be admitted that sometimes his version, though sincere, may be biased by some unique experience of his past. He may see only what he wants to see. So his version is sometimes suspect. (Naturally, the perceived integrity of an officer improves after he retires.)

The version of the threat accepted by the leaders of the administration in power is sometimes influenced by the promises made during the election campaign. If the president came into office on a platform that promised to reduce the defense budget, it is reasonable to assume that the version of the Soviet naval threat his administration accepts is something less than that of a president elected on a platform proposing an increase in the defense budget.

The books and articles of the Soviets about their capabilities have considerable effect on the perceived threat. But can those writings be trusted? What are the motives of the authors? Is Admiral Sergei G. Gorshkov, the head of the Soviet navy, writing for the NATO intelligence community, his own navy, or the leaders in the Kremlin? Does he believe what he says, or is he embarking on a sales campaign for seapower in his own country and embellishing the data in order to make his points?

Finally, one comes to the data used in the threat analysis process. An author can produce bomber gaps, missile gaps, ship gaps, fighter gaps, tonnage gaps, almost any gap desired, depending on the quality of the raw intelligence that is available. Here again, the professional analysts have considerable influence on the outcome. Their versions can vary because of the realistic restrictions in their profession and the quality of the intelligence they are asked to study. There is bound to be some guesswork involved, not all of which can be accurate.

So what is the layman or even the professional policymaker to believe? How real is the Soviet naval threat? One could draw an analogy to a professional football contest. The preseason press always contains elaborate analyses of the threats, predictions, and opinions from experts, many of whom never played football, but the real answer must emerge from the actual contest on a Sunday afternoon. Similarly, the only valid way to get a true picture of the Soviet threat would be to engage in a real-life contest. Since that is obviously out of the question, it is better to continue the debate, regardless of the motives of the debaters, and to publish the results in the hope that laymen and policymakers will have enough information to make up their own minds.

The following comments are offered in that vein. They are the views of the author, a combat commander, who has experienced in some depth the process of determining how best to fight the Soviet navy in the event of hostilities. The experiences were not theoretical exercises but the result of real-life responsibilities as the commander of the United States Second Fleet in the Atlantic and the United States Sixth Fleet in the Mediterranean. It is not contended that the conclusions are completely valid. They are no better than the data available, coupled with the abilities, experience, and judgment of the commander involved. The conclusions may be unique in that not many commanders in the history of the United States Navy have had the firsthand responsibility for seriously considering the procedures and techniques to be used in waging combat against the Soviets at sea. These conclusions, added to the multitude of opinions on the subject, may help those interested to reach their own conclusions.

In analyzing the data on the Soviet naval threat, each operational commander has his own particular technique and background, but the basic factors under consideration will not vary much from commander to commander. They might differ in order of priority and be influenced by such items as the potential location of the engagement, allied support available, and readiness of assets.

Quantity and Quality of Soviet Naval Forces

Most analyses of the Soviet navy would consider the quality of its ships. There is no question that the Soviet navy has a considerable number of cruisers, destroyers, and smaller combatants. They are in evidence throughout the world in sufficient strength to warrant attention and concern. The real issue, however, centers on their capabilities to wage a successful combat operation.

The Soviet surface combatant ship in general is relatively new, quite maneuverable, impressive in appearance, and seaworthy. It is relatively fast and well armed, primarily with defensive weapons systems. The armament and the high speed capabilities require compromises in other areas. Consequently, there is a limited amount of reload capability for the armament. Living conditions and supplies are also relatively limited. Some evidence indicates that ship construction is considerably below United States standards. Soviet ships should sink rather rapidly if hit. In addition, the armament of these ships is heavily dependent on electronics. It is not necessary to sink a ship in order to negate the major features of its combat capability. All that is required is to take counter-measures against the electronics systems, and American forces have a con-siderable capability to do that.

One aspect that should be considered is the antisubmarine warfare (ASW) capability of these ships and the Soviet navy in general. While they use the standard hull-mounted sonars, helicopters with dipping sonars, and fixed-wing aircraft with sonar buoys, they are seriously handicapped by not having any large fixed sonar arrays on the bottom of the oceans. Of course, even the United States does not have such arrays in some parts of the world, like the Mediterranean and the Indian Ocean, but the Soviet capability must suffer from that deficiency. The overall ASW capability of the Soviet navy must be considered weak, at least in relation to that of the United States and its allies.

The smaller combatants, such as the surface-to-surface missile carrying patrol boats, have proven to be effective for close-in fighting under ten miles, but they are effective only in relatively smooth seas and in coastal areas. They can be negated easily with one good strafing attack from an airplane. They cannot be considered a great threat against American naval forces, unless some gross tactical errors are made in countering them. On balance, then, the Soviet surface-ship threat is impressive. It warrants attention and respect, but it can be defeated rather easily under most conditions.

Of considerably more significance is the Soviet submarine force. The nuclear powered submarines equipped with nuclear armed ballistic missiles are most formidable. The missiles have a very long range and the accuracy is certainly sufficient to cause the destruction of a great many lives and much property. There are sufficient numbers of them to ensure that they are a real threat. Further, the American ability to negate them, while probably superior to their ability to negate America's, is still of such limited capability that they must surely be considered as the primary threat of the Soviet navy.

The Soviet attack submarine program—that is, submarines designed to destroy American ships and submarines—is also a most impressive force and will give the combat commander his greatest problems. These submarines come in several versions, the most impressive being those that are nuclear powered and equipped with short-ranged, surface-to-surface missiles. They can operate long distances from home, run quietly and deep, and have excellent speed. They can be defeated under certain conditions, but that ability is disappearing as their numbers increase and as technological improvements are added.

One version of the Soviet attack submarine that is sometimes overlooked is an older type, using diesel-electric propulsion. These have many deficiencies: slow speed, particularly when submerged, shallow depth, and a requirement for some kind of tender or "mother ship" support near their scene of operations. They are equipped only with torpedoes for armament, but the danger they pose lies in their ability to remain very quiet once on station. They are most difficult to detect when submerged. They are to be found around restricted passages such as the Strait of Gibraltar, the Sicilian straits, and so on. They will not be much of a threat in open waters or far from home, but great care must be taken in certain areas.

Of even greater concern is the quantity of the Soviet attack submarine force. While the United States probably could achieve a most enviable record in one-on-one engagements, the Soviets have an ability to saturate the American countering capability through sheer numbers alone. If there is any part of the Soviet naval threat that must be considered a real threat, it is the submarine force.

A good deal has been said about the entry of Soviet aviation into the sea-based programs. The two early Soviet carriers, under 20,000 tons displacement, and the newest one at about 45,000 tons have some impressive characteristics and indicate an appreciation of the value of sea-based air. Twenty years from now it may be most formidable, but the current capability is vulnerable. The ships, particularly those of smaller size, look top-heavy and are not stable in heavy seas. They are a fair-weather force. Even the new carrier of 45,000 tons has limitations in that regard. Although the armament is impressive in terms of engineering and design, it can be negated. The embarked aircraft, principally helicopters, are excellent but are confined primarily to the role of locating submarines. The new fixed-wing, vertical take-off aircraft, the YAK-36, has been impressively described and is an interesting start for the Soviets in fixed-wing, sea-based airpower. However, there is really no viable threat yet in any navy from vertical take-off aircraft. Technology has yet to produce the breakthroughs necessary to make those systems a realistic threat at sea. Thus, while the Soviet entry into sea-based aviation shows promise, it has a long way to go before it can be considered a real challenge to allied forces of the West.

Soviet shore-based, naval airpower is another matter. Admiral Gorshkov's ability to convince his leaders that he must have long-range, shore-based airpower in his navy, instead of relying on the Soviet air force, has enabled the Soviet navy to mount some excellent systems. Most notable is its long-range reconnaissance force. When a commander can deploy reconnaissance aircraft simultaneously in the North Atlantic, eastern Atlantic, South Altantic, Indian Ocean, and western Pacific, he poses a viable threat.

A second notable feature of Soviet shore-based, naval airpower is the high speed jet bomber, equipped with air-to-surface missiles, designed to attack surface shipping. Because of ongoing nuclear arms talks, much is heard about the Soviet Backfire bomber and its role as an intercontinental nuclear bomber. That aircraft, however, has thus far principally operated in the Soviet navy as a delivery system for air-to-surface missiles designed to sink enemy shipping. It is impressive in that role and must be considered as a high priority threat by any commander at sea within Backfire range.

The vulnerability of Soviet naval aviation stems from its need for shore bases, and denial of those bases is the easiest way to negate the threat. But if bases are provided, the combat commander at sea must worry about that threat early in the engagement and eliminate it immediately, preferably by elimination of the shore base itself. A commander in the Mediterranean, charged with supporting the southern flank of NATO but facing a fleet of Soviet navy shore-based aircraft in North Africa, would have little question about what headed his target priority list.

Soviet naval aviation, particularly the shore-based version, is a threat that can be negated, but must be counted as a valid part of the engagement problem. In an open-ocean area, it is particularly vulnerable. Soviet sea-based airpower shows considerable promise, but has probably been evaluated too highly at this point. It is presently far from comparable to American sea-based aviation.

A special note should be made of the Soviet amphibious force capability. The Soviets have produced and distributed films as well as literature emphasizing the excellence of their naval infantry. However, these forces have not been used to any extent, and there has been no public demonstration of their strength. They have no vertical airlift capability for troops and supplies. There is no integral tactical air support. In no way can they be compared to the United States Navy-Marine Corps team, and they cannot be considered a serious threat. The Soviets as yet have had no real need for such a force. If they develop a need to protect their interests far from Soviet shores and must get there by sea, then this force may develop. After all, a Soviet soldier can travel from Siberia to the southern tip of Africa by truck, while a United States marine must go 2,000 miles by ship or air just to get to one of the fifty states.

Any evaluation of a combat capability must include consideration of logistics—the supply and maintenance functions. Because the Soviets have never been required to engage in naval combat far from their shores, they have never developed any substantial resupply capability at sea. They have studied United States Navy equipment, techniques, and procedures in considerable depth and are slowly starting to duplicate some American abilities to transfer fuel at sea while steaming two ships side by side. They have a long way to go, however, before they can have a true ability to maintain their ships on station for long periods of time. Soviet combat ships are not designed to hold large quantities of supplies, including ammunition. They have limited rigging and equipment to handle large loads. Their much-touted aircraft carriers must rig cranes on deck before they can hoist supplies on board, in contrast to an integral load and unload capability of vast dimensions in American capital ships. Most Soviet replenishment operations are conducted with small craft, at slow speeds, in protected anchorages, and in fair weather. There is no airlift resupply capability.

One impressive aspect of the Soviet navy is its close ties with the Soviet merchant marine. Ships from that fleet provide much of the navy's resupply capability. This coordination must stem from the control that Admiral Gorshkov has reportedly been given over certain Soviet merchant marine ships. More of that kind of coordination and control is needed in the United States merchant maritime system.

Soviet maintenance capability away from home bases depends heavily on tenders—specially designed ships that accompany their combat ships everywhere. Although not as capable as United States tenders, they are far more numerous. There have been as many as four or five in the Mediterranean at one time. Since the Soviet combatant is limited in an integral maintenance capability, it must rely on tender support, which adds to the vulnerability of the force.

Shore bases must also be considered in evaluating the function of logistics. If the Soviets have access to such bases in the combat area, their logistics problem is greatly reduced. The threat increases the closer the Soviet combatants operate near friendly shores.

On balance, then, the logistics capability of the Soviet navy must be considered its weakest link. It is a "one-shot" navy at the moment, designed for a surprise, preemptive attack. The combat commander who can counter that preemptive surprise has gone a long way toward blunting the Soviet naval threat. In no way can the Soviets deploy and sustain a fleet at sea for long periods of time.

While logistics may be considered the weak variable in the Soviet naval threat, the Soviet ability to gather and transmit information, formulate decisions, and control and coordinate the activities of combat forces is impressive. Tactical intelligence assets range from fishing trawlers to specially designed satellites with electronic and visual reconnaissance capabilities. There are radio direction-finder networks, early-warning radar systems, long-range search aircraft, and surveillance ships that, combined with their satellite support, force an American commander to operate in electronic silence, at night, and in bad weather as much as possible in order to avoid detection or complicate the problem for the opposition. Cover and deception are part of the technique for negating the threat.

To command and control his forces, Admiral Gorshkov has developed a sophisticated system with great redundancy for reliability and centralized control. While a United States commander has more freedom of action and authority to act, the Soviets have developed a network of data links between satellites and combat commanders at sea that seems to be most effective. What is very significant is the extensive practice and assets that are devoted to the perfection and readiness of the system. The United States commander cannot count on negating this part of the threat. He must assume that the Soviets will know all about his movements and will be able to maintain control and knowledge of the situation, even under the most severe combat conditions at sea, including a nuclear weapons exchange. As far as controlling and neutralizing weapons in the combat area are concerned, the problem is less severe. The heavy reliance of Soviet weapons on electronic detection, guidance, and control makes them vulnerable in many ways. This diminishes to some degree the excellent overall command and control capability, however much the Soviet high command may know what is going on and can maintain good control of forces at sea. Overall, however, the Soviet command and control capability is worthy of considerable respect.

One of the final factors in any threat analysis is the readiness of the units to perform their combat mission. Quantity, quality, good command, and control are useless if the units are not ready. In this area the Soviet Union seems to be weak. While the Soviet units are deployed for increasingly longer periods and some outstanding global exercises are conducted about every five years, some deficiencies are worth attention.

Soviet units spend a great deal of time in port. Not many ships are kept on alert status. They rarely test their firepower. They practice the communication and coordination process a great deal, but the reliability of their weapons systems are suspect in view of their limited operational practice. The ships are immaculate and beautiful to view, but one gets the impression that more time is spent "cleaning ship" than maintaining weapons readiness.

Soviet Naval Manpower and Policy

The leadership in the Soviet navy is excellent. Admiral Gorshkov is probably the outstanding naval officer in modern times. He has convinced his country of the value of seapower. The admirals in command of Soviet fleets are also worthy of note. There has been a continuity of command and a heavy emphasis on operational experience. While academics, technicians, and program managers have their place, the command of the combat forces and the accompanying decisions are strictly a function of longtime operational experience.

The commanding officers of ships and submarines are excellent seamen, but they may be limited in numbers, since the same commanders constantly reappear. It is interesting to note that recent Soviet literature contains articles encouraging leaders in the field to "initiate" and to take more responsibility and authority for decisions at the scene of action, in contrast to the traditional views that all Soviet actions are directed from the Kremlin.

The crews of Soviet ships appear to be highly disciplined. Their appearance is superb. They are well trained, and service in the navy, though mandatory for many, is prestigious. If one steams closely alongside one of their ships it is possible to detect considerable enthusiasm for the tasks at hand and many examples of a sense of humor, even from commanding officers. On the occasion of the death of J. Edgar Hoover, a Soviet commanding officer asked an American navy commander why he was flying his flag at halfmast. When informed of the reason, he responded in a most respectful manner, stating that he sent his sympathies "although the Soviets had never enjoyed any of the same from Hoover."

The overall Soviet naval system, however, must be suspect. The trait that makes men outstanding in combat is individual initiative, an ability to react in a new way to an emergency situation that was never rehearsed or anticipated. Men trained too closely by the rule book and controlled too tightly may not respond with the initiative that is required in combat. If a commander can break the Soviet command channels and create some confusion in the Soviet ranks, a fatal weakness may develop. In general, however, Soviet naval personnel must be admired and treated with respect. As one student of the Soviet navy points out, "they are not dumb peasants." Furthermore, the leaders of the Soviet navy must be considered to be a real threat.

The Soviet threat cannot be considered in isolation. The friends that the Soviets can muster to their support can well enhance their naval threat. In some areas, such as the Mediterranean, Soviet friends seem to be disappearing. Soviet seapower in that area was greatly diminished by the loss of Egyptian ports and airfields to Soviet combat forces. In the Indian Ocean one must be concerned about Soviet bases in Yemen and the Horn of Africa because they would control access to the Suez Canal. Conversely, denying the Soviet navy use of the Suez would largely negate their threat in the Indian Ocean.

Although China dominates the Far East in the south, around the Sea of Japan in the north the Soviet naval threat is far more formidable because of the proximity to home bases and North Korea. It is this dependence on shore bases close to home that causes the Western analyst to describe the Soviet navy as "defensive" in nature. It has a limited capability to project its influence and power over long distances from home for long periods of time, and to truly control the sea. One way to greatly reduce the viability of the existing Soviet naval threat is to deny access to shore bases away from home.

The final factor to be considered is the philosophy of the Soviets toward seapower as an instrument of the state. Even superb naval forces can be negated as a threat if there is no real belief in their value and use by the Soviet leadership. Today the Soviet Union as a nation is dominated by marshals and generals. Its navy has been traditionally in a support role, defensive in nature, supporting land forces on the flanks. This must cast some doubt on the willingness of the leadership to really engage in naval warfare.

It also gives reason to admire Admiral Gorshkov for persuading the Soviet leadership to turn to the sea for resources and for trade all over the world. Although much of Gorshkov's writings must be considered propagandistic as he battles to convince his country of the importance of a blue water navy, he has been amazingly successful in that effort. The Soviets will have an increasing need for overseas trade. They are rapidly expanding their merchant marine and other resources to meet that need, and they are developing a combat force to support those overseas interests. Thus credence must be given to the Soviet intent to use the sea and to fight for their interests overseas as those interests expand. They may be cautious and reluctant to project their power and engage in conflict at this time, but the rise of the Soviet Union as a major seapower is unmistakable.

One must clearly view the Soviet naval threat as credible. Although the Soviet Union is weak in airpower, antisubmarine warfare, amphibious capability, and overseas allies, it is particularly strong in the number of submarines and in command, control, and leadership. While the threat is questionable with regard to the Soviet navy's readiness, it is increasing as the navy shifts to a strong seapower emphasis, headed by a persuasive and highly competent commander. As the Soviet navy advances from a conceptual to a combat posture, it must be constantly and cautiously reappraised, and one must ignore irresponsible evaluations from unqualified or self-serving analysts, both professionals and amateurs.

The Soviet naval threat cannot now be pictured as totally realistic, but neither can it be considered a figment of parochial imaginations. Soviet seapower is too important to world affairs to be taken lightly. Although a combat commander who believed this evaluation of the Soviet naval threat might boldly predict an overwhelming victory for United States units in a contest with Soviet forces held in an open ocean area, the outcome of a conflict waged closer to Soviet home bases would be far more difficult to predict.

The Soviet Union and
Conventional Arms Control

EDWARD C. LUCK

In his inaugural address, President Carter called for the complete elimination of nuclear weapons from the face of the earth, a goal which he voiced again one year later in his first State of the Union message. While applauding President Carter's commendable statements advocating nuclear disarmament, one may wonder whether the world really would be a safer place and whether American values and interests would be more secure unless simultaneous progress is made on limiting conventional forces as well.

Certainly wars were both terribly destructive and all too frequent before the advent of the nuclear age. Indeed, one of the reasons given for developing the atomic bomb was to provide a decisive means of ending the carnage of the second global conventional war. Since then, nuclear weapons have not been used in wartime, while conventional arms have continued to take their toll in local conflicts in many parts of the world. Moreover, conventional forces continue to absorb about 80 percent of global military expenditures.[1]

It would be short-sighted and potentially dangerous to view the Soviet-American military competition, as many American analysts have, primarily in terms of strategic nuclear capabilities, while largely ignoring the conventional balance. This tendency to focus on the nuclear equation has been exacerbated by the continual debates engulfing the Strategic Arms Limitation Talks (SALT), which at times appear more significant politically than militarily. These negotiations are generally seen in Washington—and evidently in Moscow as well—as the cornerstone of détente and as the best barometer of the state of Soviet-American relations. Yet even if SALT should finally succeed in codifying the mutual acceptance of strategic nuclear parity and perhaps in slightly lowering current numerical ceilings, the most difficult issues in the Soviet-American military competition would still remain. While attempts to limit weapons of mass destruction must be given a very high priority, these efforts should not

[1] For a more thorough discussion, see the UNA-USA National Policy Panel on Conventional Arms Control, *Controlling the Conventional Arms Race* (New York: UNA-USA, November 1976).

be allowed to distract attention from the equally important objective of curbing the many facets of the conventional arms competition.

The strategic nuclear threat holds much of the fascination of a science fiction movie. It is as horrible as it is unlikely: massive, almost instantaneous, mechanical, and largely indiscriminate warfare threatening soldier and civilian alike. The message is particularly easy to understand because the threat is directly against one's homeland. The range of threats posed by Soviet conventional forces and arms exports, on the other hand, seems much more subtle, gradual, and geographically remote. Yet conventional threats, being less risky, are considerably more likely to be carried out and present a more immediate, if less dramatic, danger.

Despite all the rarefied discussion of counterforce options and limited nuclear warfare, deterrence remains the primary purpose of the strategic nuclear forces of both the United States and the Soviet Union. Conventional forces must still carry the primary responsibility for defending territory and for furthering foreign policy goals abroad. While it is always possible that the Soviet Union could accidentally or irrationally launch a strategic nuclear strike against the United States, it seems far more probable that Soviet-American armed hostilities would result from a regional conventional conflict—in Eastern Europe, Western Europe, the Middle East, the Horn of Africa, southern Africa, northeast Asia, or Latin America—or through attempts to disrupt the sea lanes and Western oil supplies.

Analysts have often pondered which was the more decisive factor during the 1962 Cuban missile crisis, the United States strategic nuclear advantage or its decisive local conventional superiority. Soviet leaders may have learned both lessons, since the Soviet military buildup has included conventional as well as nuclear forces. And, as numerous observers have noted, there has been a particular stress on conventional forces capable of projecting Soviet military power far from home, traditionally a major Soviet weakness.

Moreover, since the Cuban missile crisis the Soviet leadership has largely abandoned its public use of strategic nuclear threats to attempt to influence the course of local conflicts. During the Vietnam war, the Soviets concentrated on supplying North Vietnam with the conventional weapons and materials necessary to carry on the war effort rather than on issuing empty strategic threats against the United States as they had in earlier years. In an era of nuclear paralysis, the conventional balance becomes increasingly important.

Assessing the Conventional Balance

The nature of the Soviet-American strategic balance has been subject to continuing controversy, with no objective and generally accepted method of calculating who is ahead or what constitutes strategic parity. Unfortunately, it appears to be even more difficult to assess, or even to define, the overall conventional balance. Unmeasurable factors, such as morale, national will, training, and quality of leadership, would no doubt play a particularly prominent role in deciding the outcome of a protracted conflict fought with conventional weapons, whether in Southeast Asia, the Horn of Africa, the Middle East, or central Europe.

The United States and the Soviet Union each deploy a wide variety of conventional armaments and forces in many parts of the world to serve a broad range of objectives and missions, not simply to deter or defend against an attack from the other superpower. The deployment patterns of American conventional forces indicate that defending the continental United States from a direct attack is not their primary mission. Nor have Soviet forces apparently been designed for such an ambitious and difficult assault across the oceans. Any serious effort to measure the overall conventional balance would entail a series of questions: which forces, where, when, and for what purpose? It should be remembered that not all of a nation's conventional forces can be reasonably brought to bear on a single point at any one time.

There are major asymmetries in the composition of American and Soviet conventional forces that greatly compound the problem of comparison. These asymmetries stem from differing traditions, requirements, missions, doctrines, geopolitical situations, technological levels, and manpower resources. As general purpose forces, conventional capabilities may be employed for a variety of missions, not all of which relate directly to comparable forces on the other side. The Soviet Union and the United States have different economic, foreign policy, and military objectives abroad that may influence the kind of forces they acquire and deploy in particular regions. Purely bilateral comparisons are clearly inadequate, since the scope of threats to their national security from third countries and the capabilities and reliability of United States and Soviet allies should also be taken into account.

In light of these complicating factors, general descriptive terms like "parity," "sufficiency," and "essential equivalence" have little meaning for the overall conventional balance, though they may apply to particular regions or weapons systems. An additional conceptual problem is the lack of relatively well-defined principles of what constitutes a stable conventional balance or an effective conventional deterrent. This raises some difficult problems for negotiating general reductions in Soviet and American conventional forces. For example, many analysts have contended that the attainment of approximate nuclear parity was a prerequisite for the SALT negotiations. Given the difficulty of applying such a concept to the conventional balance, could Soviet-American negotiations on reducing the overall size and composition of their conventional forces be undertaken without mutual acceptance that approximate parity exists at that level? Should the achievement of parity, either in the aggregate or in particular areas, be a primary goal of such negotiations, or should existing asymmetries be codified at lower levels? Would it be possible to conduct such discussions on a purely bilateral basis?

The two most frequently cited indexes of overall military strength are manpower and expenditures, which provide a gross, if somewhat simplistic, picture of the magnitude of a nation's military effort. Since about 80 percent of Soviet and American defense expenditures and at least a comparable share of their military manpower are related to conventional forces, these two indexes are clearly more relevant indicators of conventional than of nuclear capabilities. In a general sense, manpower levels indicate the overall size while expenditures suggest the quality of national military capabilities. However, there are major drawbacks to each of these indexes, and they should be applied with considerable caution to comparisons of Soviet and American strength.

Estimates of military manpower and expenditures involve serious problems of definition, measurement, and comparability. For example, how should the total number of men under arms be calculated in each country? In the Soviet Union, uniformed personnel are called upon to perform a number of functions —such as internal security, border and coastal protection, political education, construction, farming, civil defense, and running railroads—that are not required of the United States armed forces. Moreover, there are almost one million civilians directly employed by the U.S. Department of Defense, who are not counted in the manpower totals.

The level of defense expenditures may not necessarily present an accurate reflection of military capabilities. According to statistics compiled by the U.S. Arms Control and Disarmament Agency (ACDA), the ratio between military expenditures and military personnel (i.e., the amount of money spent per soldier) of the United States is the highest in the world, more than one and a half times the Soviet figure. This would appear to be the product of the relatively generous compensation levels in the American armed forces and of the technological sophistication of their weapons. Personnel costs make up more than one-half of the United States defense budget, and these expenditures are only indirectly related to military capabilities.

Even if defense outlays were a better measure of military strength, the enormous difficulties of measuring Soviet expenditures and comparing them with American outlays are well known. The uncertainties inherent in such comparisons are reflected in widely divergent estimates by reputable sources of Soviet and American defense expenditures. For example, the ratio between Soviet and American military outlays in 1975 was calculated to be 0.67:1 by the Stockholm International Peace Research Institute (SIPRI), 1.3:1 by ACDA, and 1.4:1 by the International Institute for Strategic Studies (IISS). (IISS calculations show the United States narrowing the gap in 1976 to a ratio of 1.2:1.)

Comparisons of military manpower present similar, if somewhat more manageable, problems. According to IISS, the ratio between Soviet and United States manpower in 1975 was 1.7:1, while ACDA determined the ratio to be 2.2:1. There is little doubt that the Soviet Union currently has more uniformed personnel on active duty than the United States and greater trained manpower reserves as well. However, this is not a new phenomenon, since the Soviet Union, traditionally a land power, has had a consistent edge in manpower since World War II and has fewer men under arms now than in the late 1950s. Only during the height of the Vietnam war did the United States come close to the Soviet total.

The Soviet advantage in the number of ground forces of perhaps 2:1 is bolstered by a 4:1 differential in tanks. Yet this imbalance in armored forces is partially offset by the superior quality and younger average age of American tanks and, more importantly, by a decided United States edge in antitank weapons. The two countries possess comparable numbers of tactical combat aircraft, but United States aircraft tend to have superior capabilities, particularly in payload against ground targets. Moreover, American pilots clearly have had greater combat experience.

Despite continuing improvements in the Soviet navy, the United States maintains an edge in overall naval capabilities. The Soviet Union deploys more major surface combat ships, 230 to 175, but the United States Navy has greater manpower and far more total displacement. (In other words, American ships on the average are larger.) The United States has major advantages in aircraft carriers and amphibious assault forces, while the Soviets have more attack submarines. On the water, as in the air, American forces have had much greater experience than their Soviet counterparts in carrying out military operations.

In summary, Soviet conventional forces on the whole are significantly larger, with the greatest disparity in ground forces. The United States, on the other hand, has certain qualitative advantages, particularly in naval and air forces. However, these aggregate comparisons are less important than assessments of regional balances that take into account the forces of potential allies and adversaries.

One obvious explanation of the Soviet emphasis on large ground forces is the fact that it is surrounded by potentially hostile and moderately powerful countries. As some observers have noted, the Soviet Union is the only state encircled by unfriendly Communist countries. Soviet spokesmen continually point out that their nation, unlike the United States, has already experienced the pain of foreign invasion twice in this century.

Americans, protected by natural barriers from the threat of invasion, should be careful not to underestimate the effect of these experiences on Soviet perceptions of the world. It is noteworthy, and no doubt fortunate for United States interests, that the huge Soviet army continues to be deployed entirely within the borders of the Soviet Union and Eastern Europe. Some 800,000 soldiers are massed on the Sino-Soviet border alone. The Soviets have even begun to complain about the magnitude of United States arms sales to Iran, a nation that could appear to threaten the Soviet Union only in the eyes of a paranoid observer.

There are numerous possible explanations for the presence of thirty-one Soviet divisions in Eastern Europe and sixty-four in European USSR: to maintain control over restive "allies," to provide a forward line of defense against possible invasion from the West, to influence political trends in both Eastern and Western Europe, to provide a strong platform for potential aggression against Western Europe, to satisfy bureaucratic pressures from the Soviet army, or any combination of these. Yet whatever the motivations for these large deployments, they raise difficult dilemmas for conventional arms control efforts.

First of all, it is quite impossible to distinguish whether these forces are "defensive" or "offensive," because, like most general purpose forces, they can be employed for either purpose. A good defensive posture, whether Eastern or Western, must be capable of mounting counterattacks against the aggressor. Second, it would not be entirely reassuring to conclude that the Soviets have assembled such large land forces because of a slightly paranoid view of the capabilities and intentions of their neighbors. For if the Soviets do have what Western observers would judge to be a somewhat irrational or overblown fear of invasion from the West, then it would be all the more difficult for the two sides to agree on what constitutes an equitable and stable balance of forces in Europe. Third, it is unclear how much the Soviets would be willing to reduce their conventional forces as long as China remains hostile and Eastern Europe politically unsettled.

In evaluating the Soviet-American conventional military balance, it is clearly essential to include allied forces in the calculations. Not only are there major disparities in the strength of allied nations, but also any large scale Soviet-American conflict is likely to be fought on the territory of third parties or on the high seas. In Europe, the considerable imbalance of Soviet over American forces is largely offset by superior capabilities of the United States's NATO allies compared to the non-Soviet Warsaw Pact countries. The military potential of Western Europe, in terms of population, economic strength, and technological advancement, is even more impressive. Arms limitation measures in Europe must be multilateral to be effective in the long run, and, as the deadlocked negotiations on Mutual and Balanced Force Reductions (MBFR) have demonstrated, such interalliance discussions are likely to be extremely complex. SALT, for all its complexity, looks simple in comparison.

The balance between the two alliance systems is difficult to assess, but it is generally agreed that the Warsaw Pact has a slight advantage over NATO in the European theater. IISS concludes that today there is an overall balance that makes "military aggression appear unattractive," but that "the Warsaw Pact appears more content with the relationship of forces than is NATO."[2] A June 1977 United States government study entitled "Military Strategy and Force Posture Review" reportedly termed the Warsaw Pact advantage "too small in itself for the attacker to have any expectation of quick or substantial victory." But it warned that "the chance of NATO stopping an attack with minimal loss of territory and then achieving its full objective of recovering that land which had been lost appears remote at the present time."[3]

The Soviet leadership has shown increasing readiness to provide substantial military support to friendly third world countries, though there appears to be continuing reluctance to deploy regular army units abroad. An expansion of Soviet airlift and naval capabilities has provided a greater ability to project

---

[2] The International Institute for Strategic Studies, *The Military Balance, 1977–1978* (London: IISS, 1977), p. 109.

[3] Richard Burt, "U.S. Doubts Ability to Defend Europe in Conventional War," *New York Times*, January 6, 1978.

military power farther from home, but United States projection capabilities are still far superior. Under these circumstances, arms sales have become an important element in Soviet policy toward the third world. The Soviets have generally concentrated their arms supplies in a relatively few recipient countries, frequently providing quite advanced weapons systems and relatively large numbers of Soviet or Cuban advisers and technicians. While it is difficult to compare American and Soviet arms sales, ACDA has estimated that the United States was the leading arms exporter over the past decade with almost one-half of the total and that the Soviet Union was second with 29 percent.

Approaches to Conventional Arms Control

There are three current negotiations dealing principally with conventional weapons: MBFR, Soviet-American discussions regarding Indian Ocean naval deployments and bases, and, under the auspices of the International Committee of the Red Cross, multilateral talks concerning weapons that cause unnecessary suffering or have indiscriminate effects. Though these are serious efforts, none of them is likely in the foreseeable future to produce major advances in controlling conventional arms. However, there are a wide variety of other possible approaches to limiting conventional forces, most of them as yet untested. The advantages and disadvantages of three of these approaches are discussed below.

Limitations on military expenditures appear at first glance to be an attractive way of restricting the overall magnitude of national military efforts. As experience has demonstrated, less comprehensive arms control measures do not prevent the expansion of military programs in areas not covered by an agreement. Moreover, limits on military outlays would further the important, if secondary, goal of saving resources, an objective that has largely eluded past arms control efforts. But there are serious drawbacks to the budget approach. In addition to the complex problems of definition, measurement, and comparability mentioned above, verification would be extremely difficult. There is also no guarantee that a mutual reduction in expenditures would necessarily result in a more stable balance of forces, which is a function of capabilities rather than cost.

One way of circumventing this dilemma would be to link a limitation on expenditures with a reduction in specified conventional forces or armaments. For example, an agreement to reduce Soviet and American defense outlays by 10 percent could be tied to a cutback of a certain number of armored divisions, naval vessels, or tactical aircraft, with a freeze on other forces. The budget limit would provide an overall ceiling on each nation's military efforts, while the force reduction would provide verifiable and measurable evidence of reduced military activity. By carefully choosing the forces to be limited, the agreement could reinforce military stability as well as save resources.

The apparently growing Soviet interest in naval forces capable of projecting power throughout the world may have disturbing implications for the nature of Soviet-American competition in the third world. The prospect of confrontations between Soviet and American naval units in far-flung areas of high tension is ominous. Other than in central Europe, the only place where United States and Soviet forces directly confront each other is on the high seas. Furthermore, an intense Soviet-American naval arms race would be very expensive.

Efforts should be made to limit both naval deployments in particular regions and overall naval inventories. The ongoing Soviet-American negotiations on limiting or at least freezing deployments and bases in the Indian Ocean is a good place to start the process. But these discussions should go beyond codifying the status quo and should seek to eliminate the United States and Soviet naval presence in the region. By reducing their global requirements for naval forces, such an agreement could provide a foundation for follow-on negotiations on limiting the overall size and capabilities of the Soviet and American navies. Given the asymmetries between the two navies discussed above, negotiations on limiting naval inventories would be difficult, but the potential payoff could be great. Moreover, it would be relatively simple to verify such an agreement.

President Carter has placed a high priority on reducing the global traffic in conventional arms and has promised to seek the cooperation of other major arms supplying countries, including the Soviet Union, in this effort. As a first step, he has called for a gradual reduction in United States arms sales, since this country is the leading arms merchant. So far there has been no appreciable decline in overall United States arms sales, and, until progress is made in this direction, it will be impossible to convince the other major suppliers to curb their arms exports.

In contrast to their strong commitment to retarding nuclear proliferation, the Soviets have shown little interest in limitations on the conventional arms trade. Arms sales remain a tangible means of demonstrating Soviet support for "wars of national liberation" and for furthering Soviet interests around the globe. Moreover, the Soviets are likely to be suspicious of the current American overtures in this area, particularly in light of the leading United States position in arms exports. Therefore, it is unlikely that a comprehensive agreement could be reached among the major suppliers covering all regions and all kinds of arms. Each regional situation is different and few descriptive statements apply globally. Also, the recipient countries would demand an input into any far-reaching agreement governing their only sources of armaments.

However, there are a number of less comprehensive and more feasible steps that could ameliorate the worst dangers of the arms trade. For example, the major suppliers could agree not to export certain advanced and potentially destabilizing weapons systems, such as surface-to-surface missiles, medium or heavy bombers, and the newest model fighter bombers. They could agree to consult with each other before undertaking major arms sales, particularly to areas of high tension. The principal suppliers could act in unison to encourage—or at least agree not to undermine—local efforts among recipient countries to lessen military tensions or reduce arms purchases in certain regions. Finally, they could support the initiatives to authorize the United Nations to register, publicize, and monitor all arms transfers. None of these measures would result in immediate drastic reductions in the overall volume of the arms trade, but together they would do much to alter the atmosphere of mistrust and uncertainty in which the arms trade prospers.

This brief summary of some possible approaches illustrates the inherent difficulties in attempting to control the many facets of the conventional arms race. It also suggests that there is a wide spectrum of arms control concerns that deserve far greater attention than they are now receiving. Efforts to control the nuclear and conventional arms races should be seen as complementary and reinforcing, and should be undertaken simultaneously. There is no need to choose between nuclear and conventional arms control; the United States and the Soviet Union need both.

Eastern Europe and
the Soviet Threat

ANDRZEJ KORBONSKI

Threat may be defined as a declaration of an intention to inflict punishment, possibly in retaliation. It is therefore both a menace and a warning. This concept of threat appears quite useful for the purpose of analyzing the relationship between the Soviet Union and its junior allies in Eastern Europe. After more than thirty years of Communist rule in the region comprising six countries—Bulgaria, Czechoslovakia, East Germany, Hungary, Poland, and Rumania—one is forced to conclude that it has been the Soviet threat, however defined, that has largely succeeded in achieving the four major objectives that motivated Stalin in abetting the Communist takeover of the various countries in the aftermath of World War II.

As admirably summarized by Zbigniew Brzezinski, these four goals were: (1) denying the region to countries hostile to the Soviet Union and potentially threatening the latter's security; (2) ensuring that control of the domestic political systems in the area remained firmly in the hands of elements friendly to Moscow; (3) utilizing the region's resources for the purpose of aiding Soviet postwar economic recovery and development; and (4) using Eastern Europe as a potential jumping-off point for a possible offensive against the West.[1] This is not the place to discuss in detail whether these objectives have in fact been reached in toto. Since they were formulated in the prenuclear age, one may assume that some of them are not as valid or relevant in the late 1970s as in the mid-1940s. Nevertheless, it is clear that Soviet hegemony over the region as well as Communist rule in the individual countries has remained essentially unimpaired, despite a number of crises and challenges that threatened both of them.

One can hypothesize that the single most important instrument ensuring both Moscow's hegemony and the perpetuation of Communist rule in Eastern Europe was the continued presence of the Soviet threat in its various manifesta-

---

[1] Zbigniew Brzezinski, *The Soviet Bloc*, rev. ed. (Cambridge, Mass.: Harvard University Press, 1967), pp. 4–5.

tions. This implied an awareness on the part of both the national leaders and the respective populations that any serious effort to tamper with the status quo was likely to bring about severe punishment by the Kremlin in retaliation for attempting to undermine the existing political, military, and economic arrangements in the region, laboriously constructed over the past thirty years.

As suggested above, the Soviet threat vis-à-vis Eastern Europe took several forms. Some of them, such as the military or economic ones, were quite obvious and easily identifiable. Others, whether political or sociocultural, were more subtle and less clearcut. What follows is an attempt to deal with each of these threats in turn, concluding with some speculations about the possible way in which they may evolve in the future.

The Military Threat

The military threat, which implies the willingness to use violence to preserve the existing state of affairs in the region, is obviously the primary instrument that can be used to safeguard Soviet domination of Eastern Europe. Twice in the past twenty-five years, the Soviet army was actually deployed in order to prevent the collapse of a Communist regime (in Hungary, October-November 1956) and to halt what Moscow perceived as a far-reaching qualitative change in the nature of a Communist political system (in Czechoslovakia in August 1968), which threatened to extend beyond the confines of a single country. On at least two other occasions, the use of Soviet troops was considered to prevent a mass revolt: against Communist rule in East Germany in June 1953 and to stop a changeover in the national political leadership of Poland in October 1956 that was bound to have serious domestic and international repercussions. Finally, on a somewhat different level, the sheer presence of Soviet forces stationed in Czechoslovakia, East Germany, Hungary, and Poland served as a reminder that these troops could be deployed if the situation warranted it.

Needless to say, the actual use of military force was the most drastic implementation of the Soviet threat. As a result, it was clear that the final decision to deploy the Soviet army on the territory of another country was not taken lightly by the Soviet leadership. Some evidence suggests that both Nikita Khrushchev in the fall of 1956 and Leonid Brezhnev in the summer of 1968 agonized before ordering the Soviet forces to invade Hungary and Czechoslovakia. The Soviet leadership was clearly divided as to the costs and benefits of an armed intervention, and it was finally persuaded to intervene only when it realized that a failure to take decisive action would create serious problems for the Soviet Union by weakening its authority and reducing its hegemony over the region as a whole. On the other hand, when other possible remedies were not exhausted, the contemplated use of Soviet military strength was stopped at the last minute. In this respect, the example of Poland in October 1956 attested to the obvious reluctance of the Soviet oligarchy to apply brute force, which was seen as an instrument of last resort.

The actual or implied Soviet military threat to Eastern Europe raises certain interesting corollaries. To begin with, there is the question of the threshold beyond which the Kremlin would no longer tolerate a course of action taken by an Eastern European country without recourse to arms. Obviously, such a threshold is likely to change over time according to changes in the Soviet leadership, in the general international environment, and in the overall "correlation of forces," especially between East and West. The relationship between the Soviet Union and Eastern Europe may be seen as a game in which one of the players is also the umpire capable of changing the rules at any time. Accordingly, it is virtually impossible to identify a situation that may trigger Soviet armed intervention.

Over the years, the Soviet leaders attempted on at least two occasions to define the limits of Eastern European autonomy in a way that could be interpreted as more than just a veiled warning to individual countries not to cross the threshold. In November 1956, following the crises in Hungary and Poland, Mikhail Suslov, a ranking member of the Politburo, tried to define the minimum necessary conditions of membership in the socialist camp under Moscow's leadership.[2] This was probably understood as both a warning and a way of legitimizing Soviet intervention in Hungary and near intervention in Poland. In the same vein, the so-called Brezhnev Doctrine, proclaimed with great fanfare after the invasion of Czechoslovakia in August 1968, could be interpreted as both a reaffirmation of Soviet determination to intervene again in similar circumstances and a device legitimizing Soviet aggression.

As mentioned above, the process or event triggering Soviet military intervention in a particular Eastern European country cannot be easily predicted. The question is often asked why Moscow invaded Czechoslovakia but not Rumania despite the latter's highly erratic and frequently challenging behavior toward the Soviet Union. The only sensible answer is that President Nicolae Ceausescu, though clearly a maverick on the international scene, maintained a tight and perhaps even a neo-Stalinist control over the domestic political processes in Rumania. By contrast, at least from Moscow's viewpoint, the internal situation in Czechoslovakia under Alexander Dubcek showed signs of getting out of hand, undermining the foundations of Communist rule in that country, and extending in a threatening manner into the neighboring countries. It was the perceived danger to the Communist regime in Prague, including the threat to the leading role and monopoly of power exercised by the ruling party, that finally convinced the Kremlin that armed intervention was inevitable.

The crucial factor in the decision to intervene was, of course, Moscow's perception of the events supposedly threatening its hegemony in the region. Despite many linkages between the Soviet Union and its client states, some evidence points to a misperception by the Soviet leadership of the meaning of certain processes in Eastern Europe. The situation in Czechoslovakia in the summer of 1968 was interpreted by the Soviet Embassy in Prague as leading to a collapse of Communist rule, which had to be stopped at all cost. Similarly,

---

[2] Ibid., p. 275.

the Soviet ambassador, a well-known "hardliner," not only advocated armed intervention but also promised strong support for a Soviet invasion on the part of conservative elements in the Czechoslovak ruling elite. Both perceptions were proven wrong. Communist rule in Czechoslovakia was in the process of transformation rather than collapse, and the support of Czechoslovak conservatives proved illusory when the Soviet leadership, having failed to produce a new regime sympathetic to Moscow's aims, was forced to fall back on Dubcek, whom it had attempted to oust in the first place.

By and large, however, Soviet behavior in Eastern Europe even in times of crisis has been cautious. While Moscow could not tolerate Hungary's withdrawal from the Warsaw Pact and its declaration of neutrality in 1956 without losing considerable prestige, it has frequently treated other potential challenges to its authority with benign neglect. This was true for the workers' riots and Wladyslaw Gomulka's ouster in Poland in December 1970 and for Antonin Novotny's replacement by Dubcek as Czechoslovak party leader three years earlier. Rumania's independent stance, which must have been particularly irritating to Moscow throughout the 1960s, was also largely tolerated, as was the most recent challenge to Poland's leadership in the summer of 1976. Undoubtedly, part of Moscow's caution has been due to the belief that the threat of armed intervention often had an opposite effect from that intended, as in Stalin's experience with Yugoslavia in 1948, when the threat of an impending Soviet invasion succeeded in submerging national and regional conflicts and in mobilizing the country behind Tito. The overwhelming popularity of Gomulka in Poland in the late 1950s and of Ceausescu in Rumania a decade later stemmed largely from the respective leaders' attitude toward the threat of a potential Soviet intervention.

The threat of violence can thus be seen as the Kremlin's weapon of last resort. At the same time, the continued presence of such a threat graphically illustrates the overwhelming failure of the Eastern European Communist regimes to achieve even that modicum of legitimacy that would make such a threat largely redundant. Since the local regimes are far from becoming popularly accepted, the stationing of Soviet troops, supposedly made legitimate by the provisions of the Warsaw Pact, represents a constant reminder to potential rebels in the region that any serious attempt to change the status quo in Eastern Europe would meet with a violent Soviet reaction.

The Economic Threat

Although the Soviet military threat over the years has most strongly solidified the Eastern European alliance and ensured Soviet domination of the region, in the more recent period the economic factor has begun to play an important role. As stated at the outset, one of the major Soviet objectives in seizing control of Eastern Europe after World War II was to utilize the resources of the area to promote Soviet postwar economic recovery and development. At least during the Stalinist period, the Kremlin treated the region as a colony to be exploited for the benefit of the Soviet economy. Nearly all countries, but especially East Germany, Hungary, and Poland, suffered severe economic losses by being forced to export scarce raw materials as well as capital goods to the Soviet Union at prices considerably below the world market level.

With the sole exception of Czechoslovakia, the Eastern European countries emerged from World War II operating at a fraction of their economic capacity and badly in need of foreign reconstruction aid. Since the region had minimal contacts with the Soviet Union before the war and since Germany—the traditional supplier of industrial goods to the area—was in ruins, the presumption was that the aid and eventually trade would come mostly from the West.

However, the cold war put an end to the expected expansion of Western trade and aid. The West gradually imposed its embargo on trade with the East, while the Soviet Union succeeded by various means in severely reducing East-West trade and in diverting Eastern European trade in an easterly direction. The process of trade diversion culminated in the formal establishment of the Council for Mutual Economic Assistance (CMEA) in January 1949.

During the first half of the 1950s, Eastern Europe went through a process of rapid economic synchronization accomplished essentially without the help of CMEA, which remained largely dormant until the end of the decade. The institutional synchronization was achieved by the forced imposition of the Stalinist model of industrialization on the satellite countries. The overall balance sheet in the mid-1950s showed that the various countries managed to lay the foundations for modern industrial economies, which could eventually ensure a high rate of self-sustained growth. It also showed that the region as a whole represented a major economic asset for the Soviet Union, which exploited it at will until 1956.

While Eastern Europe on the surface went through the process of industrial revolution with impressive speed, the costs proved to be very high. One of the most significant features—the importance of which became clear only recently—was the fact that the foundations for a modern industrial system were laid on a highly restricted raw materials base. In itself this was not unusual since many other industrialized countries throughout the world had limited resources at their disposal. However, the peculiar systemic and political context in which the Eastern European industrial revolution took place made this particular aspect one of crucial importance for the future development of the national economies. It meant that the individual countries, with the exception of Poland and Rumania, were heavily dependent on Soviet supplies of raw materials for their expanding economies. It also meant that they were not in a position to develop alternate sources of supply in the non-Communist world. In the final analysis it meant that they were highly vulnerable to Soviet economic pressures or threats and that Moscow would be able to maintain its control over the region without necessarily resorting to political or military measures.

As long as raw materials in general continued to be in relatively ample supply, there was no evidence that the Soviet Union used the economic threat to keep the various countries in line. Although concern was periodically voiced in some

Eastern European countries over their growing economic dependence on the Soviet Union and the need to find new outlets for their exports and new sources of necessary imports, the Soviet Union appeared willing to supply the area with increasing amounts of oil, metals, and other raw materials at prices often below those charged by other countries producing raw materials. It could be argued, however, that by the end of the 1960s Eastern Europe had been transformed from an economic asset into an economic liability for the Soviet Union.

In the early 1970s the emergence of East-West détente worked significant changes in the Communist and international environments and provided a background for two major events that underscored the rapidly rising importance of economic factors in world politics. They were the global shortage of basic fuels and raw materials and the Soviet decision to enter the arena of East-West trade in a massive way as a major supplier of raw mateials in exchange for Western technology and expertise. The problems encountered by the Eastern European countries as a result of these two developments were not greatly different from those faced by the non-Communist countries. Having become a full-fledged participant in East-West trade, the Soviet Union had to decide whether to continue supplying its Eastern European allies with ever-increasing quantities of oil and raw materials at relatively low prices or to divert some of these shipments to the West, charging much higher prices in hard currencies. For their part, the smaller Eastern European countries had to decide whether to continue expanding their trade with the West or to divert some of the Western directed exports to the Soviet Union in return for the guaranteed supplies of raw materials at reasonable prices.

This was hardly a zero-sum game, for the only winner was bound to be the Soviet Union. Most of the Eastern European countries faced unenviable choices. A decline in the volume of East-West trade would mean a reduction in the imports of Western technology that formed the basis for ambitious plans of industrial modernization in countries like Hungary, Poland, and Rumania. On the other hand, a decrease in the Soviet deliveries of fuels and raw materials would seriously hurt countries such as Czechoslovakia, East Germany, and Hungary, which were particularly vulnerable by having few natural resources of their own and no alternate sources of supply.

Although the Soviet Union appeared to be in an excellent position to apply economic pressure on Eastern Europe, it chose not to take advantage of it. To be sure, it raised the price level of major raw materials, particularly oil, traded with CMEA, insisted on receiving higher quality Eastern European commodities as payment for the raw materials, and finally forced the Eastern Europeans to become more involved in the development of new sources of raw materials and new transport facilities on Soviet territory. By and large, however, the Soviet reaction to the new circumstances can only be described as restrained. Instead of utilizing the threat of reduced raw materials deliveries, Moscow has not only been shipping increasing amounts of oil and other raw materials but has also continued to subsidize its clients by charging them prices below the world market level. The economic threat was not used in cases where it could have been applied to extract political concessions, as in Poland in the second half of 1976. Instead the Kremlin granted the Gierek regime aid and credits to bolster the Polish economy and defuse popular discontent.

This benign attitude is even more remarkable in light of the growing vulnerability of those Eastern European countries that in the past few years have accumulated huge hard currency debts. Unless these countries succeed in reducing their balance of payments deficits by either reducing their imports or expanding their exports, or both, some of them could face the possibility of defaulting on their debt repayment, and the only country that could conceivably bail them out—for a price—is clearly the Soviet Union.

While the Soviet economic hold on Eastern Europe appears formidable, it is hardly absolute. The example of the unsuccessful, Soviet-led economic blockade of Yugoslavia after 1948 must have persuaded the Soviet Union that economic warfare often backfired and that another economic boycott would not be sufficient to subdue a recalcitrant junior ally, especially in an era when East-West economic relations are much closer than in the early stages of the cold war. Moreover, there are signs that the Soviet Union itself may soon face a shortage of major fuels such as oil and thus may be forced to compete with the rest of the world for oil and other raw materials. While this will not necessarily help Eastern Europe, it will at least reduce the degree of Soviet monopoly as the major supplier of raw materials to the region.

Although potentially quite significant, the Soviet economic threat to Eastern Europe thus does not appear to be as serious as it was believed to be only a few years ago. This correlates with the unwillingness of the Soviet Union to apply its economic leverage in any consistent fashion. This situation may change, even drastically, but in the immediate future the probability of the economic threat or pressure being utilized successfully in order to achieve specific Soviet goals does not appear to be high.

The Political Threat

The concept of a political threat is not easily defined. In a sense, all threats, whether military or economic, are political in that they affect the political systems in individual countries or regions. In the absence of a better definition, it will be assumed that political threats comprise all types of nonviolent pressures that fall outside the realm of economics. This would include diplomatic threats and ideological warnings, as well as institutional, organizational, bilateral, and multilateral linkages. The Soviet Union has used all of them in the past in lieu of the more clearcut and visible military and economic threats. Contrasted with the latter two, the Soviet political threat to Eastern Europe today appears much less formidable, yet it cannot be entirely ignored. Since the military and economic threats are not likely to be used by the Soviet Union except in emergencies, the political threat may well become the preferred mode of Soviet policy toward the rest of the bloc in the foreseeable future.

In the event of deviant behavior by a junior member of the Eastern European alliance that would ultimately endanger Communist rule and Soviet hegemony in the area, the Soviet Union may well utilize diplomatic threats to restore stability and conformity in the region, with or without the help of formal and informal linkages. Before the final decision was made to invade Czechoslovakia in August 1968, Moscow used that method in an effort to bring Dubcek in line. Apart from bilateral meetings at the highest level, multilateral linkages such as the Warsaw Pact and CMEA were utilized to bring pressure on Czechoslovakia. Ideological warnings were invoked for the same purpose but without avail. In 1957 and 1958 a similar concerted action under the Kremlin's leadership threatened totally to isolate the rebellious Polish leader Wladyslaw Gomulka from the rest of the bloc and forced him eventually to abandon his independent stance in favor of conformity. In the late 1960s Moscow attempted, mostly unsuccessfully, to contain the maverick Ceausescu, while in 1971 it succeeded in forcing out the veteran East German party leader Walter Ulbricht, who opposed the rapprochement between Moscow and Bonn.

Examples of political threats used by Moscow in the past also include political blackmail and attempts to undermine Eastern European regimes from within. The former threat tended to utilize latent or existing national antagonisms in the region in order to strengthen Soviet influence. One example of the "divide and rule" method was the pressure put on Rumania, which consisted of encouraging Hungarian nationalist claims on the province of Transylvania, the perennial bone of contention between these two countries. Similarly, the uncertain status of Poland's western border provided a useful target for Soviet threats to revise the postwar territorial arrangements in favor of East Germany, which as a rule tended to be a much more obedient Soviet client than Poland. One of the favorite forms of Soviet pressure exerted on deviant Eastern European regimes was the encouragement and support of factionalism within the ruling party in order to weaken and finally destroy the regime hostile to Moscow's designs. This method was attempted unsuccessfully in Yugoslavia in 1948 and in some other countries in the 1950s and 1960s. Finally, another type of threat consisted of an official excommunication of the rebellious member of the alliance in the hope that the expulsion would force the recalcitrant regime to recant and reaffirm its allegiance. The threat failed, however, in the case of both Yugoslavia in 1948 and Albania in 1961.

This cursory review suggests that at least on the surface the Soviet political threat has not been very effective in the past in achieving Moscow's objectives. It failed to stop the rapid deterioration of the domestic political situation in Czechoslovakia in 1968, and it did not succeed in isolating Rumania from both the West and the rest of the Communist world. Nevertheless, its utility has not been entirely wasted. The fact that the Soviet Union attempted to reach its goals by nonviolent means, prior to escalating the pressure by resorting to economic and finally military threats, had considerable propaganda value in showing the Kremlin to the outside world as reasonable and eager to solve the crisis in a rational manner while its opponent appeared unreasonable and unwilling to settle the dispute peacefully. Since Moscow has always been greatly concerned about its international image, especially as a global power, various types of nonviolent threats and warnings to Eastern Europe will increase in importance in the foreseeable future at the expense of other kinds of threats.

The Sociocultural Threat

The sociocultural threat is qualitatively different from the three types of threats already discussed in that it neither aims to achieve a specific Soviet goal nor presents a direct and immediate danger to the status quo. It does not attempt to induce a process of change or to stop a process already under way. It is not directed against individuals or groups that may threaten Communist rule or Soviet hegemony in the region.

The Soviet sociocultural threat can be viewed as a gradual yet clearly visible erosion of the traditional political cultures in Eastern Europe. As a result, the national political cultures are gradually being replaced by what may be called, for the lack of a better word, the progressive "russification" or "proletarization" of the region, by which a new political culture or value system emerges from nearly sixty years of Communist rule in Russia, containing certain features of traditional Russian culture together with new values and modes of behavior imposed from above by the Communist rulers.

The new cultural traits that have been penetrating Eastern European societies since the end of World War II include such phenomena as mass corruption, thievery, growing anomie in interpersonal relations, drunkenness, and endemic absenteeism. These phenomena point not so much to a gradual disintegration of the social fabric in the respective societies as to their slow transformation in the direction of the Soviet sociocultural model, which represents the lowest common denominator.

It is clear that the rapid postwar socioeconomic development of Eastern Europe had to be accompanied by far-reaching changes in social values and mores stemming from the processes of industrialization and urbanization, improved transport and communications, and expanded educational opportunities. In the face of the massive onslaught of modernization, one would expect the traditional, largely rural Eastern European societies to be transformed rather drastically. What made the change different from that occurring in other developing countries was the fact that the impetus for change was imported from the East; largely isolated from the rest of the world long before the Bolshevik Revolution of 1917, the East had developed its own peculiar political culture and value system sharply different from those of the West.

With minor exceptions, the Eastern European countries have always considered themselves a part of the West. Hence they tended to look first at czarist Russia and later at the Soviet Union with the contempt usually reserved for culturally inferior societies. For about the first two decades following the Communist takeover, the individual countries managed to retain their national identities despite the forced imposition of the Soviet political and economic models. Even today a casual observer is able rather easily to detect sharp differences in life-styles between the Soviet Union and such countries as Hungary and Poland, but their resistance to Soviet sociocultural penetration is beginning to crumble.

In the long run, the impact of the Soviet sociocultural threat on Eastern Europe may be more dangerous than the other threats discussed earlier. The use of force or economic pressure is more than likely to galvanize active or passive resistance and to mobilize the population in defense of their respective countries and life-styles. The probable result is the rebirth of nationalism and a renewed emphasis on national identity. Both make it more difficult for Soviet influence to alter the fabric of Eastern European societies. In contrast, the penetration of Soviet sociocultural values appears inevitable in the absence of an overt military or economic threat and is bound to weaken Eastern Europe's resistance by gradually eroding the national identity and value systems of individual countries.

Conclusion

Is the Soviet threat to Eastern Europe, however defined, real or imaginary? Before answering this question, it should be made clear that this particular threat is qualitatively different from Soviet threats directed at other areas of the globe. In the latter case it may be assumed that Moscow's ultimate goal is to change significantly the domestic political system of the given country or region and its international status in the direction favored by the Kremlin.

This may range from the establishment of a Communist regime friendly to the Soviet Union to a withdrawal of the country from a Western-sponsored alliance system. The thrust of the Soviet threat is obviously different in the case of Eastern Europe, where the individual countries are being ruled by Communist regimes closely allied to Moscow. Hence the purpose of the threat is not to bring additional states into the Soviet orbit but to prevent those already controlled from leaving it. Of the four separate Soviet threats to Eastern Europe, the military one appears most formidable, followed by the economic and political ones. The sociocultural threat belongs to a different category, although its long-run impact may be just as important as the other types of threat.

It may be argued, however, that in recent years and especially since the invasion of Cezechoslovakia in 1968 Moscow's attitude toward its Eastern European allies has been characterized by considerable restraint and absence of overt or covert threats. There is, for example, no evidence of Soviet pressure on Poland during the systemic crises in December 1970 and June 1976. There are indications of reduced Soviet intimidation of Rumania despite the latter's frequently erratic behavior. To be sure, the Kremlin did not hesitate to use political threats to depose East Germany's Ulbricht, and it also attempted to use economic pressure to extract concessions from Hungary in the early 1970s. But by and large the use of overt threats or pressures represented an exception rather than the rule.

In particular, Soviet economic policy toward Eastern Europe has been indicative of the new approach, characterized by restraint rather than outright pressure. Especially in the most recent period of raw materials scarcity, the Soviet Union was in an excellent position to utilize its monopoly position to exert economic pressure on the region. Yet, except for raising the prices of oil and other raw materials, it has not used its economic strength to increase its influence over the region. On the contrary, it has not only continued to subsidize the local economies but also utilized economic aid and credits, without attaching any visible political strings, to support a regime that found itself in economic difficulties, such as Poland in the second half of 1976.

In view of the range of options available to Moscow, all this can be interpreted as a testimony to the growing political sophistication of the Soviet leadership. It was apparently willing to pay the price of heading an important political, military, and economic alliance. This is a fairly new development that may yet prove to be short-lived and illusory. Nevertheless, it does represent a major departure from past patterns of Soviet behavior toward Eastern Europe that only a short time ago were based almost exclusively on the application of a variety of threats.

It must be made clear, however, that this does not mean that the Soviet threat to Eastern Europe today is a myth rather than reality. The fact that the Soviet Union has chosen to use persuasion or incentives in the last decade to maintain its hegemony over the region does not mean that military or economic threats are no longer instruments of Soviet policy toward Eastern Europe. The history of the last thirty years has amply demonstrated that the Kremlin would not hesitate to use force to achieve its objectives. Moreover, fear of the use of the Soviet military might in asserting Moscow's hegemony is responsible for preserving the Soviet bloc. Therefore, it would be a serious mistake to conclude that the Soviet threat to Eastern Europe has become a myth. Insofar as Eastern Europe is concerned, it is still very real.

Yugoslavia and Soviet Policy

SIR DUNCAN WILSON, G.C.M.G.

It is now about thirty years since the Yugoslav break with the Cominform and the gradual development from 1949 to 1953 of an identifiable "Yugoslav way to socialism." It cannot be long before Tito dies or retires from active politics, and the equilibrium that he has established both within Yugoslavia and in its international relations will then be endangered. At home he has managed, if not to solve Yugoslavia's "nationalities" problem, at least to contain it and also to achieve a working balance between a fairly liberal economy and a fairly restrictive political system. His foreign policy has involved an even more acrobatic balancing act. He has developed strong economic links and tolerable political relations with Western countries. At the same time, the formal political monopoly enjoyed in Yugoslavia by the Communists has made him acceptable to the Soviet leaders.

The price Tito long had to pay for this was to be the target, as an embodiment of "bourgeois revisionism," for Mao's radicals in China; but now he has been welcomed in Peking as a national leader who has always known how to stand up to the Russians. As one of the original leaders with Nasser and Nehru of the "nonaligned" nations, Tito has also enjoyed the status of an honorary Asian or African in the continuing "North-South" debate between the developed and developing countries of the world. This status is not very welcome to the Soviet government, which is even less liberal than the Western powers with economic aid.

Can Tito's successors continue this virtuoso act? Will the Soviet government allow it to continue? And if not, what action can or will the Soviet government take to prevent them from doing so? The importance of these questions to the Western alliance is so obvious that there is no need to dwell on it. Before they can be answered, however, some historical analysis of the development of Soviet-Yugoslav relations over the past thirty years is necessary.

The break between Yugoslavia and the Soviet Union in 1948 was in the first instance a conflict of personalities, and the personality of Tito has remained an important factor in Soviet-Yugoslav relations. Stalin disliked his independence. He was a national leader who had not been imported in the wake of the Soviet army, however much that army had helped him in 1944 and 1945. Moreover, he had pursued a course disagreeable to Moscow on various domestic and foreign issues between 1943 and 1948. If there was a parallel case in the Communist world, it was that of Mao Tse-tung. Tito's deviations, and this is an important point, were never in a liberal democratic direction. His faults in Stalin's view were that during World War II he pursued a domestic policy of Communization without regard to the Soviet need not to frighten off the Western allies and that after the war his policy toward neighboring countries seemed liable to lead the Soviet government into a major East-West confrontation. Stalin, probably misled by his advisers, thought that Tito was too big for his boots and that, if it came to a choice, enough of Tito's colleagues would place their loyalty to Moscow above their loyalty to him. This was a momentous miscalculation. Tito's successful resistance to Stalin in 1948 vastly increased his prestige outside as well as inside Yugoslavia. It had as great a mythical value as the wartime exploits of the Partisans and gave the Yugoslav Communists a self-confidence that has remained an important factor in Soviet-Yugoslav relations.

Since 1948 Yugoslav independence has been to some extent institutionalized. In the four years before the death of Stalin, the essential steps were taken to develop a new economic system and a new political theory within Yugoslavia. On the economic front, even without a blockade from Eastern Europe, which in 1947 had accounted for most of Yugoslavia's foreign trade and the essential supplies on which their ambitious plans were based, the overcentralized economy and overdetailed plans would probably have collapsed. In 1950 the hectic drive toward agricultural collectivization that had been undertaken after 1948 as a proof to their own faithful that the Yugoslav leaders were exemplary Communists had been brought to a standstill by stubborn peasant resistance. At the end of 1950, arrangements were made with the United States and other Western governments for a regular supply of economic assistance. Thus the transition was eased toward something closer to a market economy and the recognition of profit as an important incentive.

Another vital step for the Yugoslavs was the evolution of a new ideological position within the Communist framework. When it became clear that there could be no accommodation with the Cominform powers under Stalin, at least the lower ranks of the Yugoslav Communist Party found it hard to be simultaneously anti-Stalinist and Communist. At this stage Yugoslav ideologists, primarily Edvard Kardelj and Milovan Djilas, set out to prove from plenty of available data that Stalin represented "bureaucratic" and "hegemonistic" tendencies alien to the essence of Marxism and Leninism. The Yugoslav party was the true believer; the Communist Party of the Soviet Union (CPSU) was the heretic. Then Yugoslav practice began to be adapted to this new tenet; there was some administrative decentralization, less arbitrary activity by the secret police, and some public diminution of the more obvious party privileges. Most important of all, the campaign for the collectivization of agriculture was officially canceled, and the "private" status of peasant farmers was tolerated.

However, simply to oppose arbitrary domestic policy and support the export of a certain kind of revolution was not in itself an inspiring program. The theorists were encouraged to find a more positive idea with which the Yugoslavs could illustrate their claim to be the true heirs of Marx and Lenin. As a result the law on workers' self-management was announced by Tito in June 1950, and workers' councils began to be formed throughout Yugoslav industry. Any idea of a purely syndicalist state was firmly precluded by the Basic Laws passed at the end of 1951, which provided a rigid framework for the operation of the new councils; and the monopolist party remained able to run workers' councils as well as parliamentary assemblies. Nonetheless, the rudiments of a new system existed, and the Yugoslav Communist Party at its Sixth Congress in November 1952 took some formal steps to adapt itself to the new situation. As a sign of new times, the party was rechristened the League of Yugoslav Communists (LCY). It undertook to dissociate itself from the direct administration of the country and to become instead the conscience of society, which should prevent the blind pursuit of particular interests by workers' councils or local committees. The LCY pledged itself, in its own official phraseology, to use "persuasive" and not "administrative" means.

By the spring of 1953, therefore, the distinctive elements of a "Yugoslav way to socialism" were becoming visible—administrative decentralization, some play for incentive and the profit motive, the LCY as social conscience rather than an organ of dictatorship, cautious links on a national basis with the Western powers, and the LCY links with "progressive forces" all over the world. In March 1953, however, Stalin died, and thus the negative foundation, so to speak, of Yugoslav policy was removed. Since then there has been a continuous dialectic in Yugoslavia between the main proponents of the comparatively liberal ideas evolved in 1950–53 and those who, mistrusting the social and political implications of these ideas, thought that the Soviet Union after Stalin was likely to develop along less bureaucratic and hegemonistic lines and were generally anxious to draw as close as possible to the Soviet Union without sacrificing Yugoslav independence.

Again, the position of Tito has been crucial. His instinct has been to throw his weight against "reformers." It was he who had the greatest confidence in the reforming intentions of Khrushchev, and he who most disliked lack of discipline in the LCY and signs of "rotten liberalism" (i.e., Western influence) in Yugoslav society as a whole. But he could also sense better than anyone else the reality of Soviet threats to Yugoslav independence. He would not abandon the"Yugoslav way" as he saw it. He could appreciate the economic necessities that had stimulated the "liberal" Communists in Yugoslavia to action, and he backed them effectively when circumstances forced him to do so. For many years the dialectic between the two wings of the LCY, with Tito hovering as long as possible above the argument, was the main key to internal developments in Yugoslavia. It was also for a long time the key to the pattern of Soviet-Yugoslav relations.

From Stalin's death until 1970 this pattern involved a succession of rapprochements and estrangements—attractions to and repulsions from the pole of Moscow. In 1953 Tito wanted to leave the door open for a reconciliation with Stalin's successors. He sincerely hoped for and expected "positive social developments" in the Soviet Union, away from bureaucracy and hegemony. One of his motives in disciplining Djilas early in 1954, and rejecting any idea of political pluralism at home, was to prove to Khrushchev the quality of his Communism. The year 1956 was the time of closest reconciliation between the Soviet and Yugoslav leaders. Khrushchev adopted some Yugoslav ideas at the Twentieth Congress of the CPSU, distancing himself some way from Stalin and admitting the concept of "different ways to socialism" and "peaceful coexistence." Communism, he argued, did not need revolution to triumph in bourgeois or social democrat countries. When Khrushchev decided later in 1956 that the leadership in Eastern European countries would have to be changed in order to give some wider reality to these ideas, Tito for a few months could regard himself as Khrushchev's main adviser, and his former ambition for a dominant role in Eastern Europe began to reemerge.

The revolution in Hungary in November 1956 and the Soviet counteraction blasted these hopes. They also introduced a new factor on the scene of European Communism—China—as a powerful supporter of centralist discipline. A brief phase of Yugoslav repulsion from Moscow ensued, while Khrushchev tried to come to terms with Mao. The new Yugoslav party program introduced at the Seventh Party Congress in the spring of 1958 expressed far more interest in "self-management"—intranational and international—than the Chinese and, at this stage, Khrushchev could tolerate. But by the summer of 1959 the Chinese had badly overplayed their hand. Khrushchev began to recoil from policies that he styled "adventurist," and the way was open to a second reconciliation with Yugoslavia by 1962. This was facilitated by a dangerous overheating of Yugoslavia's "self-managing" economy at this period, which led to a short-lived attempt at recentralization and tighter social control by the LCY.

At the same time a new factor in Yugoslav foreign policy began to have an effect on Soviet-Yugoslav relations. In the mid-1950s Tito had conceived the idea of "nonalignment" as adding a moral element to Yugoslav foreign policy and increasing Yugoslavia's international importance. His close personal links with Nasser and Nehru enabled him to join and sometimes lead the group of nations outside NATO and the Warsaw Pact. They did not wish to become embroiled in a cold war that might easily turn into a hot one, and they felt that the money spent by the "blocs" on armaments could be better used for development aid. In 1960 and 1961, however, Tito's emphasis on "nonalignment" worked strongly for the Soviet Union. "Decolonization" was the main theme of the Asian and African leaders at this period. On this issue the pressure both at the United Nations and at "nonaligned" summit conferences was entirely on the Western powers and served well the general purposes of the Soviet leaders. This was in fact the period, 1961–62, when Tito nearly lost his international balance and toppled over toward the East.

This trend ended in 1964 for economic reasons. The brief "recentralization" had been a failure, and the LCY decided formally at its Eighth Congress that the only way out of Yugoslavia's multiple economic difficulties was a fundamental economic reform, which would allow market factors to have much freer play internally and which would adapt the structure of the Yugoslav economy more closely to the world market. State and party relations with the Soviet Union remained good, despite the fall of Khrushchev in 1964; but the economic reform carried out in the summer of 1965 involved ever closer links with the Common Market countries in particular and a period of growing Western influence in the social and intellectual as well as the economic life of Yugoslavia. The policy of reform was opposed, not least for these reasons, by many "conservative" or centralist Communists, up to the highest level of the LCY. Tito had much sympathy for them, and Yugoslav history might have been very different had they displayed more caution. But their opposition to economic reform assumed the proportions of "fractionalism" or conspiracy by Vice President Aleksandar Rankovic, and in June 1966 Tito felt bound to act decisively against it. Rankovic was indicted largely for the misuse of his capacity as head of the secret police. His fall was accompanied by startling revelations of their corruption and by commitments to a much higher standard of legality in the future use of their powers. Whatever Rankovic's connections with the Soviet leaders, and there is some evidence that they were quite close, the circumstances of his fall worked in favor of closer approximation of the Yugoslav social pattern to Western standards.

Even so, formal relations with the Soviet government remained good, especially on foreign policy issues. Then, however, in 1968 the "Prague spring" supervened. The Czech economy was decentralized, the Czech Communist Party was transformed, and an effort was made to give a "human face" to socialism. These changes met with Tito's open and wholehearted approval. Perhaps he saw in them a sign of the direct influence of Yugoslav ideas in Eastern Europe. He welcomed the fact that Alexander Dubcek, unlike Imre Nagy in 1956, made no attempt to loosen formal ties with the other Warsar Pact countries. Nonetheless, the Soviet leaders decided that the new regime in Prague was a threat to their imperial interests and invaded Czechoslovakia in August 1968. For some weeks the Yugoslavs thought that the clock was being turned back twenty years. Tito's public position was that there was again a serious threat to Rumanian and Yugoslav independence, and he made it clear that the Yugoslavs would defend themselves.

Tito had his own domestic reasons for invoking national unity against a foreign threat, and the immediate scare soon passed, but the Soviet invasion of Czechoslovakia marked another important turning point in Soviet-Yugoslav relations. State and party links have indeed been restored to normality. There has often been an appearance of cordiality in the exchange of high-level visits, and foreign policy interests have often coincided, particularly over East-West détente and the Middle East. But it has been hard even for Tito to detect in the Brezhnev regime the "positive social tendencies" that he welcomed under Khrushchev. And the "Brezhnev doctrine" of 1968—the idea that the Soviet government had the right, or duty, to intervene if "socialism" is ever threatened in a "socialist" country—has made any formal reentry into the socialist camp even less attractive to Yugoslavia than before.

Meanwhile, within Yugoslavia the dialectic between liberal and conservative Communists continues and will continue after Tito has departed from the political scene. It has indeed become inextricably mixed up with other questions and is both more complicated and less important in itself than it once was. The main point, however, is that it will not be easy for any new Yugoslav leader to reverse the elaborate machinery of self-management, as finally formulated by the 1974 constitution and the 1976 Associated Labor Act. Formulation, particularly of such a complicated kind, may not mean so much as practice, and to describe Yugoslav practice adequately months of study on the scene would be necessary. The author can only make the broad, and doubtless arbitrary, judgment that self-management has not only been institutionalized in Yugoslavia, but is also a working system.

No doubt it does not work as it should. The average man's time, energy, and goodwill are unlikely to qualify him to be such a completely active citizen as the system prescribes, participating in an overlapping network of committees as producer, general consumer, consumer of social services, and so on. He probably still prefers to spend time in maintaining his personal links with the food-producing countryside, perhaps staying at his weekend cottage, perhaps in doing a spare-time private job. And the good factory director will no doubt have his own unofficial ways of making the elaborate economic system work. But the model does work somehow, and there is genuine participation from the factory floor upwards in making it work. Thus, it will be harder after Tito's disappearance than before to modify it from above in a centralist sense, and this in itself is an important factor in Soviet-Yugoslav relations.

The new internal equilibrium reached within Yugoslavia in the last five years has in fact resulted largely from the "nationalities crisis" of 1971 and 1972. Racial tensions between the ex-Austro-Hungarian and the ex-Ottoman parts of Yugoslavia were quite effectively contained during the first fifteen years of the Communist regime, but played an increasingly important part as power was transferred from the center of the federation and as the problem of economic development came to the fore. The crucial question was whether to invest in success, as evidenced in the comparatively highly developed industries of Croatia and Slovenia, or to create new sources of wealth in the less developed republics of Macedonia, Montenegro, and Bosnia.

This dilemma had its reflection in internal Yugoslav politics and not least in the dialectic between liberal and conservative Communists. It also tended to spill over into the field of foreign policy. To put the matter oversimply and crudely, Croat and Slovene Communists tended to favor more economic independence for the developed republics, less intervention by the central organs of the LCY, closer links with Western countries—particularly with those on their borders, which absorbed so much of their labor surplus—and hence increasing divergence from the Soviet model. The less developed republics preferred a more centralized system of investment, less laissez-faire, and more political power to the LCY. If this involved more general regimentation of society, it was all the more likely to be acceptable to the Soviet Union.

At the end of 1971 Tito was faced with something very like a breakaway movement on these issues in Croatia. To the outside observer, Yugoslavia already resembled a confederation of republics much more nearly than a federal state, and Croat representatives in Belgrade seemed already to have brought much of the federal machinery to a halt. This, however, was not enough for Croat nationalists obsessed with historical claims to independence and with the conviction that Croatia contributed economically much more to the Yugoslav federal government than it could ever get back from it. On the second point, at least they carried with them most of the prominent Croat Communists, including the prime minister, Savka Dabcevic-Kucar, who seemed to have thought that she could successfully tame the nationalist tiger.

Meanwhile, the extreme nationalists were suspected of links with Croat émigré organizations in Germany, and of being in touch through them with Soviet agents. One way or another the Soviet government hoped to profit from this crisis of the Yugoslav state. Tito revealed in 1971 and 1972 that Brezhnev had offered him aid in dealing with Croat separatism. Here was a new element in the pattern of Soviet-Yugoslav relations, one that could reappear in a highly destabilizing form. Tito's energetic action at the end of 1971 defused the "nationalities crisis." Yugoslavia has become, under the 1974 constitution, an even more confederate state than before. Its economy still inclines toward the West, especially the Common Market; but in the last five years Yugoslavs have also managed to increase their trade with Eastern Europe, as a reinsurance against a recession in the West and the application of restrictions on their exports. The political line of the LCY has correspondingly hardened, and some brakes have been imposed on what might be called the "Occidentation" of Yugoslav society.

Brezhnev has also made some contribution to the present comparatively even state of Soviet-Yugoslav relations. He has declared more than once, most recently during President Tito's visit in September 1977, that the Soviet Union will respect Yugoslav independence. He has also adopted or tolerated various foreign policy positions that Yugoslavs support. They had long been in favor of something like the Conference on Security and Cooperation in Europe (CSCE) held at Helsinki in the summer of 1975 and of the broad agreements of principle that were reached there. Since the "review" conference in 1977 was to be held in Belgrade, the Yugoslavs had some proprietary interest in the successful codification of those principles of "peaceful coexistence" that they themselves had long advocated. The Soviet leaders can, moreover, count on the Yugoslavs not to press too hard on questions of human rights, such as "Basket Three" of the Helsinki package. There were too many skeletons, though minor ones by Soviet standards, in their own cupboard, and Tito himself has always been ready to take a Soviet-type stance on Western interference in the internal affairs of other countries.

Another vital question on which the Soviet government has moved nearer to the Yugoslav position has been that of Eurocommunism. The acceptance of the doctrine of "different ways to socialism" in respect to Asian and African countries, or even for Western European countries without a strong Communist party, was one thing. The application of this doctrine to the Warsaw Pact countries, or to countries like France and Italy with strong indigenous Communist parties, was quite another. Theoretically, however, the Soviet government accepted at the Berlin Conference of European Communist Parties in July 1976, a degree of independence for them that the Yugoslavs had preached and illustrated since 1952.

At the risk of oversimplication, it may be said that in the last five years Tito has achieved a new type of equilibrium, or has allowed it to take shape, both on the Yugoslav internal front and in Soviet-Yugoslav relations. In both cases there is a sort of implicit bargain. Internally, a considerable amount of freedom is allowed to market forces, to private economic initiative, and to the satisfaction of consumer needs. This freedom is based on the implicit understanding that the highly complicated forms of "total self-management" are generally observed, as defined in the legislation of 1974 and 1976, and on the further conditions that the LCY retain its political monopoly and exercise it from time to time in a restrictive sense against, for example, neo-Marxist philosophers whose famous magazine, *Praxis*, ceased publication in 1975, and artists and authors who conspicuously deviate from the canons of "socialist realism." It should be added that, even in these respects, Yugoslavia remains a very open society in comparison with the Soviet Union.

In the field of foreign affairs the implicit bargain with the Soviet Union seems to be that Yugoslavia follow its own "way to socialism" as defined above, provided that it does not propagate it too actively among the member countries of the Warsaw Pact and provided that on a reasonable number of important issues of interstate foreign policy the Yugoslav government backs the Soviet line.

Thus, the former regular pattern of attractions and repulsions between Belgrade and Moscow has been modified in the last five years and has been succeeded by some rapprochement and a new state of Yugoslav balance between East and West, inclining more to the East than in the years 1966 through 1970. Tito has preserved an almost ostentatious equilibrium in his public actions. On the one hand, he has made it impossible for the Marxist-humanist periodical *Praxis* to continue publication—no "rotten liberalism" for Yugoslavia. On the other hand, there are occasional arrests and trials of "Cominformists"—people who want to rebuild the LCY on a centralized Soviet model and have perhaps been recruited by Soviet agents for this purpose—and a first visit to Peking in September 1977 to balance the immediately preceding visit to Moscow. Thus if Tito has attained an equilibrium between East and West, it is hardly a static one. It is still marked by swings to one side or the other, even if these are smaller than in the past, and it is very much the expression of his own personality.

Will this equilibrium last after Tito's death or retirement? What are the basic issues that will then determine Soviet-Yugoslav relations? The Soviet interests are fairly clear, and it is the Soviet side of the relationship that is likely to be the more stable of the two under Brezhnev or his immediate successors. Whatever social and economic forces are at work in the Soviet Union, it is likely to remain for some time a highly centralized state, hostile to the comparatively liberal and "capitalist" democracies of the West, and with a Communist party enjoying a monopoly of effective power.

The word *enjoying* is used advisedly. There is no sign that the Soviet leaders are prepared to forgo their political monopoly, and their extreme reluctance to do so is increased by their essentially imperial position in Eastern Europe. Whatever might happen in their own country, the Soviet leaders know that in the other Warsaw Pact countries anything less than a Communist political monopoly would probably involve an anti-Communist political revolution. This is what Soviet troops fought to prevent in Hungary in 1956 and in Czechoslovakia in 1968. There is little doubt that in the same cause they would be sent to fight again. Even if they have learned nominally at least to accept some diversity among Western European Communist parties, this does not necessarily apply to the countries of the Warsaw Pact. And if "peaceful coexistence" with the West is necessary for some time, the qualification remains that it should not involve the cessation of "ideological war"; in less abstract terms, economic and technical contacts must not involve exchange of political ideas or the risk of political infection.

Yugoslavia is, of course, one obvious source or potential source of such an infection. And here it is the very existence of Yugoslavia, as an Eastern European Slavic state outside the Soviet system, which is the crucial issue. It is doubtful whether Poland and Hungary in 1956 or Czechoslovakia in 1968 paid much attention to the details of Yugoslav experiments in self-management. But the existence of an independent Yugoslavia was in itself an encouragement for them to evolve their own national models, and the Yugoslav foreign policy of "nonalignment" has encouraged Rumania to practice a sort of "nonalignment" even from within the Warsaw Pact, symbolized by its maintaining diplomatic relations with Israel and by its special link with China. It could even be argued that Yugoslavia is more troublesome to the Soviet Eastern European empire as an independent Communist state than it would be if, by some unlikely conjunction, it developed a multiparty system and closer political links with the West, though the Soviet leaders would do their best to prevent such a development.

Yugoslav independence remains in any case an offense in the eyes of the Soviet Union, and it is strongly interested in getting Yugoslavia back into the "socialist camp" as a comparatively obedient satellite. The main benefit would be political, and primarily local in Eastern Europe, though the political blow to the West would also be severe. The military bonus could also be considerable if the Soviet Union gained access to ports on the Adriatic and drove a wedge between the countries of NATO's southern flank. The risk of immediate armed reaction from the West it might calculate to be small, after the example of Czechoslovakia. But it must also think that the political and economic fruits of East-West détente, such as it is at present, must be sacrificed. And the local risks arising from Yugoslav reactions might escalate if the return to the "socialist camp" were not effected smoothly. On the other side, a tolerable sort of Soviet coexistence with Tito's Yugoslavia has been achieved, limiting the effects of Yugoslav independence. The Czech example is still a warning to other Communist states of Eastern Europe that they cannot enjoy too much independence, and Tito himself has been ready on some vital issues to meet urgent Soviet requests, such as the overflight and refuelling of Soviet aircraft during the Middle East crises of 1967 and 1973. Obviously, then, a vital point for the Soviet leaders is to estimate how far Tito's successor or successors will continue on such issues to lean toward the Soviet Union.

On the Yugoslav side the basic issue now, as in 1948, is simply that of independence. Whatever Khrushchev may have said in 1956, or Brezhnev in 1976 at the Berlin Conference of European Communist Parties, about the permissibility of "different ways to socialism," Tito's successors as much as Tito himself will be well aware of the dangers of the bear hug. The "socialist camp," as Tito said to Khrushchev, sounds uncomfortably like something with barbed wire around it. Reentry into it would certainly force any Yugoslav government to pursue a much less individual foreign policy and to impose tighter internal discipline. The close economic links forged with the West would be broken, and the economic cost of the total "reorientation" of Yugoslav foreign policy would be high.

On the internal front, too, considerable risks would be involved. It would need determined leadership and a strong uniform party to impose on Croatia and Slovenia, with their vital economic interests in the Western connection, a totally pro-Soviet policy. Tito had enough trouble in 1971 and 1972 in scotching the threat of Croat separation. It proved on that occasion that the Yugoslav army and secret police were loyal to the center and could not be split up into "Republican" units with "Republican" loyalties. No doubt steps have been taken to ensure that this remains so, but the strain involved, e.g., on Croatian generals in acting for the federal government against a revived movement for Croatian independence, should not be underestimated. It might not be easy for Tito's successors to suppress such a movement without some such "fraternal aid" as Brezhnev offered to Tito in 1971. On the other hand, it is hard to imagine that such aid could be accepted without grave risks to the internal stability of Yugoslavia, up to and including a mass popular reaction such as took place in March 1941, when the Cvetkovic government signed its pact with Hitler. And this in turn could precipitate a major East-West confrontation over Yugoslavia, unless the Western will and capacity for resistance were already undermined.

The Yugoslav as well as the Soviet leaders could therefore calculate that, in the present general East-West political climate and relation of forces, any attempt to incorporate Yugoslavia in the "socialist camp" would be fraught with danger. A crisis situation can, however, be envisaged that would start with the resurgence of national tensions in acute form within Yugoslavia. Would this force Tito's successors to recentralize at any cost, including the cost of accepting Soviet aid? And, if so, would it not be in the interest of the Soviet leaders to foster such a situation? Might they not be tempted to establish a new foothold in Yugoslavia by covert encouragement on the one hand to "Cominformists" (conservative centralist Communists) and, on the other, to extreme and disruptive nationalist movements that could serve as an excuse for centralist action?

Again, however, Soviet leaders must consider that, at least in the present state of East-West relations, this could be a dangerous game. It could especially be so when Tito, with his unique personal prestige, is no longer on the political scene and when separatist movements in Yugoslavia could conceivably lead to the separation of Croatia, Dalmatia, and Slovenia (the old constituents of the Austro-Hungarian Empire) from the rest. These unlikely separations could occur only after the collapse of central leadership in the Yugoslav army, secret police, and LCY. But unless Soviet penetration of these is greater than is expected at the present, the Soviet leaders have to consider this risk and the consequent possibility that the West would profit as well as Moscow from separatist movements that developed too much activity. It seems likely, then, that the Soviet leaders will for the present prefer the long-term chance that Yugoslavia will ultimately gravitate toward them as a whole to any gamble involved in encouraging separatist movements and then intervening to suppress them.

As for the Yugoslavs themselves, any possible successors to Tito will be well aware of what is at stake for themselves and their country. There is only one quarter from which their independence will be threatened, and this they know well enough, whatever they may say. No successor to Tito will have his prestige or, for some time at least, his practice in international maneuver. Equally, however, none will have his particular emotional interest in reconciliation with Moscow or will be tempted to sail quite so close to the East wind. To that extent their task will be easier than the one Tito set himself, and they will know from the example that he set in 1948 and 1968 that a serious threat from the East can be a great unifier of their country. Thus the outlook over the next few years is for no substantial change in Yugoslav-Soviet relations unless Western weakness or expressions of disinterest lead the Soviet leaders to overconfidence and induce despair on the Yugoslav side.

Southern Africa: Testing Détente

RICHARD E. BISSELL

Southern Africa has one feature common to both Soviet and American perceptions: the region is equally remote geographically from both superpowers. Beyond that, it has served only as a focus of conflict during the last several years for the two powers—to the point that some observers have cited it as an illustrative failure of the pursuit of détente with the Soviet Union.

The relationship between the Soviet-American détente and events in southern Africa has suffered from a number of myths. As so often happens, when a myth is repeated often enough, it takes on the character of a fact in the public mind. In mid-1977, for instance, a study prepared for the House International Relations Committee could say in all confidence that "Soviet intervention in Angola clearly threatened détente." At the same time the report stated that "the Soviets perceived no such contradictions; they justified intervention." M.A. Suslov, a member of the Politburo and chief ideologist of the Communist Party of the Soviet Union, has explained the absence of perceived contradictions in Soviet attitudes toward détente: "The principle of peaceful coexistence between states with different social systems, as is well known, has nothing in common with class peace between the exploiters and the exploited, the colonialists and the victims of colonial oppression, or between the oppressors and the oppressed." *Pravda* phrased the same argument differently: "The policy of peaceful coexistence and the relaxation of tensions in relations between states with different social systems—a policy which is generally recognized in our time—cannot be interpreted as a ban on the national liberation struggle of the peoples who oppose colonial oppression or as a ban on the class struggle." The principal question to be answered in this essay, then, deals not only with objective Soviet actions in southern Africa and their general trends, but also with the American reaction as conditioned by the détente atmosphere generated by the Nixon-Kissinger diplomacy. If a major purpose of détente, after all, was a lessening of Soviet-American tensions in all parts of the world, can one say that Soviet and American leaders have been equally responsible in restraining conflicts in southern Africa? The answer to that question could be useful in assessing the utility of linking various issues within the one negotiating framework of détente.

Soviet Involvement in Southern Africa

There are four reasons for Soviet interest in southern Africa: (1) political—the effort to dislodge traditional Western powers from an area of influence; (2) economic—the attraction of raw materials common in southern Africa; (3) ideological—the historical pursuit of Marxist-Leninist goals to create other socialist societies; and (4) strategic—the global competition involving the "imperial" Soviet Union in which key sea passages such as the Cape of Good Hope assume great importance, particularly when the United States is denied access to them.

Without attempting to attribute greater or lesser strength to these various reasons, one can say that southern Africa has offered an uncommon opportunity to pursue all four purposes at the same time. In many cases, the Soviet Union has found that the third world offers opportunities in which one purpose will contradict another. In the Middle East, for instance, gaining political advantage with an indigenous government can mean sacrificing the local Communist party. Southern Africa, the record will show, offers few such contradictions for Soviet policymakers.

Soviet interest in southern Africa prior to 1970 was virtually nonexistent. Within South Africa, a Communist party had existed for a number of decades, but it was banned by the government and was therefore largely in exile. The Soviet projection of power and influence did not attempt to reach that far south. The Khrushchev record of attempting to seize opportunities in black Africa was certainly not one to encourage imitation. In Ghana, after much investment of time and effort, most of the Soviets were ejected from the country with the fall of Kwame Nkrumah in 1966. With somewhat more success, they remained in Sekou Touré's Guinea, where they have obtained secure access to air and naval facilities to conduct surveillance of the mid-Atlantic Ocean region. But southern Africa never offered comparable opportunities before 1970. The economies of southern Africa were firmly linked to mining and trading networks centered on Britain, South Africa, and Portugal. Support facilities were insufficient to attempt the regular projection of Soviet power into the area. And the one major prestige project supervised by a non-Western power during this period, the Tan-Zam Railroad, was constructed by the Chinese.

The only real opportunity open to the Soviet Union was the construction of relationships with the various nationalist guerrilla groups attempting to overthrow regimes in Rhodesia, the Portuguese colonies, and South Africa. Considering the unpredictability of the guerrilla leaders, however, the Soviet Union found it worthwhile to give only minor amounts of cash and small arms. Their realistic evaluations could hardly justify more: the chances of guerrilla success in the near future were very slim, the American intelligence services had more influence on some major guerrilla leaders (Joshua Nkomo of Rhodesia, Holden Roberto of Angola, and Eduardo Mondlane of Mozambique), and the guerrilla movements in the only real prize of the region (South Africa) were manifestly incompetent in the face of South African power.

By the early 1970s, then, the Soviet Union appeared to take on the attributes of a capitalist state in its relations with southern Africa: it was more interested in trade agreements than socialist revolutions, engaged in the creation of state-to-state relations with black Africa, and content to condemn white-ruled governments in the United Nations while trading in embargoed Rhodesian chrome for substantial profits. The dramatic changes to occur in Soviet policy in the wake of the Portuguese revolution of 1974, then, were to shock much of the world not so much because of their long-term historical significance but because the Soviet Union had shown little interest in southern Africa before 1974.

The current role of southern Africa as a testing ground for détente stems primarily from the change of power in Portugal in 1974 and the decision of the new military rulers to grant independence to the African colonies. In Mozambique, where the Mozambique Liberation Front (FRELIMO) had reigned as the supreme liberation movement for some time, the transition to power did not involve outside help. The Soviet Union had a cordial relationship with the new rulers, stemming primarily from arms provisions over a period of years, but so did China, several African nations, and those who had provided social assistance (the Scandinavian states and private citizens of the United States, among others). The Soviet Union and the Eastern European states did become increasingly involved after the independence of Mozambique, but this was due primarily to the need for law and order. This need, precipitated by the Rhodesian border problems and the unrepresentative nature of the FRELIMO regime, was satisfied mostly by a large East German security force. Even if there had been greater Mozambique interest in Soviet cooperation, the attention of the Soviet Union was being totally distracted by Angola.

The Portuguese authorities had planned to grant independence to Angola on November 11, 1975, and the events there did more than simply transfer power to a black government. The emergence of the Popular Movement for the Liberation of Angola (MPLA), with the contribution of Cuban and Soviet arms and advisers, brought into question the extent of Soviet aims and tactics in southern Africa and elsewhere.

During the first half of 1975, most observers only gradually became aware of the drift of events in Angola. The three liberation movements—the MPLA, the National Union for the Total Independence of Angola (UNITA), and the National Front for the Liberation of Angola (FNLA)—were not cooperating. Political factions based on geographic and tribal factors developed as the MPLA moved into the capital of Luanda. The FNLA, supported by Zaire and the United States, controlled the northern part of the country, while UNITA, led by Dr. Jonas Savimbi and supported by neighboring Zambia, occupied the south. By the end of June, however, events began to move more rapidly. The Soviet Union shipped in 100 tons of light arms in April; in May and June weapons arrived in seven ships (four Soviet, two East German, and one Algerian) on Soviet orders for the MPLA.

The first crisis came in July, when the MPLA utilized its advantageous position in Luanda to eject the other liberation movements from the capital and to announce that it alone would succeed the Portuguese authorities in November. Such a premature attempt to seize power by the MPLA prompted a round of decision-making by each of the outside powers with an interest in the conflict.

The initial United States response was to propose confidentially to the Soviet Union a withdrawal from the conflict of all non-African powers. When rebuffed in that effort, Secretary of State Kissinger turned to the Central Intelligence Agency to provide covert aid to the FNLA and UNITA. While such a move was opposed by many of the bureaucrats in the African Affairs Division of the State Department, the secretary of state apparently felt that the demands for aid were more insistent, particularly when endorsed by African leaders close to the scene, including those of Zaire, Zambia, and South Africa. American aid increased noticeably after July 1975.

It is beyond doubt that Kissinger initially attempted to use the diplomatic atmosphere of détente to defuse the situation. The Soviet Union either could not or would not respond to the Kissinger initiative. Since the entry of other Communist states, such as Cuba, did not appear until the late summer of 1975, it can be assumed that the Soviet Union still had a free hand and chose not to respond to Kissinger at a time when the Soviet Union appeared to hold all the bargaining chips. Kissinger's response, in using covert CIA channels, was designed to communicate privately to the Soviet Union the extent of America's willingness to defend its interests, while publicly maintaining the détente relationship.

In Luanda, the MPLA consolidated its hold with substantial aid from the then radical Portuguese government and from various Communist governments. Since the first Cuban troops arrived in early September, it appears that Castro had decided to send substantial troop support toward the end of July. Some form of coordination between the Soviet Union and Cuba existed, for the buildup of weapons that could be operated only by non-African troops began in late summer, as shipments from Black Sea ports and Algeria grew in volume. What cannot be determined is whether Cuba or the Soviet Union took the initiative in such a large-scale commitment. It was obviously in both their interests to support the rise of the MPLA, but such an involvement of conventional troops clearly carried a number of risks—and perhaps even jeopardized détente.

The interest of the Soviet Union in the events developing in Angola depended, in addition, on an unusual factor: the position and role of the Communist Party of Portugal (PCP). The PCP, in contrast to a number of other European Communist parties, has consistently followed the Soviet line, both during its existence underground when it was suppressed by the Salazar dictatorship and after its emergence as a legitimate political force in 1974. The role of the PCP, indeed, was critical during the first eighteen months after the Portuguese coup; its power was proven to be an illusion only in the 1976 elections in Portugal. But in regard to Angolan developments, the role of the PCP was significant. The PCP, after all, had a major influence on the Socialist army leaders governing Angola during the transition to independence. It was they who allowed the ships from the Communist nations to dock in Luanda and transfer arms to the MPLA without risk to the Soviet donors. Without such a legitimate means of infusing its influence into the Angolan scene, it is unlikely that the Soviet Union and Cuba would have been involved to such an extent. Important, too, was the attitude of the Portuguese regime to the MPLA. In July, when the MPLA showed its determination to monopolize power in Luanda, the Portuguese army stood back, acknowledging the implicit transfer of political power to indigenous forces before independence. The MPLA was the most attractive nationalist group to many Europeans, being relatively well educated, urbane, and multi-racial in its leadership. Thus the Soviet Union was not dealing with a band of guerrilla insurgents. Its arms and advisers were being shipped to a government-to-be. In Soviet perceptions, the diplomatic gamble was far less than the world made it out to be. The MPLA's leader, Dr. Agostinho Neto, was a confirmed product of the PCP, the arms and advisers could be shipped into the Luanda harbor on invitation and without risk, and Angola had the hard currency source (Cabindan oil) to pay for the arms once independence and power were won.

By November, Soviet support for the MPLA regime was wholehearted. The Soviet Union's clients followed its lead on November 11, 1975, and recognized the Angolan government; besides the Eastern European bloc, this group included Somalia, Congo, Mozambique, North Vietnam, Algeria, Guinea, and Cuba. When Moscow attempted to apply similar pressure on Uganda's mercurial president, Idi Amin, to recognize the MPLA, he expelled the Soviet ambassador. The break in relations lasted only six days, November 11-17, when the ambassador returned to apologize. At the same time, American intelligence sources indicated that Soviet military advisers were not in Angola itself. The field work was being left to the Cubans.

With the escalation of the conflict in November, the American government attempted once again to lower the stakes, except that in contrast to its tack in July, when Secretary of State Kissinger had offered the Soviet leaders a carrot, it chose in November to use the stick of détente. In his Detroit speech of November 24, Kissinger warned that the United States could not "remain indifferent" to Soviet and Cuban intervention. Such a decision to "go public," however, failed on two scores. The Communist powers ignored his protests, and the American people were alerted to growing CIA involvement in a foreign conflict, which many fallaciously compared to the Vietnam experience. The secretary's problems were compounded by the beginning, on November 27, of a South African public appeal for American aid to UNITA and the FNLA. Such appeals, combined with public notice of China's withdrawal of aid to the FNLA at the end of November, helped to polarize American debate, with most strength going to the "no aid" faction.

Discussions in the United States over possible aid to the other factions were increasingly affected by the desire to avoid supporting the losing side. The secretary of state finally tried to isolate the Angola question from that of détente in order to avoid imperiling the Strategic Arms Limitation Talks then under way. The only successful diplomatic moves by the United States related to the use of airports in various countries by Cuban troop planes. Most countries—Guyana was an exception—complied with American requests to exclude the Cuban planes, obliging the Soviet Union to use long-range IL-62s for the Cubans.

When the FNLA and UNITA became inactive in January 1976 (temporarily as it turned out), Soviet intervention in the region became more dramatic: several Soviet naval vessels were semipermanently stationed off the Angolan coast; the Soviet fishing fleet in the South Atlantic, with the usual complement of electronic monitoring ships, was expanded, particularly in South African waters; and well-based rumors of discussions between the MPLA and the Soviet Union spread regarding Soviet base rights in Angola.

At the same time, several possible ominous developments did not occur. There was no large-scale infusion of Soviet personnel, since 10,000 to 15,000 Cubans remained to ward off the revived UNITA threat. Gulf Oil remained as the operator of the Cabindan oil concession, thus providing the Angolan government with hard currency for development purposes, and the Soviet Union did not justify its Angolan intervention as a unilateral right. Instead it maintained that it had acted in response to the South African intervention in southern Angola on behalf of UNITA. The accuracy of such a historical argument need not be discussed here. Suffice it to say that the claim for a justified intervention reflected a degree of concern about international opinion.

The Lessons of Angola

Such a Soviet justification did little to pacify a rapidly emerging state of alarm in the United States, Western Europe, and China. What most distressed the informed observers in those countries was the demonstrable ability and willingness of the Soviet Union to intervene successfully in a region so logistically distant, the large-scale transfer of military equipment by air and ship, the coordinated supply of that equipment by clients and satellites, and the use of Soviet sea power to protect convoys of merchantmen in the South Atlantic. The financial cost to the USSR was considerable. The direct costs are difficult to measure since much equipment was outdated from the Soviet army's point of view, and indirect costs such as the break-off of the Cuban-American rapprochement must be considered as well.

With the proven expansion of Soviet military capabilities came statements by Soviet leaders to the effect that Soviet participation in the third world "struggle" was fully compatible with détente. The clear deterioration of the political climate created by détente, as understood by the American side, was clearly occurring in the margins, that is, the third world. To some American observers, the Soviet Union appeared to interpret détente in a convenient fashion. It meant stability and noninterference where consolidation was to the Soviet advantage, i.e., Eastern Europe, but détente allowed the systemic struggle to continue where it was to the advantage of the Soviet Union, as in southern Africa.

The public reaction in the United States was clear-cut. During the election year of 1976, *détente* became a dirty word, the policy was disavowed by President Ford, who was seeking reelection, and the secretary of state turned his attention to southern Africa to regain the initiative for American diplomacy. American foreign policymakers had no choice but to accept the Soviet rules of the game; southern Africa was a realm of competition, not cooperation. Since the American public had understood détente to mean increased cooperation, American diplomatic leaders were seen to have failed. Although Kissinger had wished to "manage the emergence of the Soviet Union as a superpower," he appeared to have succeeded only in making Soviet leaders aware of the rights, but not the responsibilities, of being a superpower. Only historians can measure the ultimate impact of irresponsible Soviet actions in delaying futher agreements arising from the Strategic Arms Limitation Talks (SALT) and expanding the conservative coalition on SALT in the Senate. But it is already clear that the initiatives of the Carter administration with regard to arms limitation have been hamstrung by the legacy of the Angolan confrontation.

Also important, though, is the apparent lesson learned by the Soviet Union in southern Africa: that the West is unable to confirm or terminate its historical relationship with South Africa, which paralyzes Western diplomacy and thus allows the region to become a playground for the Soviet Union. One can judge the Soviet attitude only by its subsequent actions, and they point to increasing involvement. In Mozambique, the government of Samora Machel has been liberally supplied with East German and Cuban advisers, and the latter have been given the duty of flying the eighty to ninety MIGs shipped in during 1977. Mozambique has excluded virtually all influences that are not tied closely to the Soviet Union. This applies to Chinese as well as Western influences. The formerly pro-Western government of Zambia is now a major transit center for Russian advisers and arms to the Patriotic Front of Rhodesia, whose only common element appears to be Soviet support. Without that support and its implicit prohibition of internecine warfare, the Patriotic Front leaders, Joshua Nkomo and Robert Mugabe, would long ago have been carrying on a war between themselves. Finally, the Soviet Union appears to consider itself an arbiter of strategic developments in the region, taking upon itself the responsibility to watch over the growth of South African weapons developments. A major incident in August 1977 is highly illustrative of the new state of affairs.

Détente in Southern Africa, 1977 Style

It has been known for some years that South Africa not only had the capability to produce all the materials for nuclear weapons, but was also probably fabricating a crude nuclear device in case it became militarily isolated. Since such a nuclear weapon would be highly inefficient in the southern African military environment, few observers took such a development to be a qualitative threat to stability in the region. It was reasoned, after all, that South Africa would fall not by external invasion, but by internal erosion of law and order.

Thus it was something of a shock when, in early August 1977, Brezhnev sent a personal message to President Carter, reporting that Soviet spy satellites had revealed plans of the South African government to test an atomic bomb in the South African Kalahari desert. The photographs revealed a structure of a design and configuration often used elsewhere for testing nuclear weapons. The Soviet Union, in its role as the arbiter of peace in southern Africa, also notified France, Britain, and Germany that something needed to be done about this South African development. What the Soviets complained about was the impact that such a test would have on proliferation of weapons and general "international peace and security." The Soviet Union had said little when India demonstrated its nuclear capability. So part of its concern must have derived from anxieties about facing a nuclear opponent in southern Africa.

The response of the United States was straightforward. It asked South Africa for an explanation and for a commitment not to test any nuclear weapons. After considerable argument between the Western nations and South Africa, the latter did publicly state it was not going to conduct an atomic test, but it refused to commit itself as to the future. From the South African perspective, if it had been planning a test, the Soviet demarche had clearly accomplished the same purpose as an actual test. The world now believed that South Africa possessed the atomic bomb. If it had no such bomb, it now had the deterrent value of what is sometimes called "Israel's closet bomb." Whether or not it exists is immaterial; South Africa is now considered a nuclear power.

A further response by the Carter administration, however, betrayed a continuing desire to link the distant issues of southern Africa and détente. Following the episode, Zbigniew K. Brzezinski, assistant to the president for national security affairs, leaked a full account of the Soviet-American cooperation in the South African bomb episode to the major American newspapers. The apparent purpose was to prove that détente was alive and well and that the misunderstandings between the Soviet and American leaders on other Soviet-American issues during the first half of 1977 were being put aside. In effect, if détente had been derailed in southern Africa, it could be recreated there.

One must consider, though, the effect of the episode on southern African politics. The United States was pressed into a confrontation with South Africa by the Soviet Union, and it was a dispute that alienated both the leadership and public opinion in South Africa, an important actor in any negotiated settlements in the region. In addition, the Soviet Union demonstrated its role as the guardian of the black states in southern Africa, a role affirmed by the willingness of the United States to undertake measures against South Africa at the initiative of the Soviet Union. The United States has not prevented the proliferation of nuclear weapons, since all now believe that South Africa possesses "bombs in the closet."

The episode reflected, too, an unusually strong Soviet penchant for unilateral measures. The original message to President Carter indicated that the Soviet Union would let loose a verbal barrage against South Africa two days later in *Pravda*, and did the United States wish to join in the condemnation? It was clear that such a public trumpeting of South Africa's intentions would do grievous damage to the American diplomatic initiatives concerning Rhodesia and Namibia, in which South African participation was essential. It was not in the Soviet interest for such negotiations to reach fruition. The unilateral Soviet approach reminded some observers of the Soviet measures in the Middle East during the 1973 war, when the Soviet Union threatened to intervene to prevent the annihilation of the Egyptian army, an intervention that was deterred in large part by Kissinger's intention to undertake a countervailing American response. In the South African case, the Soviet Union suggested once again that its definition of "consultation within the détente framework" involved the Soviet Union's determining its response to a given situation and then informing the United States of its intentions without allowing scope for negotiation. Such a Soviet attitude appears merely to add one more layer to the game of competitive power politics, rather than introducing true cooperation.

The Death of Détente Linkage

The passage of three years of prolonged confrontation between the Soviet Union and the United States in southern Africa with only episodic attempts at cooperation is casting doubt on the wisdom of linking the future of détente to political and military developments in distant regions such as southern Africa. In 1977, a year when many submerged approaches to foreign policy finally surfaced after years of Kissinger, it was clear that Americans of several points of view were basing their southern African policies on an anti-Soviet perspective. The willingness of the Carter administration to face up to southern African problems forthrightly did little to generate a unified American view. Indeed, the foreign policy community appeared highly polarized, although joining in the long-term purpose of reducing Soviet influence in southern Africa.

One group of Americans called for the reinforcement of the Kissinger tilt toward white Africa. The major economic interests of the United States, some strategic materials, and transit routes were said to be best safeguarded by quiet support of the South Africans. Implicit in this approach was the encouragement of the UNITA forces in Angola in tying down Cuban units and Soviet aid in an unending jungle guerrilla war, in effect waging a "Vietnam war" against those who supported North Vietnam against the United States. The tenuous hold of black governments in southern Africa encouraged this approach, as did the obvious instability of the black nationalist groups, as shown by the internecine warfare of the Patriotic Front of Rhodesia and the jailing of over a thousand opponents by Sam Nujoma, president of the South-West Africa People's Organization (SWAPO). Moderate African leaders, such as Félix Houphouët-Boigny of the Ivory Coast and Ngwāzi Dr. H. Kamuzu Banda of Malawi, encouraged such an approach, for their anti-Communism and desires for economic growth outweighed their distaste for South African racial policies.

The other section of American opinion argued that the best American attack against Soviet influence was the development of close working relationships with black African governments most prone to Soviet blandishments. The key African magnets in this case were Nigeria and Tanzania and their potential influence on the political leaders of the guerrilla movements of southern Africa. This policy was described as a need to recognize long-term American interests, that is, the increasing role of Nigeria as a major supplier of American oil and the goal of nonracial democratic societies throughout the continent.

The importance of both ends of the opinion spectrum was their common goal of rolling back Soviet influence throughout the continent. The emissaries of the Carter administration, including Andrew Young, argued for the natural role of American free enterprise in southern Africa, the basic irrelevance of Soviet social and economic theories, and the need for the United States to regain the initiative seized by the Soviet Union in 1975. In this manner, several shades of informed American opinion accepted the reality that southern Africa witnessed only the competitive aspect of détente and that the political contest between the two nations would continue—if not on the central European front, then in the margins of the Western political world.

The events in southern Africa did much to demonstrate the character of the Soviet-American détente. The potential for cooperation can be constructed much like a common denominator. The calculated interests of both sides can create a détente when those interests coincide. But as the Soviet Union demonstrated in southern Africa, where Moscow defines its interests as competitive with those of the United States, American optimism about the détente relationship is bound to be sorely bruised. The United States, or at least Congress and the public, expected cooperation across the board from the Soviet Union. The durability of détente thus depends on the expectations of both sides in constructing such a relationship. The fact that détente was sold to the American foreign policy community as a reduction in competition ultimately resulted in its weakening. It is thus ironic that a region so far from the essential interests of the Soviet Union and the United States could serve to cripple Soviet-American cooperation across a wide range of common pursuits. It is clear, with the advantage of hindsight, that Secretary of State Kissinger's attempt to use the leverage of détente to limit the Soviet role in Angola served only to weaken détente; he used a twig to move a boulder, and the twig gave way. It may eventually be clear, as well, that the recent attempts of the Carter administration to use the joint Soviet-American action on South Africa's nuclear test to recreate détente was an equally futile exercise. The test of the proposition will come when the United States identifies an interest of its own in peril and seeks out the cooperation of the Soviet Union in supporting an American initiative to save the United States's interest. The United States has not yet seen any measurable support from the Soviet Union for American initiatives in southern Africa.

These considerations are not aimed at denigrating the concept of détente. At the same time, the recent American fascination with the concept of interdependence, combined with the clear global reach of the United States and the Soviet Union, has led many observers to conclude that all international issues are linked. The desire for extensive, indeed global, cooperation with the Soviet

Union has sometimes blinded Americans to the fact that the Soviet Union is an equal negotiating member in this partnership. Although the Soviet Union excludes some areas of international life from the cooperative search for stability, the United States cannot force it to accept the American perspective. During the last eight years of détente, little more than the general principles were delineated by the Soviet and American negotiating partners. Future years will determine, in the context of specific international challenges, the exact ground rules for the conduct of détente in each problem area and in each region.

The United States and the
Soviet Union in the Middle East

O. M. SMOLANSKY

As the effort to get Israel and the Arab states to the conference table gathered momentum after the inauguration of the Carter administration, the heated public debate on the prospects for peace in the Middle East was marked before October 1977 by considerable restraint on one important issue—the possible role to be played by the Soviet Union. There was, to be sure, general recognition of the Kremlin's annoyance at being excluded from previous attempts sponsored by the United States to settle the Arab-Israeli dispute and of Moscow's determination to remain an active Middle East power, a determination reinforced by the Soviet Union's geographic proximity to the region, its extensive interests there, and its role as cochairman of the Geneva conference on the Middle East. There was also a reasonably widespread awareness of the fact that peace in the Arab-Israeli sector is unlikely to prevail without Soviet acquiescence.

Nevertheless, though rarely stated publicly, the prevailing attitude in American, Israeli, and even Arab policymaking circles appeared to favor, if not outright exclusion of the USSR from the ongoing negotiating process, at least its confinement to a "formal" or "procedural" role. The reasons for this reluctance to grant the Soviets a "substantive" part varied from one group to another, but the denominator common to most was a basic mistrust, often combined with dislike, of the Soviets and of their ultimate intentions.

In the West, memories of the cold war have understandably been dying hard. We have been conditioned by years of crises and by our perception of Moscow's role in the Korean, Vietnamese, and Angolan conflicts; by the occasionally fierce military, political, and economic rivalry between the superpowers; and by simple repugnance toward the Soviet dictatorial regime. The Kremlin, for all its obvious interest in curbing the arms race and normalizing political and economic relations with the West, particularly with the United States, has not helped its cause by expanding its military and political presence into areas outside the Communist orbit and by continually emphasizing the vapid propaganda line that "ideological competition" between the "socialist and capitalist systems" must go on regardless of any other considerations.

In the particular case of the Middle East, generalities are augmented with specifics. It has been correctly noted in the West that the Soviets have been on the defensive since their eviction from Egypt in July 1972, with the result that their political positions in the Arab world are presently weaker than at any time since 1955. Why, then, it is legitimately asked, should the West draw the USSR back into the mainstream of Arab politics and, in so doing, assist Moscow in recovering the ground lost by its own ineptitude and inability to "handle" its Arab clients? In addition, the superpowers have been engaged in occasionally bitter competition since 1955 for the allegiance and good will of the Arab states. Now that the West is clearly on the ascendant, the argument goes, it makes little sense to help restore the Soviets to their former position of eminence. Would they not engage in a new round of competition in the future?

In Israel, on the other hand, memories of vital Soviet support during the war of independence have long since faded and have been replaced by the painful awareness that Moscow's massive military, political, and economic backing has turned the Arabs into a serious adversary and has contributed, however indirectly, to the outbreak of three major regional conflicts. Thus, the desire of some Israelis to exclude the USSR from the negotiating process and the possible eventual peace settlement is also easily understandable. The Soviets may be safely assumed to be ready to lend the Arabs their full moral and diplomatic support. In short, with the Kremlin involved, the Israelis expect nothing but additional trouble, an opinion shared by many knowledgeable observers in the West.

In view of these considerations, it may come as something of a surprise that among the Arab "confrontation states" of Egypt, Syria, and Jordan, as well as Saudi Arabia, there also appears to be little enthusiasm for introducing the Soviets into the negotiations. On closer examination, however, this Arab attitude is not all that astonishing. The conservative, anti-Communist, and solidly pro-Western outlook of the Saudi and Jordanian monarchs is too well known to require elaboration. It is true that King Hussein has periodically flirted with the Kremlin, but his decisions to do so have been invariably occasioned by Amman's determination to exert additional pressure on both the United States and Jordan's oil-rich Arab benefactors. President Anwar al-Sadat's anti-Soviet views, conditioned by both his Moslem orthodoxy and his experiences with the Kremlin leaders, are also a matter of public record. His expulsion in 1972 of most Soviet military advisers, without even attempting to secure any quid pro quo from a delighted Washington, testifies among other things to the depth and sincerity of his anti-Soviet sentiments.

The Syrian attitude, which bears the strong personal imprint of President Hafez al-Assad, is more difficult to gauge. Cool and calculating, Assad has maintained his Soviet connection even though during the traumatic days of the Lebanese war the USSR took strong public exception to the Syrian role in that conflict. The necessity of maintaining a working relationship with

Moscow is dictated, in the Syrian view, by the exigencies of the Arab-Israeli conflict and inter-Arab politics. Nevertheless, because Assad also did not trust the Soviets he apparently shared the preference of his Egyptian, Jordanian, and Saudi counterparts in having the Carter administration take the lead in searching for a diplomatic resolution of the Arab-Israeli dispute. Since the Carter administration before October 1977 showed a willingness to prod the reluctant Israelis into some of the concessions sought by the moderate Arabs, they saw no reason to complicate an already confused situation by insisting on immediate Soviet inclusion in the negotiating process. Finally, all the Arab leaders have been acutely aware of Moscow's inability to extract any concessions from Israel. The United States has been and remains the only power capable of such action.

Soviet Influence in the Middle East

These arguments are serious, and they have some validity in the context of past Western, Israeli, and Arab experiences with the Soviets. Nevertheless, it may be in the interest of the parties directly concerned to draw the USSR actively into the processes of seeking and subsequently maintaining peace. Before the case is examined in detail, however, several basic assumptions underlying this argument should be stated. First, it is presumed that peace in the Middle East is a high priority of United States, Israeli, and Arab foreign policy and that it is in the national interest of all concerned to see the conflict resolved. Second, the Arab-Israeli problem is unique in world politics in many important ways. Therefore, attempts to settle it should ideally be based on the positions of the parties directly involved and should not be unduly influenced by such extraneous matters as larger Soviet-American competition.

Thus, in this instance, the linkage approach to superpower relations should not be invoked. Under Nixon and Ford it proved impossible to make the state of Soviet-American relations contingent on Soviet cooperation in resolving regional conflicts. There is no reason to believe that linkage, if attempted, would be any more successful under President Carter. It is unrealistic to assume that Moscow would abandon superpower competition in one part of the world for the sake of achieving agreement in another. Conversely, United States attempts to upstage the Soviets outside the Middle East or even in other parts of the region—now seemingly accepted as part of the superpower relations during the period of détente, in which the Carter administration's basic attitude toward the USSR combines cold war competition with limited forms of cooperation[1]—should not blind Washington to the desirability of achieving its basic objective of peace in the Middle East. Third, the Soviet Union has been active in Middle East affairs since 1955 and has given no indication that it intends to abandon this effort. Barring an all-out war, Moscow's presence in the area can only be eliminated in one of two ways. One would be through the settlement not only of the Arab-Israeli conflict but also of all the other intraregional

[1] See Hedrick Smith in the *New York Times*, July 8, 1977.

disputes. Anyone even vaguely familiar with the Middle East will instantly recognize that such a fortuitous state of affairs will not occur any time in the near future. Hence, even if the United States miraculously succeeded in resolving the Arab-Israeli dispute on its own initiative and without Soviet cooperation, other serious political difficulties will remain and new ones will arise, creating a politically heated situation that an embittered Soviet government could exploit.

Another possibility would be for the USSR to withdraw unilaterally from participation in Middle East politics. This course of action has much to recommend it from the standpoint of objective Soviet interests, but it is unrealistic to expect the Kremlin to take such a step in the light of its extensive investment in the area as well as its proclivity to "prove" itself as a superpower capable of playing an active role in the important arenas of world politics.

In the meantime, the USSR retains a degree of leverage in Syria, which is dependent on Soviet weapons, and should not be written off completely in Egypt. Should Sadat's gamble on the United States fail, he or his successors will have little choice but to resume closer cooperation with the Soviet Union. Put differently, the Kremlin leaders well realize that their potential for influencing the affairs of the Arab-Israeli sector has recently been significantly circumscribed but not totally eliminated. Since political "successes" in the Middle East are usually preludes to "failures" (and vice versa), Moscow can reasonably expect eventually to regain influence following its present disfavor. In any event, as bad as the situation may now be, the Kremlin is not likely to panic. All it has to do is to wait for events to unfold and for things to go wrong, as they usually do. In this sense, it may be in the United States interest to co-opt the Soviets now, inviting them into the negotiating process rather than excluding them from it. Should the USSR rejoin the game at a later stage independently of Washington's wishes, it may be expected to arrive in an adversary capacity. This turn of events would not be in the interest of the United States.

Soviet Participation in Middle East Negotiations

The assertion that the effort toward an Arab-Israeli peace settlement should proceed in cooperation with the Soviet Union is based on the assumptions that, given the right circumstances, Moscow might well play a constructive role and that, for this reason, it would be in the interest of all concerned to avail themselves of the Kremlin's assistance. Conversely, peace may well prove unattainable without Soviet cooperation.

Specifically, drawing the Soviet Union into the negotiation and implementation processes has certain advantages. It would significantly diminish Moscow's propensity for disruption and for capitalizing on differences that are bound to arise in any attempt to settle the Arab-Israeli dispute. It would severely weaken the impact of the "rejectionist front," including important elements in the Palestine Liberation Organization (PLO), and perhaps, in the long run, reduce Soviet influence with the PLO, Iraq, and Libya, which reinforce the Soviet position in the Arab world. It would improve the chances for the ultimate success of the peacemaking effort by denying the moderate Arabs the opportunity to turn to a dissatisfied superpower should they, for whatever reason, become disenchanted with the United States or Israel. Finally and ironically, it would use the Kremlin to help settle the Arab-Israeli conflict that has been one of the primary sources of Soviet leverage in the Middle East.

In addition, it must also be borne in mind that Soviet consent will be needed to implement any new international agreements dealing with the freedom of navigation in the Straits of Tiran and Babal-Mandeb as well as in the Gulf of 'Aqaba. Such agreements must form an integral part of any meaningful peace settlement. Moreover, Moscow's cooperation as a coguarantor of peace along with the other great powers is indispensable in controlling the flow of modern weapons to the Middle East. Without such a comprehensive international agreement, the large-scale arms traffic into the region will continue, enhancing the likelihood of future disruptions.

Conversely, the Soviet Union's exclusion from the negotiation and implementation processes would have important negative consequences. While it is not in a position to prevent a peace settlement if the parties directly concerned decided to enter into one, the Kremlin can severely complicate or even disrupt the process when serious problems arise to divide the Arabs and the Israelis. Syria and even Egypt can be expected to use their Soviet connection if they conclude that Arab interests are not being adequately considered by either Israel or the United States. It is equally unlikely that, once this occurs, the Soviets will not involve themselves in these negotiations, whether or not the West and Israel approve. For, in the final analysis, in international affairs the parties to a dispute are those that conceive themselves as such and have the ability to influence significantly its outcome. The Soviet Union meets both of these qualifications, and, if it rejoins the Arab-Israeli conflict under the circumstances described above, it may be fully expected to do so from an avowed adversary stance.

In short, while the temptation to exclude Moscow from, or limit its role in, the Arab-Israeli negotiating and implementing processes is all too understandable, the question is strictly practical. Can and will the Soviets facilitate achievement of a stable peace in the Middle East? If approached in a realistic fashion, there is little doubt that Moscow can help settle the Arab-Israeli dispute. The real problem revolves around the Kremlin's willingness to help bring peace to the conflict-ridden area. No categorical answer can be given to the question of the Soviet Union's ultimate intentions. At the same time, there is some reason to believe that the USSR may cooperate with the United States, the Arab countries, and Israel.

For one thing, knowledgeable Russians are fully aware that Moscow's current position in the Middle East is extremely weak. In the 1970s the Kremlin has suffered very serious setbacks in Egypt, Sudan, Somalia, and, to a lesser degree, in Syria. At the same time, with the exception of Libya and Ethiopia, the Soviets have been unable to attract major new clients. This turn of events has left Moscow's position in the Middle East and northeastern Africa anchored in Iraq, Libya, the People's Democratic Republic of Yemen (PDRY), and Ethiopia (a new "convert"). It is not an enviable situation; given the bitter rivalry between Addis Ababa and Mogadishu, the "acquisition" of Ethiopia may well turn out to have been a costly mistake. Torn by political dissension and economically crippled, Ethiopia is not likely to develop soon into a major asset, while the loss of the established naval and air facilities in Somalia has dealt a major blow to whatever ambitions the Kremlin may have had in the Indian Ocean area. Libya, the PDRY, and, to a lesser extent, Iraq are volatile and unpredictable. As clients are wont to do, all three have utilized the USSR to further their own interests. None would hesitate to dissociate itself from the Soviets should it, for whatever reason, decide that reliance on Moscow no longer serves a useful purpose. Aware that their ties with these Arab states are fragile, and increasingly entangled in Ethiopia, the Soviet leaders may adopt a much more flexible role in the Arab-Israeli sector.

Moreover, the USSR appears to have concluded that the Carter administration genuinely desires peace in the Middle East and is determined to resolve the conflict. Therefore, if American diplomatic efforts are successful while the Soviet Union stays out of the negotiating process, Moscow's relatively weak position is likely to be undermined even more. Since the Kremlin is deeply concerned about the deterioration of its positions in the Middle East and northeastern Africa, it is likely to accept a genuine offer to participate in the search for a peace formula. Further, by being a part of the process, the USSR would realize positive benefits associated with official United States recognition that the Soviet Union is a superpower whose status in the Middle East equals that of the United States. The attainment of this objective has been one of Moscow's long-term but frustrated goals.

It is fashionable in the West to object to this reasoning on the ground that, its official statements to the contrary notwithstanding, the Soviet Union does not want a genuine settlement of the Arab-Israeli conflict. Indeed, perpetuation of tension is said to constitute a major source of Soviet influence in the Middle East. However, though historically correct and emotionally satisfying, the argument may no longer be valid. It fails to take into account Moscow's more recent experiences in the Middle East and northeastern Africa. As alluded to above, far from having increased its influence in the Arab "confrontation states" since the 1973 war, the Soviet Union has in fact suffered a number of significant setbacks. In the process, the Kremlin leaders have become acutely aware of their limited influence on events in the Middle East. Moreover, the Soviets know that encouraging hostilities might easily lead to an outbreak of another war and hence to a possible superpower confrontation.

Another Middle East war would also likely result in an Arab oil embargo. Many would argue that such a sharp deterioration of Arab-Western relations, coupled with the imposition of enormous economic hardships on the "capitalist" world, is in the interest of the USSR. Upon closer examination, however, this does not seem to be the case. First, the Soviet Union is not likely to benefit from major economic dislocations in the industrial West, on which it now heavily depends for the import of badly needed technology, capital, and other high priority items. Second, it is hard to imagine that the Soviet Union would join an Arab oil embargo, as petroleum exports to the West now constitute its most significant single export item and hard currency earner.

However, if Moscow continued to export oil to the West in the face of an Arab embargo, it would clearly establish itself as an opponent of the Arabs. The Kremlin would in fact be actively undermining the Arab cause that it has openly claimed to uphold—an untenable position that the Soviet leaders will go out of their way to avoid. Finally, the view that the USSR favors turmoil and is opposed to peace in 1977 rests on a fundamental misreading of the Soviet objectives in the Arab-Israeli sector. Throughout all the convolutions of Moscow's Middle East policy since 1955, the one common theme that emerges is the Kremlin's quest for full superpower status and consequent recognition that its interests must be considered in whatever regional arrangements are reached. To obtain this objective, the Soviet government may be counted on to make some concessions and to cooperate constructively in efforts to settle the Arab-Israeli conflict.

Another objection to this line of reasoning revolves around a different set of premises. Many Western analysts argue that, if Moscow's position in the Middle East and northeastern Africa is in fact as weak as intimated above, there is no reason for the United States to rush to the Soviet Union's assistance by conferring on it the status of an equal partner in American efforts to settle the Arab-Israeli dispute. It is obvious that Washington's policy in this matter must be weighed in the light of United States objectives and interests in the region. Specifically, if it appears that the United States can single-handedly bring the opposing sides to a mutually acceptable and lasting agreement, it might be argued that there is no need to accommodate the Soviet Union. However, the assumption that this country, despite its considerable leverage in Israel and the Arab states, can in fact do all these things on its own is open to question. The first and most immediate question is the Carter administration's willingness to force a settlement on those parties that, for whatever reason, are reluctant to accept solutions favored by the United States. It is impossible to predict whether and to what extent Washington would seriously consider applying pressure on the different protagonists. That pressure would be required should be obvious. In the recent past the atmosphere has been charged with emotion over the meaning of such concepts as "defensible borders," "the Palestinian homeland," and the "catalyst" role of the United States.

Second, even if the Carter administration were willing to use its influence fully to achieve a settlement, the resolution of substantive problems, such as the future status of Jerusalem, the West Bank, and the Gaza Strip, is likely to create dissatisfaction on both sides. Some disgruntled Arabs will feel obliged to look elsewhere for moral, political, and possibly military support. This turn of events would once again provide the Soviet Union with an entry point into the Middle East.

Third, most analysts overlook the possibility, not so remote, that some moderate or conservative Arab governments might be replaced by other regimes more militant and therefore unhappy with the role played by the United States or with the provisions of a prospective United States-inspired peace settlement. Again, the resumption of relations with Moscow would be a likely point of departure for their foreign policy. A dissatisfied Soviet government may be fully expected to seize on such opportunities to reestablish itself in an area from which it had been deliberately excluded by the Americans.

Finally, there remains the crucial problem of arms supplies to the Middle East following a peace settlement. It is often assumed in the West that a "reasonable" settlement will "produce peace." Put differently, it is believed that the signing of an agreement and the eventual establishment of political, economic, and cultural contacts between the former adversaries will eliminate their quest for national security. This is an unrealistic assumption. To look at but one specific example, it is unlikely that Saudi Arabia would discontinue its massive military buildup even after the settlement of the Arab-Israeli conflict, for Saudi arms purchases are motivated only partly by Arab-Israeli relations. In these circumstances it would be unrealistic to expect Israel to lower its guard. However, as long as Israel maintains or even increases its military strength, the neighboring Arab states are bound to follow suit no matter what some of their present leaders may presently be saying. In short, even under the best of circumstances, no Middle East leader with a sense of history will entrust the security of his nation to a piece of paper even if it is reinforced by demilitarized zones, a United Nations or other military force, and great power guarantees of the inviolability of the new frontiers. This is not to discount the importance of all these steps as an inducement to Israel and the Arab states to sign a peace treaty. Rather, it is intended to point out that, as long as there is no effective international agreement limiting weapons shipments to the entire region, an arms race is bound to continue. In an area as volatile as the Middle East, arms races in the past have meant wars of increasing intensity. Thus, without a comprehensive international agreement limiting arms exports to the Middle East, war is still a likely eventuality, and no international agreement excluding the Soviet Union makes any sense at all. One way or another, Moscow is likely to remain a factor in the Arab-Israeli equation.

United States Policy and Soviet Participation

Notwithstanding periods of "peaceful coexistence" and "détente," relations between the United States and the Soviet Union since 1945 have been marked by mutual suspicion and rivalry that have brought them to the brink of a nuclear holocaust. Military, economic, and political competition between the superpowers is likely to continue in the foreseeable future and will include occasional crises and even wars by proxy provoked by their respective clients pursuing their own national interests. At the same time, as in the past, Washington and Moscow are likely to cooperate in instances where their respective interests converge, such as in matters dealing with arms control and trade.

In this general framework, leaders of the United States and the Soviet Union have had and will continue to have varying options for dealing with such problems as may arise. Broadly speaking, they will in each instance have the choice of either escalating or defusing tensions and of helping to settle crises when they arise or maintaining them at a dangerous level. Since increasing levels of competition may entail undesirable consequences for all concerned, one may hope that the latter practice will be used selectively by both sides. The temptation to score gains at a rival's expense must be weighed against the likely negative long-range consequences of potential short-run "victories." Nowhere is this process more obvious than in the Middle East.

In general terms, it could be argued that the foundations on which United States "successes" have been based are just as ephemeral and transitory as those of the Soviets before 1972—to a significant extent, the United States is at the mercy of regional and local forces over which no outsider has sufficient unilateral control to ensure its privileged position. More specifically, in the Arab-Israeli sector, the Carter administration seems to have locked itself into a "no-win" situation. Having publicly enunciated principles on which peace between Israel and its Arab neighbors is to be established, the United States has abandoned its previous role as mediator and has emerged as an arbiter of a "fair" peace settlement. In the process, Washington has raised the expectations of the Arab states and the PLO and has placed itself on a collision course with Israel where the victory of the Likud party has strengthened Prime Minister Menachem Begin's determination to hold on to the West Bank territories occupied in 1967. By advancing its own relatively detailed peace formula, the United States has thus contributed to the hardening of the antagonists' positions and, in so doing, has detracted from the chances of reaching a lasting peace settlement.

How the Carter administration will extricate itself from this unenviable position will only gradually become evident. One likely consequence of what has been aptly described as the president's "open mouth" diplomacy will be a serious alienation of Israel (and of the influential Jewish community in the United States) and, if the West Bank and the Gaza Strip are not ultimately "delivered," of the Arabs as well. If so, the Soviet Union will have been provided with an opportunity once again to strengthen its positions in the Arab world.

Washington clearly desires peace between the Arab states and Israel, but the issue is its ability to settle the conflict. It is this writer's contention that, as a result of its official policy, the Carter administration has not only retarded whatever chances there might have existed for an early settlement of the Arab-Israeli dispute but has also undermined its own ability to serve as an impartial mediator in the negotiating process. Thus it becomes apparent that, contrary to earlier expectations, Washington will not be in a position to "engineer" a

Middle East accord by its own devices. Given this basic premise, the answer to the question of whether the United States should continue to go it alone in an effort to resolve the Arab-Israeli conflict, or whether a belated attempt should be made to draw the Soviet Union into the process as a full-fledged member of the "settlement team," seems clear. Both the cause of peace in the Middle East as well as United States national interests dictate the second approach.

September 15, 1977

Postscript

Two important events have occurred since this essay was written. One was the Soviet-American declaration, made public on October 1, 1977, pledging an accelerated effort to convene the Geneva conference before the end of the year. The other was President Anwar al-Sadat's dramatic visit to Israel. In the joint statement, the superpowers undertook to help overcome Arab-Israeli differences and agreed that the peace conference should ensure "the legitimate rights of the Palestinian people," establish "normal peaceful relations" in the region, and provide for international guarantees of the final border settlement. Since the declaration both recognized "the legitimate rights" of the Palestinians and neglected to refer specifically to the Palestine Liberation Organization (PLO), it was an obvious effort at a compromise and attested to the seriousness of Washington and Moscow in seeking a peaceful resolution of the Arab-Israeli conflict. The statement did not imply superpower collusion to impose peace in the Middle East but rather reflected a recognition on the part of the Carter administration that no comprehensive peace settlement could be achieved without the cooperation, or at the very least the acquiescence, of the Soviet Union. In dissociating itself from the efforts of its Republican predecessors to keep the Soviets out of the Arab-Israeli settlement process, the Carter administration took a wise and courageous step.

At the same time, the United States's efforts to work out compromises that would be acceptable to all concerned parties encountered serious problems. By October, it became obvious that attempts at reconvening the Geneva conference in late 1977, according to a timetable worked out in Washington earlier in the year, were bogged down in procedural matters. The handling of the question of Palestinian representation at Geneva clearly indicated the enormity of the problems that lay ahead once the peace conference reconvened. It was Sadat's realization that he was running out of time while the United States seemed unable to persuade Israel and Syria to make the necessary concessions that prompted him to take matters into his own hands. By going to Jerusalem, he attempted to get to the heart of the Arab-Israeli problem by cutting through the maze of procedural issues and establishing a working relationship with the government of Prime Minister Menachem Begin. Since Begin also had serious misgivings about Washington's policy, the visit took place and instantly elated many Israelis and Egyptians. As a result, the Middle East situation has undergone a major qualitative change. After some four years of concerted United States efforts to bring peace to the Middle East, the initiative has passed from Washington to Cairo and Jerusalem. Moreover, the carefully wrought improvement in Soviet-American relations on this issue has been temporarily shattered as a deliberate consequence of the rapprochement between Israel and Egypt.

At the time of this writing, it is impossible to predict all the consequences of the Sadat-Begin initiative. Nevertheless, it is obvious that in moving on their own the two leaders have unmistakably indicated their dissatisfaction with the Carter administration's leadership in the peacemaking process. In so doing, they have demonstrated once again that although outsiders in the Middle East do have a very important part to play, they cannot always control events and are typically at the mercy of local forces.

Some observers might conclude that the Sadat-Begin initiative invalidates the Carter administration's earlier efforts to include the USSR in its attempts to effect a Middle East settlement. However, while the final outcome of the new scenario is beyond prediction, one thing seems clear. No effort to achieve peace in the region that fails to recognize the Soviet Union as an "interested super-power" is likely to meet with long-range success.

December 15, 1977

The European Military Balance

JOHN ERICKSON

Assessments of the "military balance" are by reputation notoriously difficult undertakings, seemingly governed by metaphysical rules all their own in spite of the appearance of statistical rigor. It is generally accepted that what American usage calls "bean counts," the simple aggregation of men and machines, furnishes little real guide to the nature of the balance prevailing in the European theater, or elsewhere for that matter. The measurement of military force must be, of necessity, relative and comparison made essentially between those force levels that mutually determine each other. Obviously, force levels enter into this discussion from the outset, but the aggregate of military power must include deployment patterns, the cogency of military doctrine, "tactical technology" (command and control systems, concepts of organization), and, in the last resort, resource relationships (although simple price evaluations and comparisons do not always reflect the full value of the resources committed and expended).

The point about aggregate military power can be made with some dispatch. It is extremely rare, for example, to find any public discussion of the European military balance that includes any exposition of Soviet order of battle (forward deployment) in east-central Europe. Soviet capability thus remains merely statistical abstraction: there can be no excuse for official secrecy to cover this lacuna, for presumably the Soviet high command knows where its own divisions are located and is aware of the fact that 2nd Guards Tank Army, for instance, is deployed in the Group of Soviet Forces in Germany. In regard to public opinion and public awareness, such lack of specific information serves merely to fuel a gloomy fantasy of overwhelming, all-pervasive Soviet strength or a comforting fiction that no real threat exists. Thus, political (or popular) perceptions collide at once with professional appraisals of the balance. Of the two, it is the former—for all its vacuity—that may be of decisive importance, the perceived balance that holds sway throughout the European body politic. Certainly, this perceived balance (paradoxically enough, only imperfectly perceived) induces in European opinion that strange but established cyclical pattern of complacency coupled with extreme, even hysterical, alarmism.[1]

Soviet Military Capabilities in Europe

An obvious starting point must be the detail and the impact of the Soviet military buildup, widely reported and variously interpreted, including the freakish views set forth by at least one commentator who sees a whole new "tactical revolution" in Soviet military thinking, a commitment to "daring thrusts," and a daunting array of superregiments loosed upon an unsuspecting Europe.[2] This can be disposed of at once: such an interpretation is born of sheer mistranslation and a failure to identify what are basically traditional Soviet military clichés compounded of bombast and hyperbole. There has not been any basic revolution in the Soviet view of the organization and conduct of theater operations in Europe; the reality is grim enough without the frippery of this kind of invention. High force levels have been an integral element of Soviet military policy in Europe for the past three decades and more, with forces deployed forward never falling below twenty-five to twenty-six divisions and reaching thirty-one divisions at present (that is, if the Southern Group of Forces in Hungary can be counted in this force, a not unreasonable assumption).

Soviet doctrine with respect to its theater forces has not altered in its essentials, namely, the commitment to wage and to win a European campaign at all levels of weapons. That latter qualification, *all levels of weapons*, assumes considerable military significance. The problem of the "net assessment" of Soviet capability is complicated by the odd admixture of strategic problems with tactical ones in Soviet operational thinking—the selection of major thrust lines, the form of operations, the allocation of the air effort, and the timing of the introduction of nuclear weapons, to mention only some of the most prominent items.

To put this somewhat colloquially, the Soviet command is competing as much against itself (or the terms of its perception of Soviet shortcomings) as against NATO as such. Some of this can be seen in the buildup that has proceeded over the past few years. Clearly, Soviet forces in the European theater were deficient in mobile battlefield cover for columns on the move (hence the SA-8 and SA-9 SAM systems), Soviet artillery with its previous resources could not muster so high a number of guns for fire preparation, and there was a shortage of rifle (motor-rifle) units on the main axis or axes of advance where armor was to be committed. Flank cover for attacking columns has been increased, organic air defense has been expanded (with much greater overlapping coverage), and artillery resources (with ammunition) substantially augmented.

[1] On optimism versus pessimism in balance assessments, see *Assessing the NATO/Warsaw Pact Military Balance* (Washington, D.C.: Congressional Budget Office, 1977).

[2] See P. A. Karber, "Die taktische Revolution in der sowjetischen Militärdoktrin," *Europäische Wehrkunde*, no. 6, Juni 1977 and no. 7, Juli 1977, or "The Tactical Revolution in Soviet Military Doctrine," BDM Corporation, March 1977.

As a consequence, both the Soviet tank division and the motor-rifle division have been increased in strength, with the motor-rifle division (which has 266 tanks) now falling only marginally behind the tank division proper in tank strength (the tank division having 333 battle tanks).

The net result in gross numbers has been some 130,000 men added to the manpower strength of Soviet divisions deployed forward in east-central Europe, a 40 percent increase in tank strength, and substantial qualitative and quantitative improvement in artillery holdings, though the most dramatic leap has been reserved for multiple rocket launchers. Meanwhile, regimental artillery in motor-rifle formations has also been increased. Artillery command and radar reconnaissance vehicles have been introduced to improve the capability of artillery to provide effective fire support in the course of high-speed offensive operations. In addition, a new and powerful "gunship" helicopter introduced in growing numbers can furnish direct fire support, antitank capability, and assault transport facility.

Pride of place in this program bids fair to be the new Soviet main battle tank, the T-64 (refined into the T-72) to replace the T-62. Equipped with a 125-mm smooth-bore gun, this new tank weighs some forty-one tons and develops a speed reported at sixty miles an hour (though more realistically estimated at forty miles an hour). Over a thousand of these new tanks have been introduced into Soviet armies in East Germany, while an even more advanced model is reported to be under test. But even as the equipment scales increased in all Soviet formations and regiments, the capacity for further absorption is substantially diminished, signifying that either organization must be changed, new units created, or reserve stockpiles vastly expanded. Even at this stage of a simple catalogue of increased equipment scales, the question of organizational concepts and operational doctrine—not to mention command and control—intrudes on any assessment.

The numerical tally would not be complete without reference to the buildup in what Richard Burt has called "Eurostrategic weapons," Soviet medium and intermediate range ballistic missiles (MRBMs and IRBMs), with the older SS-4s and SS-5s now being replaced by the MIRVed SS-20, of which some 300 are now targeted on the European landmass. At the same time, Soviet air capability has grown apace both in terms of quality and quantity, with newer models (such as the MIG-23 and the SU-19) introducing increased payload and range and facilitating for the first time offensive air operations into the depth of the NATO theater.[3] Equally, the modernization of the IRBM force with its wider coverage of targets releases Soviet tactical air resources for a greater variety of missions.

There are two main time-frames in which to view this buildup, the first over the whole decade (1967–68 through 1977–78) and a shorter, more intense period embracing the past five to six years. According to gross figures, the net balance

[3] See Robert P. Berman, *Soviet Air Power in Transition* (Washington, D.C.: The Brookings Institution, 1978), chap. 4, on "potential wartime roles."

between NATO and the Warsaw Pact results in an advantage across the board for the latter: an advantage in total manpower (1:1.2, a disparity not offset even by including French forces in the Federal Republic of Germany in Western totals), the same disparity in combat manpower, an advantage of almost 3:1 in main battle tanks (6,500 NATO tanks as opposed to over 16,000 in the Warsaw Pact arsenal), 1:2.5 superiority in artillery, and 1:2.4 in tactical aircraft.

Considered in these terms, there is no overwhelming degree of Warsaw Pact superiority, particularly if one adopts the Soviet operational requirement of a minimum advantage of 3:1 in armor and between 5:1 and 8:1 in artillery, with the same high ratios for tactical aircraft. In round figures, the Warsaw Pact forces enjoy a 2:1 advantage over NATO forces, which implies a certain risk for the West but not inevitable defeat and disaster. Indeed, recent Soviet reappraisals of the requirements for sustained combat capability as well as the very numerical buildup just examined suggest that this advantage does not translate immediately into operational superiority. High rates of anticipated battlefield loss, vastly increased ammunition expenditure rates in high intensity operations, and logistical complexities cannot be ignored in this equation. For example, using Soviet "norms," a Soviet motor-rifle division would have expended most of its manpower and much of its weapons and equipment after five days of high intensity operations, even as the commander is required to maintain sufficient resources to carry out a final, successful assault at the close of this period. Obviously, something must be changed, and change is in the direction of providing for a more extended campaign, which falls somewhere between the short- and long-war thesis.

Given this ratio of advantage in favor of the Warsaw Pact, does this effectively dispose of the central problems inherent in the European military balance? The answer must be an equivocal no in view of the relationship between quality and quantity—also a form of "balance" in its own right—and the underlying trend in Warsaw Pact military programs toward faster modernization combined with greater numerical expansion. New battle tanks brought into the European theater augment rather than replace the older machines, which go into storage. The large-scale introduction of modern combat aircraft has not resulted in any reduction in numbers, for this is a one-for-one replacement program. Thus, while retaining the same nominal order of battle, Soviet air regiments and divisions have increased their strength by at least 25 percent. Trainers also have a combat capability, so they should not be discounted.

These figures and the configurations of modernization programs can only represent part of the problem. It is necessary at this point to attempt to construct a different estimate of the prevailing balance (or lack of it). Perhaps the best approach is to consider the "deployed threat" and the "deployed response" as some measure of military-political realities. This comparison is also better in that it attempts some estimate of initial combat capability and the role of combat readiness, all in the light of the fully developed Soviet capability to launch a high-speed armored offensive with little or no warning time. Warning time becomes one of the most important and one of the most complex problems to admit into the analysis of the balance. First, however, one must look at the main deployment patterns of both NATO and the Warsaw Pact, patterns that are the product of long historical development and that cannot be so easily changed, if only for political and financial reasons.

Deployment Patterns

On NATO's central front, six of the seven nations committed to joint defense have delegated responsibility for operational planning and control to integrated NATO commands. The exception is France, which maintains one corps (2nd Corps) on the territory of West Germany and one corps in northeastern France but whose forces are not integrated into NATO. The forces of the Central European Command comprise twenty-six divisions (assigned by Belgium, the Netherlands, the United Kingdom, Canada, West Germany, and the United States) and some 1,400 tactical aircraft. This major command is divided in turn into the Northern Army Group and the Central Army Group. NATO air forces come under Allied Air Forces Central Europe, established in 1974 to centralize control of air elements, in place of two distinct tactical air forces. The northern flank is covered by Allied Forces Northern Europe, responsible for the defense of Norway, Denmark, Schleswig-Holstein, and the Baltic approaches. Allied Forces Southern Europe, commanded by an American admiral, is charged with the defense of Italy, Greece, and Turkey as well as securing communications in the Mediterranean and safeguarding Turkish territorial waters in the Black Sea. Air forces come under AIRSOUTH, together with two naval commands (NAVSOUTH and STRIKEFORSOUTH).

Soviet forces in east-central Europe form their first echelon from the three Groups of Forces (Germany, Poland, and Czechoslovakia), to which a fourth could be added, the Southern Group in Hungary. Soviet forces in East Germany comprise twenty divisions (ten tank, ten motor-rifle, and one artillery division), Northern Group in Poland two to three divisions, and Czechoslovakia (Central Group) five to six divisions. The first group of forces has its own air army in support, as has the Northern Group, while the Central Group has at least two air divisions available. Forward deployed Soviet strength thus amounts to a minimum of twenty-eight divisions (or thirty-one to thirty-two, counting the Southern Group); in all, sixteen tank divisions and fifteen motor-rifle divisions.

Put another way, these resources are sufficient to mount between eight and ten breakthrough operations across the face of the central front as a whole. Reinforcement (or a second echelon) can be provided by at least three westerly military districts—Carpathian, Baltic, and Belorussian. The Leningrad Military District would presumably provide forces for operations on the northern flank, though it could also furnish amphibious and airborne forces for operations in the Baltic. This second echelon could furnish eight armies—thirty-one divisions—with eleven divisions drawn from the Carpathian, ten from the Baltic, and ten from the Belorussian Military Districts, in addition to at least two airborne divisions. Three air armies would also be used in support.

Difficulties arise at once in discussing the force levels of non-Soviet Warsaw Pact formations operating with the Soviet forward attack echelon. Nominal order of battle may well not mean much in reality, for gross numbers do not represent actual capability and operational effectiveness. In the "northern tier" (East Germany, Poland, and Czechoslovakia) of non-Soviet forces, some thirty-one divisions are available on paper—six, fifteen, and ten respectively. Much would depend on the type of operations envisaged by the Soviet command. The only non-Soviet Warsaw Pact forces directly subordinated to Soviet command are two East German corps (two tank and four motor rifle divisions). However, it is open to much argument whether Soviet operational planning sees an extensive role beyond the German border for these troops. They could be held back deliberately to contain the West German "counterthrust" aimed at Berlin. A plausible explanation is that non-Soviet formations would be used in specialist roles (like the Polish 6th Airborne Division or the Polish amphibious brigade) or else bonded into special battle groups, drawn from earmarked formations and units whose standard of training and equipment is well known to Soviet planners and commanders. Meanwhile, all the non-Soviet air defense forces (interceptors and SAMs) come under the overall direction of the Soviet Air Defense Command, which has a deputy commander for the Warsaw Pact area.

The Soviet assault first echelon (combining Soviet forces in East Germany with the Northern Group and elements of the Central Group) without reinforcement on any scale could amount to at least twenty-five divisions, possibly supplemented by select non-Soviet Warsaw Pact formations which might well not exceed ten to twelve divisions. There are certain distinctive features that mark out this grouping in relation to present deployment. Unlike NATO forces, Soviet formations do not appear to be obliged to make substantial transits to move their war stations. Even in their peacetime configuration, Soviet *armies* are facing NATO *corps*, a fact not without significance even allowing for the differing strengths in NATO and in the Warsaw Pact. For example, the Soviet 3rd Shock Army deployed about Magdeburg can field 55,000 men, 1,198 tanks, 1,100 infantry combat vehicles, backed by at least 18 SCUD missiles and 408 guns, an artillery strength that can be substantially increased by drawing on available resources.

NATO's maldeployment has been the subject of much discussion, and a shift toward more rational deployment must clearly enter into any discussion of the prevailing balance. To move to what might be presumed to be operational war stations, NATO formations are inevitably involved in quite a complex pattern of cross-movements: I Netherlands Corps must move the greatest distance, I German and I British Corps are involved in north-south movements, I Belgian Corps must move east, III German Corps is more favorably placed save for one brigade, V United States Corps is in a position comparable to III German Corps save for one division, and II German Corps faces complicated movement with one of its divisions. It has been estimated that even under favorable conditions, given an optimum rate of movement,[4] the positions designated under the "forward defense" plan could only be manned after a considerable time span.

There is also the balance, or the imbalance, of the main NATO commands. The Northern Army Group is committed to the defense of a front stretching for some 125 miles, facing potential Soviet thrusts along both sides of the Helmstedt-Dortmund autobahn, striking into the north German plain along a so-called tank highway. The Central Army Group holds a front of almost 375 miles, defending the Palatinate from any thrust aimed from the Thuringian bulge and thus slicing through West Germany at its narrowest point. A further complication could be an extension of this front to the southeast in the event of any Soviet irruption through Austria. To stiffen the defense against an armored attack aimed against the north German plain, an American brigade is presently earmarked to move there in order to bring an American presence into the area. French forces are deployed on both sides of the Rhine, and it is a matter of surmise for friend and foe alike at what point they would join operations in the European theater.

Though deployment patterns in the abstract convey little of actual effectiveness, the problem of NATO's maldeployment and the capability of its forward deployed forces, particularly its antitank capability, have recently come in for considerable attention. Combat readiness and initial combat capability must be weighed heavily in the balance, while the counterweight is rapid reinforcement. The several multinational corps in the NATO area do not maintain their wartime strength in peacetime and have been held in conditions of "graduated availability." Only the combat elements, the brigades, are at war strength in terms of personnel, but to bring corps and divisions to a full state of readiness means drawing on support and supply personnel who should be at their stations either before or after the move to war stations. Thus, lack of support troops combined with unfavorable deployment could have a serious effect on operational readiness, which can be even further affected by the lack of standardized equipment distributed within the various national units. Soviet divisions deployed forward in east-central Europe are all maintained as Category A formations, that is, with at least 85 percent of their manpower and 100 percent of their equipment, vehicles fuelled and stocked. Divisions forming the strategic "second echelon" are Category B, with most of their equipment but only two-thirds of their manpower. Category C divisions, held in the hinterland, have various holdings of equipment but only a quarter of personnel. It is worth noting, however, that the personnel missing from the Category A divisions—ten to fifteen percent—are also support troops and specialists, though with rapid air transport it would not be difficult to "top up" these formations. Even Category B divisions could be used in an emergency without major reinforcement, or might move on prepositioned stocks and stores.

---

[4] British gunners in Germany must transport their nuclear warheads a distance of ten to fifteen miles to the guns in secret deployments in the forward area, but it has been suggested that this road movement will be severely hindered by refugee traffic.

This "readiness-reinforcement ratio" obviously comes very near to the heart of the problem for NATO and the Warsaw Pact alike. Such a ratio governs combat readiness, initial combat capability, deft deployment, full combat support, and logistical efficiency combined with flexibility induced by high degrees of standardization. With respect to the latter, the Warsaw Pact enjoys a long-standing advantage with standardized Soviet equipment in all military establishments, not to mention a common tactical doctrine and standard training practices. Yet by a curious transmogrification, this standardization, taken as it is almost to the *nth* degree, does not produce flexibility. On the contrary, standardization on this scale and with this degree of thoroughness breeds rigidity, to judge by a variety of Soviet and non-Soviet complaints. That is connected in turn with the manpower-training aspect, for "training" is so often the repetition of a series of drills or rehearsed procedures. Inflexible command and rigid discipline are also standard practice. In a recent exercise a Soviet motor-rifle battalion commander found himself in need of fire support but did not call on available helicopters because the plan did not specify helicopter support.[5]

There is almost total artificiality in trying to examine comparative readiness-reinforcement ratios, if only because any political reality is missing. This is also to assume that operations will begin and will continue for some sustained period in the conventional mode (though the Soviet ability to launch a theater nuclear offensive is not to be underestimated). In addition, it should be admitted that the Soviet capability to use chemical weapons, possibly on a selective tactical basis, is far in advance of NATO's provisions for chemical warfare. Despite these qualifications there appear to be three contingencies that could illuminate relative strengths.

First, in the event of an in-place unreinforced attack, with strategic surprise playing a vital role, attack orders would be issued some seventy-two hours in advance, thus cutting NATO warning time to a maximum of forty-eight hours. Soviet and select non-Soviet divisions already activated under the guise of military exercises, duly notified under the "confidence-building measures" stipulated by the Helsinki declaration, would amount to thirty-five formations. The addition of at least two Soviet airborne divisions, with Czechoslovak divisions used in part in the first echelon of the Central Group, would be possible. The Southern Group might also be committed to the whole operation. This in-place unreinforced offensive would encounter some eighteen NATO divisions, a 2:1 ratio in the Soviets' favor. The present American reinforcement rate over a period of ten days is little more than one division and forty tactical air squadrons, while the Soviet command could draw on immediate short-range reinforcement from forces of the Baltic, Belorusian, and Carpathian Military Districts, all over a period of three to five days.

Second, NATO might confront a full-scale Warsaw Pact deployment during a period of tension. While increasing warning time appreciably, this factor would be offset by full and complete deployment at war stations, with Category B

---

[5] This is a Soviet critique of a battalion exercise. See Lt. Col. A. Zakharenko, *Krasnaia Zvezda*, August 5, 1977.

divisions brought to a greater state of readiness and even set in motion to designated staging areas. First and second echelons would be fully manned, extra resources being drawn from non-Soviet Warsaw Pact forces. The command and control procedures would be adjusted and the logistical requirements met more fully. A minimum of sixty to sixty-five divisions would be brought into play. NATO would have some three to five days of warning time and could counter with twenty-five to twenty-six divisions, with the expectation of reinforcement within a two-week period of three divisions from Belgium, the United Kingdom, the Netherlands, and possibly French forces. Over the same period, the Warsaw Pact total force could amount to over eighty divisions.

Third, the premeditated all-out offensive, the least likely contingency, would dispense almost entirely with surprise. NATO's warning time would more nearly meet its classic configuration of twenty-three days. Such an offensive would involve the full mobilization of the Soviet strategic reserve and forces from the seven westerly military districts, as well as six airborne divisions, producing a Warsaw Pact force in the region of ninety divisions. The NATO response, given orderly mobilization, would be on the order of thirty or more divisions.

These figures are wholly arbitrary, though each contingency can be subject to close statistical scrutiny, and are intended to be a mere indication of scale. The general conclusion, however, must be that Soviet combat readiness is of a higher order than that prevailing within NATO, that the combat readiness of non-Soviet Warsaw Pact formations is a moot point, and that rapid reinforcement on a considerable scale is eminently feasible within the Warsaw Pact. Much then hangs on the argument about outcomes, a short campaign versus a more protracted one, though what cannot be disputed is the critical nature of timely warning orders during a period of political tension and the dispatch of reinforcements without delay. Also crucial would be NATO's ability to increase its initial combat capability to a point where any Soviet offensive would suffer a high initial loss rate—and it would have to be prohibitively high.

All this has so far ignored air capabilities. Warsaw Pact air forces presently enjoy a numerical superiority over NATO of 2.4:1, though reinforcement would reduce this imbalance to 3:2 at a stroke. Comparing air capabilities is no easy task, nor is the conversion of air capability into an equivalent "ground forces output" in terms of destructiveness, casualties inflicted, and the like, complicated yet again by the very different developments within the NATO and Warsaw Pact air forces. NATO developed long-range, deep-strike tactical aircraft, while until recently the Warsaw Pact discounted long-range and heavy payloads, concentrating on air defense and limited ground support. This situation is now changing with some rapidity as new long-range aircraft come into front-line service with Soviet air armies. The massive investment in battlefield mobile defenses, SAMs, and antiaircraft guns and interceptors forces NATO to assign substantial resources to suppression, while deep-ranging Soviet strike aircraft pose a major problem to NATO's own air defense systems. NATO also suffers from the fact that lack of depth diminishes the deployment area for air units, while the insufficient number of air bases results inevitably in too great a density of occupation and complications in the management of air traffic control, radar operations, and supply facilities. With at least ninety airfields at their disposal, Warsaw Pact air units could also operate from dispersed natural sites serviced by mobile systems. But the introduction of advanced combat aircraft places limits on this mode—hence the lengthening of runways, expansion of fuel depots, and a hardening program for aircraft shelters, with at least 1,500 available.

Though Soviet air resources in the European theater are considerable, they would also be severely stretched (again, if one assumes a conventional mode in the initial phase of operations). An initial air strike would almost certainly be mounted, with Frontal Aviation supported by medium bombers of the Long-Range Aviation air force. The first echelon would be used to clear corridors through the NATO air defense system, with antiradar missiles for suppression and destruction of NATO's SAM sites, followed by wide-ranging strikes against NATO air bases, as well as nuclear installations (storage sites and launchers), and key command and control centers, a complex targeting plan that would inevitably reduce the intensity of the attack on NATO air bases. (Knocking out an air base requires a heavy tonnage of bombs; so it is no easy task.) For operations beyond the range of Frontal Aviation—targets in the United Kingdom, for example—Long-Range Aviation could commit the Backfire, TU-22, and TU-16 bombers, using the SU-19 to strike at airfield defenses and employing the longer-range MIG-23 "Flogger-B" as escort fighter. All this is to say that the Soviet air force must realize a high degree of success in a relatively short period of time, all in the face of increasing losses that would be considered worthwhile if NATO sortie rates could be held down, NATO's nuclear capability severely damaged, and command and control disrupted. The residue of air resources would be committed against any NATO counterattack against a Soviet breakthrough, a task that would include holding off NATO reserves from the battlefield. The growing force of helicopters adds to the direct fire resources of the ground forces. But present ground support is evidently in something of an experimental phase in Soviet operational thinking, and an aircraft not unlike the wartime *Shturmovik* may yet be needed.

The operational commitment of Soviet tactical aviation, even when supplemented by Long-Range Aviation, is heavy and demands a high sortie rate, with operations carried out under strictly centralized control. In spite of the numerical advantage, the Soviet air forces must operate within quite narrow margins. A limited number of independent air operations must enjoy a high degree of success, with a premium on the outcome of preemption. For both sides, management of the air battle is crucial. In NATO there is a pressing need to protect targets open to the initial Soviet air strike, to cope with targets at low altitude, and to combine the air battle for limited air superiority with the suppression of Soviet ground-based antiair defenses. The introduction of airborne warning and control systems (AWACS) would presumably double warning time from the present ten minutes for the detection of Soviet takeoff. Performance, of course, remains a disputatious point. With 116 men per aircraft in the U.S. Air Force in Europe (aircrew, maintenance, and handling) and only 67 men per aircraft in the Soviet Air Army in East Germany, there is less reliance on tactical air in Warsaw Pact forces (but greater investment in ground-based air defense systems). The Soviet bloc also suffers from a lower rate of aircraft utilization, including training time, with Warsaw Pact pilots only rarely achieving the twenty hours a month attained by NATO pilots. It is little wonder, therefore, that there have been growing complaints in the Soviet air force over the inflexibility of training schedules and the rigidity of training patterns.

Although the "air balance" is narrower than the gross figures would suggest, Soviet airpower is undergoing both expansion and diversification. The traditional formula of NATO quality offsetting Warsaw Pact quantity no longer holds. On the other hand, in a much wider context, the quality versus quantity aspect of the balance involving the whole range of advancing military technology may well be shifting in NATO's favor once again with the advent of precision-guided munitions (PGMs). Here the United States enjoys a significant advantage in target sensors, guidance systems, and warheads. To oppose Soviet armor and its numerical superiority, there are also new antiarmor ammunition for the new American XM-1 battle tank and a new high velocity gun. The neutron bomb might become a major addition to NATO's armory, which is also augmented by bomblets and antitank cluster munitions. But once again it is useful to bear in mind the possible counter. A Soviet offensive might concentrate on PGM systems as high priority targets in an initial attack.

Conclusion

Obviously, the ramifications of the military balance in Europe go both deep and wide. There is, for example, the whole issue of the relationship of the flanks to the center, a subject in itself, as is the role of naval forces and the balance at sea. There is an obvious explanation for the preoccupation with the central front in Europe, but the flanks—north and south alike—could be the scene of actions, initially indeterminate, which then spill over into the central and main front. The greatest imbalance in this context is undoubtedly in the north, which is also the location of the most powerful concentration of Soviet naval force, the Northern Fleet.[6] On the southern flank, NATO forces do not face comparable numerical inferiority, but existing (and reinforced) Soviet forces could operate with greater flexibility.

The gross numbers involved in looking at the European military balance, whether this be a matter of forces in being or after reinforcement, bear out a consistent Warsaw Pact advantage of 2:1, rising to 3:1 in the light of the Warsaw Pact's speedier reinforcement capability. On closer inspection, however, this advantage is neither so decisive nor so expansive as some would have it.

[6] See J. Erickson, "The Northern Theater: Soviet Capabilities and Concepts," *Strategic Review* 4 (Summer 1976), pp. 67–82.

Put briefly, the "balance" viewed in grand terms is depressingly imbalanced, yet the narrower the focus, the more tenuous this disparity becomes. The real point of contention is how either side would fare in a more protracted campaign. With equal plausibility a case can be made for success attending either side. However, it is reasonably plain that NATO forces require some repositioning, some restructuring, and not a little reequipping. Soviet ground forces are currently optimized in terms of organization, weapons, and support, the only alternative now being for the Soviet command to amass reserve stocks and thus combine shock power with sustained combat capability.

The deterrent power of NATO forces still holds, but the margins are narrowing appreciably. On the other hand, the Warsaw Pact forces have derived and continue to derive much political advantage from visibly high force levels. From that point of view, the "political balance" has tipped against NATO and the "perceived balance" (to use another of these terms) is not in NATO's favor. This is a matter of political will and a certain financial sacrifice, neither of them particularly common commodities in Western Europe. For the moment, the balance holds up much as it has for some years, but there are the beginnings of a shift or a slide that could all too rapidly assume ruinous proportions. Mere tinkering will solve nothing.

Soviet Economic Capabilities and Defense Resources

JOHN P. HARDT

Although the Soviet Union's massive military establishment projects its power throughout the world and into space to influence the course of world events, its economic and technological power is limited. Efforts to reduce the technological lag of its civilian economy and raise the standards of living of its people—so important to a dynamic, modern economy—tend to fall short of Soviet plans and expectations. Moreover, the future economic and technological base of Soviet power does not match projected plans for military growth. Today, the Soviet Union is a dominant economic power only in central or Eastern Europe. For the future, the Soviet Union will remain a military power without the necessary economic base if it continues its emphasis on economic autarky.

If it were prepared to reorient its priorities and methods, this modern Sparta might join the Western industrial countries as a member of the elite group of economically and technologically advanced nations. Indeed, the Soviet resource base in energy, metal, and other natural resources provides a better underpining for development than that possessed by the current economic giants of Europe, Asia, or North America. Thus the formula of economic interdependence whereby Soviet resources would be wedded to Western technology is an attractive and officially accepted program for future development. Indeed, there are precedents for this. The early Bolsheviks argued for joining the "Machine Shops of Germany" with the "Granary of the Ukraine." This earlier combination was to be attained, to be sure, by the spread of Communist revolution, whereas the current development of economic interdependence is to result from negotiation and understanding. In this scenario, détente gives hope of entente, Stalin's world of two markets becomes one market, and the spirit of the Helsinki Final Act is carried forward.

It is well known in the West that the Soviet Union has continued to expand its military arsenal. Perhaps less appreciated is the fact that it is also committed to a policy of economic interdependence designed to improve the overall Soviet economic and technological position. The image that appeals to some Soviet leaders is the postwar economic miracle of Japan. During the 1950s, that Asian economic giant was able effectively to transfer technology from the more advanced industrial countries of the time and build on Western technology with minimum political and economic intervention from foreign states or multinational corporations. Some Soviet leaders find this formula especially appealing. A key aspect of the Japanese formula that has escaped much public attention, however, has been the small military burden—approximately 1 percent of its gross national product—that Japan sustained during this period. The comparable Soviet figure is 13-15 percent.

The central questions are: Can the Soviet Union attain the position of an economic and technological superpower while retaining its eminent position as a military superpower? How will efforts to introduce Western technology benefit or change the Soviet economic and political system? What margin of influence may Western nations or organizations have on the course and impact of economic interdependence and technological change in the Soviet system? However these questions are answered, certainly policies of both East and West in security and economic affairs are in conflict. The opportunities and risks in the policy of economic interdependence are central to East-West relations.

Dimensions of Soviet Power

It is important to consider the burden of military resource claims and the Soviet leaders' perception of their priority. The Leninist formula for economic development, as expounded by Stalin, primarily emphasized the creation of an economic base for developing future military programs, including current production as well as stockpiles of military equipment. This approach was largely mission-oriented in the sense that the overtaking and surpassing of military support bases of Western industrial countries and the development of Soviet military arsenals were directly related to a presumed security threat. Indeed, the German invasion of the Soviet Union seemed to validate this priority. The continuation and expansion of Soviet postwar power was also mission-oriented in the sense that it was to be the political base both for projecting Soviet power abroad and retaining power within adjacent territories. Stalin's views were often made quite clear on the direct political relevance of Soviet military power. (He claimed, for example, that in Italy the Communist takeover was unsuccessful because the Soviet army had not proceeded far enough.) Presently, the development of Soviet strategic forces, the naval outreach, and the conventional buildup of strength on the China border, carried out under Stalin's successors, appear to have a political mission, albeit with more diverse goals than the arms buildup of the 1930s.

In dealing with the economic and technological capability of the Soviet Union, it may be useful to consider economic missions more than comparative balances. For years one could say, in comparative terms, that the Soviet economy was about half the size of the American economy in terms of goods and services produced, that it spent approximately as much as the United

States on national defense, and that the Soviet technological efficiency in the civilian pursuits was about one-third to two-fifths of that in this country. In measures of GNP per capita and energy production per capita, the Soviets are similarly less advanced than the United States and most of the Western industrial countries. It is more useful, however, to consider the economic and technological purposes of the Soviet economy. In doing so, one finds that the relative quality of resources and approximate parity of military technology offer a more useful basis for assessing the purposes of the Soviet leadership.

There are signs that the Soviet leaders are becoming increasingly aware of the disadvantages inherent in their pattern of technological development. The progressive slowdown in their economic growth rate, the sharply rising capital requirements for incremental outputs, and the increased need for attractive consumer goods to provide incentives for a scarce labor force have all underscored the need to improve economic efficiency for civilian as well as military purposes. It is also clear to Soviet leaders that the economic base for future power requires a modern, technologically advanced civilian economy in order to support future generations of military programs.

Economic Modernization: Sputnik to Détente

In the late 1950s, a state of euphoria brought on by the successful launching of Sputnik and reasonably successful economic programs led Khrushchev to adopt a policy of both "guns and butter." His seven-year plan, initiated in 1959, stressed broad economic modernization along Western lines in energy, metals, transport, agriculture, and other consumer-related sectors. It also involved overtaking and surpassing Western standards for food, housing, and other measures of consumption. This entire program was to proceed while the Soviet Union moved toward equivalence with the United States in the political use of military power.

Bad weather and overcommitment of resources caused economic failures and resulted in a reexamination of these ambitious modernization and consumer targets. The failure of the Cuban missile venture, by which Khrushchev hoped for political projections of equality on a narrow strategic military base, led to a reappraisal of military programs by Khrushchev and his successors.

Late in 1964, Khrushchev's successors, Leonid I. Brezhnev and Aleksei N. Kosygin, moved toward a selective policy of economic interdependence in the world economy. The historic decision to build passenger cars with industrial cooperation from the Italian company, Fiat, symbolized the change. This acceptance of selective Western involvement in developing automotive transport marked the beginning of a policy of economic interdependence as a necessary ingredient for Soviet modernization. Brezhnev and Kosygin had apparently concluded that if some improvement in the Soviet consumer's lot was to be forthcoming, selected areas, such as Western style passenger-car production and increased meat output, must be singled out for special attention. They adopted a policy of selective consumerism in lieu of the Khrushchev program of across-the-board economic modernization and improvement in living standards.

The Fiat plant became a featured project of the Eighth Five-Year Plan (1966-70). This project was to be the forerunner of further developments with Western companies in the automotive field. The Kama River truck plant became, in turn, a key project involving Western technology in the Ninth Five-Year Plan (1971-75). This plan further broadened the selective concept of Western-style economic modernization and consumerism. In the expanded scope of technological change the development of energy, metal production, agricultural processes, and computer applications were to be some of the key sectors for Western involvement in Soviet modernization.

The full political and economic implications of the Fiat venture within the Soviet economy are not yet clear. Still, its relative success may have encouraged a broadening of modernization priorities, or it may have reflected merely the deepening economic problems of the Soviet economy and its resistance to improvement without efficiency measures and technology imported from Western sources. As one Western observer put it, the Soviet leaders may have decided to stop denying themselves the advantages of Western economic and technological interdependence. In any case, the advantages of economic interdependence have been illustrated by the "economic miracles" of the advanced Western industrial nations. The Soviet leaders were encouraged by the prospects held out by the agreements with the United States following the 1972 summit meeting that forecast improved trade facilities and the availability of long-term, low-interest government credits. The formula discussed for the West Siberian natural gas project, "North Star," was especially attractive in that the multibillion ruble project was to be supplied with plant and equipment from the United States on a priority basis for development of the pipeline, and with liquefaction and energy transport facilities with no repayment required until after the facilities were operative. The sequential payback arrangement was then to be at reasonably favorable terms from the output of future gas generated in the new facilities, developed largely with Western technology and facilitated by Western credit. Although this project involved the reallocation of domestic Soviet investment resources within the Soviet plan, it posed no significant problem in terms of diverting hard currency from other projects or incurring onerous debts that might influence short-term import policies.

The Soviets apparently hoped that government credits and large multibillion-dollar project financing, as discussed in 1972 and 1973 for the North Star project, might also be forthcoming from Western European countries as well as Japan. Their hope was for such projects as Japanese assistance on long-distance transmission of petroleum from the Tyumen Province in West Siberia to the Pacific and joint development of Yakutia natural gas, an agreement with the West Germans for joint development of the massive, modern Kursk metallurgical capability, and a variety of smaller projects to be concluded with the French, the United Kingdom, and other Western European countries.

By its actions restricting trade preferences and access to Export-Import Bank facilities, the United States Congress eliminated the possibility that the North Star formula might become a standard American vehicle for financing and facilitating large-scale Western technology transfers to the major Soviet projects, especially in resource development. Subsequently, parallel projects under discussion with Germany and Japan were revised from the earlier pattern of long-term, preferential financing to that of more conventional commercial and businesslike terms akin to those elsewhere in developed economies.

As preparation for the Tenth Five-Year Plan (1976-80) proceeded, however, leadership interest continued in technological transfer, various forms of economic interdependence, and a broadening of sectors of priority for modernization involving Western technology. This interest was dampened by hard currency trade deficits and rising debts. Emphasis is still being given to various modes of financing, and these financing ventures all give priority to those that provide returns or repayment out of products developed from imported technology in specific projects. So-called compensation agreements, i.e., projects financed by purchase of products from completed enterprises, became the vogue. This new formula also includes industrial cooperation characterized by royalties, quality control, and other aspects of Western managerial involvement and is expected by 1980 to account for as much as 40 percent of Soviet-American commercial relations. All these institutional arrangements improve the prospects of effective technology transfer and ease the hard currency deficit problem.

Notwithstanding the significant increase in the economic growth and overall performance of the postwar economies of Western Europe and Japan associated with technology transfers, one must note significant differences in the projected Soviet pattern. Unlike the industrial nations of Europe and Japan that had developed economic infrastructures on which a broader and technologically more modern economy could be built, the Soviet economy is narrowly geared to military-industrial needs. Whereas the Western industrial nations were short of natural resources and unskilled labor, the Soviet economy is self-sufficient in most materials and unskilled labor required for a modern economy. Unfortunately these material resources and unskilled labor are poorly located for serving new Siberian industrial centers, and costs for their development are significantly higher than those required to develop earlier resource bases.

Aided by the development of the transnational corporations, the economic institutions of the Western industrial nations were well suited for technology transfer, absorption, and adaptation, while the Soviet economic system has tended to resist technological change, especially when related to Western systems of management. Whereas both Western and Soviet economic development plans aim at improving capital efficiency and labor productivity by increased capital and technology per worker and improved incentives from increased availability of consumer goods, the accommodation of measures of efficiency and incentives is especially difficult in the Soviet system. Finally, while accepting some military claims on their technologically advancing economies, none of the Western industrial nations, including the United States, has accepted the burden of defense that the Soviet economy has consistently borne. The theoretical prospect for a significant improvement in economic performance through technology transfer is certainly possible in the Soviet economy. It is a process that might get under way in the period of the current (as yet unpublished) Fifteen-Year Plan, one for which the rich Soviet resource base in energy, metals, timber, and so on may be helpful. Nonetheless, the five areas of uniqueness noted above make such a miracle unlikely in the near future.

Balance Sheet on Economic Modernization at the Outset of the Fifteen-Year Plan (1976–90)[1]

Several of the specific projects the Soviets have adopted in their long-term effort to elevate their general economic and technological capability to the relative level of their military power deserve closer attention. The Soviet economic plan includes a number of large multibillion ruble projects involving long gestation periods and significant Western technological imports. Some of the major projects include automotive plants like the passenger car facility at Tolyatti and the truck plant on the Kama River, the Baikal-Amur railroad development (BAM) in the Far East and East Siberia, agricultural investment programs (including the opening of new nonblack soil lands and construction of storage and transportation facilities), integrated energy development programs (including new primary energy sources as well as transmission and utilization facilities), metal processing and development projects, computer systems for national economic reporting, planning, and enterprise management, and tourist facilities, including hotels, airlines, and other facilities aimed at the 1980 Olympics. Each of these new projects, initiated during the preceding ten years, will continue to generate increasing demands for Western imports as well as expanding civilian requirements for domestic investment resources. The Soviet leadership continues to accord high priority to these projects and clearly expects significant and favorable results from them. Western analyses of the impact to date of imported technology suggest that the Soviet leadership has correctly assumed that Western technology could be a major factor in accelerating economic performance.

Whatever the Soviet leadership's expectations, there are several potentially disturbing factors in the formula for recent success in these Western-oriented projects. A primary problem is cost, the diversion of resources from other priority projects, including military programs. These priority projects may place very high demands on scarce Soviet resources, including skilled man-

---

[1] See Holland Hunter, M. Mark Earle, Jr., and Richard B. Foster, "Assessment of Alternative Long Range Soviet Growth Strategies" and Murray Feshbach and Stephen Rapawy, "Soviet Population and Manpower Trends and Policies," *Soviet Economy in a New Perspective,* ed. John P. Hardt (Washington, D.C.: GPO, 1976).

power, for building effective facilities to increase the output of finished goods. Especially resource-demanding is the construction of the economic infrastructure for raw material development in the far reaches of Siberia. The cost, for example, of adding facilities for delivering oil and natural gas to Soviet markets from the permafrost regions of Siberia is many times the comparable cost of oil production or gas development in the older regions. Every one of the major projects placed by the Soviet leadership on its priority list of multibillion ruble complexes primarily requires interrelated investments and long gestation periods before showing effective economic results.

A second disturbing feature for Soviet decision-makers is the requirement of the systems-transfer as well as process-transfer of technology. The transfer to the Soviet Union of managerial expertise may be the primary factor in the success of these priority projects in economic development systems. It may also have disturbing political and institutional side effects. The new variations in party and economic control represent special exceptions and relaxations in traditional political and economic controls. These current variations in administration reflect the pattern of technological absorption of these new priority projects into the Soviet economy. To date, the small-scale replication of Western-type management and control within the Soviet bureaucracy has been treated as an exception. In the future, if these exceptions are spread to many projects, the changes may influence the system itself. At stake in these two aspects of effective technology transfer are priority in resource allocation, particularly the traditional priority of military or heavy-industrial claimants for high quality resources, and the traditional dominant role of the party and the governmental bureaucracy at all levels of the Soviet economy.

Financing imports of technology has also proved to be a problem. The terms on which the Soviet leaders once hoped to obtain credits and technology from the West to support their economic modernization programs have not met their expectations. Financing large-scale projects such as the North Star on long-term, favorable terms with sequential payback has not materialized. In its place, the Soviets have been required to accept short-term competitive rates with concurrent payback for projects of lesser scale, such as in mineral fertilizer and metallurgy development. Poor harvests in 1972, 1975, and 1977, together with the adverse effect on Soviet exports of the Western recession and the impact of Western inflation on Soviet import prices have made persistent balance of payments deficits a major factor in limiting trade with the West. The level of Soviet indebtedness reached in 1976 after a serious trade deficit in 1975 appears to have compelled the deferral of many contemplated additional long-term projects. Furthermore, there have been negative effects on a number of the project areas noted above for which Western technology is critical. The major deferrals include delays in production of Western automobile and truck models in the Soviet Union; in development of the power-consuming industries and resource development industries in East Siberia and the region around the Baikal-Amur railroad; in the development of the agribusiness complexes required for modernizing the feed grain livestock industry; in the development of long distance AC and DC transmission facilities for bringing cheap hydro- and coal-generated power from Siberia to European Russian markets; and in importing transmission, exploration, extraction, and other facilities for petroleum and natural gas complexes to meet the projected plan of both onshore and offshore output increases. Further deferrals include delays in the Kursk metallurgical project for pelletizing and direct metal reduction; in the introduction of an effective, computer-assisted national economic reporting system; and in completing facilities for tourist expansion for the 1980 Olympics.

The costs of further Soviet equivocation in opting for Western cooperation to achieve economic modernization are high indeed if the expensive multibillion ruble projects are not brought to a level of effective production in the context of the Fifteen-Year Plan. The gestation periods are long in any event for these major projects, so central to future Soviet performance, but the possibility for converting facilities, once the commitments are made, is very small. Regional energy, metal, and transportation facilities are sunk costs. The returns come only after completing the economic complexes that provide them.

Likewise, decisions to allocate investment resources to long-term defense projects have become increasingly difficult to reverse. With respect to strategic weapons systems, modern naval developments, and even equipping modern conventional forces for the China border, the options for conversion of economic resources from the military to the civilian sector have become increasingly limited over time. After the Cuban missile crisis the gestation period from the decision to embark on a strategic weapons buildup to actual deployment may have been a decade or more. Writing at the time, this observer noted that "Premier Khrushchev is using up today, in weapons systems decisions, many of the options of his successor and preconditioning the resource allocation pattern that will be his successor's inheritance."[2] That observation in 1962 is even more relevant in 1977 to the pattern of resource decisions. Once taken, the decision between guns and butter is irreversible within the period of the Fifteen-Year Plan.

The Economic Dilemmas of CMEA and the Warsaw Pact

The Soviet policy of economic modernization and emphasis on consumerism defined the limits within which the smaller countries of the Council for Mutual Economic Assistance (CMEA) could adopt their own new economic strategies. The new Eastern European strategy emphasizes selective modernization, using Western technology and managerial techniques. Eastern European efforts in the 1960s to achieve modernization on a broad front proved unacceptable and therefore unmanageable to the Soviets. The attempted Czech application of a broad policy of modernization was forcibly stopped by the intrusion of Soviet tanks into Prague. The Prague approach to economic modernization on a broad front proved difficult to manage for most Eastern European

---

[2] John P. Hardt, "Strategic Alternatives in Soviet Resource Allocation Policy," *Dimensions of Soviet Power*, ed. Leon Herman (Washington, D.C.: GPO, 1962), p. 19.

countries. In its place the Eastern European countries adopted a strategy of selective emphasis on growth areas and economic reform in specific mechanisms and sectors for the first five years of the 1970s.

The Eastern European countries embarked, though unevenly, on large long-term projects for developing selective sectors with special emphasis on Western technology transfers. They also adopted a consumer oriented program designed to provide increasing incentives, but these also generated substantially increased expectations. A modern industrial structure, an accelerated rate of economic growth, and especially an increase in visible consumption, including availability of meat and other quality products, became a normal feature of Eastern European economic policies.

In 1975 the Eastern European leaders and planners were probably surprised when the Soviet Union, in the wake of the significant increase in world energy prices, radically changed the terms of trade with its Eastern European partners. In 1973 and 1974 the price of Soviet oil was about one-fourth of that set by the Organization of Petroleum Exporting Countries (OPEC) and could be paid through export of goods not necessarily marketable outside of CMEA. In 1975 this situation was revised by a planning arrangement whereby the prices paid to the Soviet Union by the end of the decade would close the gap with the current OPEC prices and presumably increase the requirement of Eastern Europe to make "hard" goods deliveries to the Soviet Union. The Soviet bargainers in the annual trade agreements also sought and apparently obtained enhanced cooperation and investment from Eastern European economies in joint CMEA projects such as the Orenburg natural gas pipeline and other Soviet resource projects. Soviet planners had been pushing each of these projects for some time as they had the advantage of being a part of the Soviet domestic economy. One is tempted to wonder whether the Soviet use of the energy lever in these unequal negotiations has brought an increase in the military production burden on the Eastern European countries, as well as in their share of other Warsaw Pact military costs.

One might expect the Eastern Europeans to reduce their imports from the West in the face of pressing new requirements from the Soviet Union and irreducible, increasing requirements in their domestic economies. But modernization and improved consumer performance are tied to the elimination of bottlenecks in Eastern European plans that only Western imports can provide. By the end of this five-year plan period, hard currency imports to the Eastern European countries from the West may increase from $17 billion in 1976 to as much as $28 billion in 1980. The indebtedness of the Eastern European countries has risen sharply, although unevenly. Poland was the pacesetter; its debts increased from less than $1 billion when Edvard Gierek replaced Wladyslaw Gomulka in 1970 to over $10 billion in 1976, in convertible currencies.

One question in this context is why the Soviet negotiators do not extract the maximum short-term economic returns from Eastern Europe. The Soviets are probably sensitive to the political vulnerability of the Eastern European Communist parties and desire to benefit from increasing long-term productivity of the Eastern European economies. The Soviets provided about 1.3 billion rubles in credit to the Poles in the fall of 1976 after the price riots of the summer, presumably to keep Polish party leader Gierek in power. It appears that the Soviet leaders view Gierek as the best possible prospect among Polish political leaders. Combining Soviet and Polish interests, Gierek is acceptable to Soviet leaders as long as he can control his party. In the longer term, the Soviet Union will either benefit or suffer from the ability of the Eastern European economies to produce more "hard" goods or products that can be sold under world market conditions. If they are politically committed to Eastern European economic plans, they might wish to maximize their long-term economic returns from this continued alliance or at least minimize the Eastern European burden on the Soviet economy.

Political stability in Eastern European countries has been shaken by the response of their people to the human rights provisions of the Helsinki agreement. In the German Democratic Republic and Czechoslovakia, the reactions and public demonstrations of leading citizens, at considerable personal risk, suggest the extent of the impact throughout Eastern Europe of the human rights aspects of these agreements. Effective consumerism, or the economic improvement of the citizen's lot, is one of the party's important counterweapons in maintaining political stability. Indeed, economic performance is linked to stability in other ways. The agreements, long sought by the Catholic Church, to have churches built in new Polish towns was a concession that seems to have a political and economic rationale. The fear of political instability in Eastern Europe appears to make the Soviets cautious in pressing their advantage. It may also account for the buildup of Warsaw Pact forces in recent years as a mechanism through which Soviet control can be reasserted if necessary by force.

One factor in assessing current Soviet choices between short-term military goals and long-term economic improvements is the age of its leadership. The Brezhnev era has been characterized by consensus and status quo policies. Soviet acceptance of global economic interdependence must be assessed against this resistance to change.

The succession to Brezhnev may not be followed immediately by a firm, stable leadership. A turbulent transition may follow his political or physical demise. Whoever eventually succeeds him will take over his long-term commitments to competing military and economic programs. The worst of policies would then be one of equivocation. The Soviet leaders may be free to choose, but they are no longer free *not* to choose, and the consequences of their choice will have to be accepted, on the whole, by Brezhnev's successors.

Western and Soviet Options

Commercial relations between East and West may be promoted or restricted through government action. Western governments are following both policies, restricting trade by tariffs, quotas, and other nontariff barriers, including licensing, and promoting trade by government credits, trade facilities, and subsidies. The avowed purpose of such restrictions is to protect the domestic producers and labor force while denying potential adversaries economic and technological resources that would significantly enhance their military capability. Restrictions intended to protect the interests of domestic producers are of particular interest during times of economic recession when foreign competition threatens domestic employment and production. Licensing of industrial products is employed when production processes are believed to enhance the military capability of a possible enemy. Trade promotion, on the other hand, is intended to provide new foreign markets for domestic producers, thereby permitting large-scale, more efficient operations and possibly maintaining low unit costs and prices while profits rise.

Government loans and guarantees tend to reduce the risk of dealing in uncertain Eastern markets, to reduce credit charges, and thus to make Western exports more attractive to Eastern importers. These measures are designed to facilitate Western exports to the East while other measures tend to restrict imports. It is an uneven commercial policy for developing the national interests of either Western or Eastern nations.

Credit policy poses special problems in East-West commercial relations. As credits are made easier, the resulting trade deficits lead to increased indebtedness. This process is exacerbated as the policies and priorities of Eastern nations tend to encourage imports and have difficulties in providing goods and services that would attract hard currency. The rapid accumulation of Eastern debts to a level between $40 billion and $50 billion in recent years is the outgrowth of this situation. Restriction on Western licensing of exports that otherwise might enhance the Eastern military-support economy adds uncertainty to the relationship. Measures intended to restrict exporting through control of products and processes that might bolster Soviet military capability are unevenly applied by the United States, as well as by other nations of NATO and Japan. The inclusion in the unilateral United States control list of export items not included in the list of embargoed commodities mutually agreed on by the members of the Coordinating Committee (COCOM)—an informal group consisting of NATO member states (except Iceland) and Japan—attests to this discrepancy. The list of commodities (such as certain computers, nuclear reactors, aircraft, and electronic equipment) that the United States may effectively control or deny, however, is now much shorter. Moreover, the effect of American limitations on the export of strategic technology diminishes as the capability of Warsaw Pact military production increases. To determine what production processes might significantly contribute to the military capability of a foreign power is a complex question. There is also the problem of identifying critical bottlenecks in the Soviet economy that may be released by technical breakthroughs achieved with the aid of Western technology. The United States Defense Science Board has attempted to unravel these complexities. As a member of NATO, however, the United States should not adopt such policies nor should any other NATO powers without consulting other North Atlantic partners.

In Europe two highly integrated groups face each other with conflicting economic and security priorities. The European Economic Community is highly developed economically and technologically and has minimal barriers among its members to the useful flow of goods, services, and civilian technology. Degrees of specialization in industry, agriculture, and transportation have been worked out to conform with concepts of comparative advantage. The Warsaw Pact is a highly integrated military organization with standardized modern equipment, closely integrated forces, and unified command structures. Europe also has two less integrated, less efficient groups facing each other: the North Atlantic Treaty Organization (NATO) and the Council for Mutual Economic Assistance (CMEA). NATO suffers from lack of integration and standardization. Considerations of sovereignty and national interest often reduce the areas of common efforts and burden sharing. The same kinds of problems plague CMEA.

The state of integration of the respective economic and military organizations of Eastern and Western Europe illustrates the traditional difference in priorities. The Soviet Union and its Eastern European allies now seem to recognize that problems of an economic nature inherent in CMEA need to be addressed and remedied. Likewise, NATO nations express a need for more effective integration and a closer relationship between economic and security policy. A common Western policy toward the Eastern nations on economic and security matters is a newly important item on the agenda. Certain areas for consultation derive from the problems posed for the NATO alliance by the combination of Soviet economic potential and military power. Among these are the need for continued and vigorous consultation about a common NATO policy on export licensing and technology transfer to the East, considering not only trade but bilateral cooperative exchanges as well as differentiation of NATO's posture between the Soviet Union and its Eastern European allies; reappraisal of Western policies on tariff and nontariff barriers to Eastern trade, including quotas, determination of market disruption, and dumping; consideration of a coordinated Western credit and financing policy toward the East, reexamining concepts of competitiveness and considering conformity with reporting requirements of the provisions for economic cooperation of the Helsinki agreement; and a broader framework of multilateral Western consultation to interrelate bilateral East-West relations and cope with political, economic, and security questions.

Western policy on economic interdependence is important, but the major determinant in long-term Soviet economic and technological performance is its military policy. If the Soviets choose to stay on their current course of military superpower augmentation, they must defer or forgo the option of joining the Western industrial nations as an economic superpower. If economic interdependence and modernization continue to be a priority aim of the Soviet leadership, their country may, in time, join the Western industrial nations as an economic superpower. This would probably require a budgetary emphasis on, and accord a higher priority to, economic modernization rather than military augmentation. It would also require an expanding program of Western technology imports that could affect both the economic and the political aspects of the Soviet system.

Should the Soviet Union become an economic superpower, it might also become economically competitive with Europe, Japan, and North America in the world market for industrial goods. Its leaders might be less inclined to focus global competition on areas where Soviet military competitiveness was dominant. This type of qualitative shift would make Moscow's long-term slogan of peaceful coexistence more meaningful.

This essay is based on an address delivered to NATO commanders at the Supreme Headquarters Allied Powers Exercise (SHAPEX) at Mons, Belgium, on May 12, 1977, to be published as "Soviet Economic Potential and Military Power" in *NATO Review*, March 1978.

Human Rights and Détente

DIMITRI K. SIMES

Human rights will undoubtedly remain an integral part of the Soviet-American relationship. There is little chance that the Kremlin will be able either completely to suppress dissent or to undertake a far reaching relaxation of domestic controls. Consequently, political repression in the Soviet Union will continue, and inevitably the dissidents will search for Western support, their main if not their only hope at this stage. The American public, including a significant section of the Congress and the media, strongly sympathizes with the brave men and women challenging Moscow's oppressive practices. Public pressure in support of the Soviet dissidents cannot be discounted by those who formulate official United States policy. The experience of recent years demonstrates that Congress simply will not allow any administration, regardless of its intentions and preferences, to ignore the Soviet human rights record as a factor in its relationship with the United States.

At the same time, as far as the Soviet regime is concerned, even the most cautious and indirect involvement on behalf of the dissidents represents unwarranted interference in its domestic affairs. Not only are the United States's efforts to help members of the Soviet opposition groups perceived as a threat to the system, but they also have a certain spillover effect on other spheres of the Soviet-American relationship. From the Soviet point of view, American criticism of the Kremlin's treatment of its citizens amounts to questioning the very legitimacy of the regime. As the Soviet leadership sees it, détente with the West, and with the United States in particular, is supposed to strengthen the Kremlin's international positions and improve the performance of the troubled Soviet economy through investments, credits, and technology transfers. This in turn could, at least to some extent, help avoid an unpleasant choice between guns and butter and enhance the stability of the system while avoiding major reforms. To a degree, the Kremlin perceives détente as a substitute for internal innovations. Western pressure to force the Soviets to relax their domestic controls challenges the basic Soviet philosophy of détente as a form of "peaceful offensive" against the West. In this context it is not surprising that the Soviet leadership reacts strongly to American efforts to establish greater reciprocity in the ideological struggle. Distrustful of Soviet citizens, Moscow knows too well that it, and not Washington, has to fear the open competition of ideas.

It is possible to argue that there is no reason for the Kremlin to be so defensive about Western criticism of the Soviet human rights performance. After all, despite numerous difficulties and shortcomings, the Soviet system demonstrates an impressive degree of stability. The experience of the last decade shows that the government is not seriously threatened by the dissent that failed to attract any real domestic constituency except among alienated intellectuals and some minority groups. The dissidents make the Soviet leaders uncomfortable, but they do not represent a realistic threat to the survival, or probably even the stability, of the system.

Nevertheless, Moscow becomes extremely nervous over any sign of Western sympathy for the dissidents. The precise reasons for this are unknown. Most likely they differ, in some respects, from one Soviet bureaucracy to another. The foreign policy establishment is probably most concerned with the impact of publicity about Soviet repression on the regime's image abroad. The Soviets assert that criticism of alleged human rights abuses in their country is simply a cover for those who want to undermine détente and launch production of new weapons systems. Whether Soviet officials and commentators believe their own charges is not entirely clear. However, there is indeed a connection between the American public's perception of the Soviet Union and its willingness to spend money on defense. Exposure of Soviet persecution of dissidents also reflects badly on Western Communist parties and encourages further distance between Moscow and the Eurocommunists.

The Soviet ideological and domestic security apparatus may be concerned that Western solidarity with the dissidents could enhance their standing in Soviet society. Aware that their appeals find a response in the White House, the protesters could become bolder in their challenge to the authorities. Pragmatic and insensitive Soviet leaders probably have difficulty accepting that the American president can be genuinely concerned with the plight of citizens of a foreign, especially a hostile, country. As one perceptive observer put it, "the Soviet rulers cannot possibly view the issue of 'human rights' as simply one aspect of a larger ideological debate. For them it represents a clear and present danger."[1] This danger is not necessarily as serious and real as the more paranoid members of the Politburo see it, but there does seem to be a consensus among the Soviet elite that the administration's human rights diplomacy is not something that can be easily dismissed as a minor nuisance.

This is not meant to suggest that the Kremlin's angry response should discourage the United States from defending basic principles of humanity. It would be unrealistic to expect that all American initiatives would be equally acceptable to the Soviet leadership. Such harmony rarely exists even between allies, to say nothing of major political, ideological, and military rivals. There is no reason to overemphasize Moscow's distaste for the administration's

---

[1] Irving Kristol, "Detente and Human Rights," *The Wall Street Journal*, April 15, 1977.

human rights posture. American policies are designed to pursue United States interests as long as they bring desirable results in opening Soviet society. As long as Soviet irritation with them is not strong enough to override Moscow's interest in other mutually advantageous arrangements, there is no reason to be overly concerned about the Kremlin's anger. The question is not so much how the Soviet regime feels about the new American emphasis on human rights, but what this emphasis means for the promotion of human rights in the Soviet Union, as well as for the general status of the Soviet-American relationship.

Human Rights in the Soviet Context

In order to appreciate the complexity of dealing with human rights in the Soviet context it is important to remember that the traditional Russian attitude toward individual liberties differs greatly from the ideals of Anglo-Saxon civilization. Rights of citizens were always considered secondary to the interests of the state. Anarchy, resulting from unlimited freedom, was more feared than abuses of power. Collectivism rather than individualism was a dominant force in Russian political philosophy before the Revolution.

Russians have never lived under a truly democratic government. The short period after the collapse of the czarist regime and before the Bolshevik take-over was not so much a democratic interlude as it was an intensive struggle between different authoritarian forces. Significantly, while both the Bolsheviks and their right-wing autocratic opponents managed to develop impressive popular constituencies during the civil war, the moderate liberal elements found themselves almost totally isolated and failed to display any real muscle.

Even dissidents courageously protesting Soviet repression frequently display remarkable intolerance of even minor disagreement. According to George Kennan, "our experience with Soviet defectors had shown us that however such people might hate their Soviet masters, their ideas about democracy were primitive and curious in the extreme, consisting often only of the expectation that they would be permitted and encouraged by us to line their recent political adversaries up against the wall with a ruthlessness no smaller than that to which they professed to be reacting, after which they would continue to rule, with our help, by their own brand of dictatorship."[2]

Surely most, if not all, modern Soviet dissenters would be outraged at any suggestion that there are similarities between their perceptions of democracy and the Kremlin's. Yet there are strong indications that such similarities do exist. Examples of the dissidents' autocratic thinking range from their attitudes toward repression outside the Soviet borders to bitter debates among themselves. Alexander Solzhenitsyn, for instance, had warm words for Franco's rule in Spain. According to *Kontinent*, a leading émigré journal, there are no political

---

[2] George F. Kennan, *Memoirs, 1950−1953*, vol. 2 (Boston: Little, Brown and Company, 1972), pp. 96–97.

prisoners in Greece and Chile. This statement was made while the Greek Black Colonels were still in power.[3] Solzhenitsyn clearly prefers authoritarian rule as long as its leaders accept "their responsibility before God and their own conscience," a kind of authoritarianism with a human face.[4] Outraged by repression in the Soviet Union, the exiled writer is unhappy about the "surplus" of freedom in the West. The dissidents often seem to be incapable of political compromise. When the Medvedev brothers, two dissidents with reputations beyond reproach, challenged a common opposition community view regarding the wisdom of indiscriminate Western pressure on the Kremlin, they were called traitors and even agents of the KGB. The intolerance evident in some dissident writings raises disturbing questions about the strength of their commitment to democratic ideals.

Needless to say, the dissident movement includes quite a few individuals whose perception of democracy is close to the Western tradition. Andrei Sakharov is one case in point. Yet one wonders whether these liberals represent a mainstream of dissident thinking. Even more importantly, there is serious doubt whether they can rally public support in a society that has had little opportunity to develop a taste for freedom and that for centuries has accepted repression as a way of life.

The fact that some dissidents are undemocratic does not mean that repression directed against them is any more justified than if they were devoted supporters of Western liberal values. Neither does it mean that they do not deserve the sympathy and encouragement of the West. But the strength of authoritarian views among the dissident community serves as a reminder that in trying to change Soviet repressive practices, the West is dealing not just with the Kremlin but also with the power of Russian autocratic political tradition and the prevailing philosophy of Soviet society that to a degree is shared even by those brave people who oppose the regime.

Dissident Goals

Rational discussion of Soviet dissent is an extremely difficult task. It is not that the data are unavailable. Rather, the problem is the enormous emotional involvement many Western commentators and social scientists have with the Soviet opposition. Objective attempts by some students of Soviet society to evaluate the political philosophy, personal values, and tactics of the Soviet opposition frequently meet with strong disapproval and even hints that those who, with whatever intentions, express less than total admiration of the dissidents are doing the KGB's work. As a result, the study of dissent has become almost a total monopoly of scholars with a prodissident bias. Serious analytical studies of the Soviet opposition are still in the minority. Even more importantly, they have little influence on American public perceptions of

---

[3] *Kontinent*, no. 2, 1975, pp. 468–69.
[4] Alexander Solzhenitsyn, *Iz-Pod Glyb: Sbornik Statei* (Paris: YMCA Press, 1974), p. 26.

Soviet dissent, which are generally dominated by black and white stereotypes of stupid, corrupt, and oppressive Soviet officials on the one hand, and heroic, selfless, and brilliant protesters on the other. The real situation is more complex than that.

The most popular model of Soviet dissent among American students of Soviet affairs assumes that while protesters may argue among themselves and commit minor tactical errors, as a rule their objectives are extremely noble and worthy of unquestionable Western support. According to Leonard Shapiro, "of course, Solzhenitsyn is not on the side of anyone or anything—except truth, justice and freedom under the law."[5] The trouble is, however, that perceptions of truth, justice, and freedom vary from one individual to another, and the Russian writer who received the Nobel Prize is no exception. His views on the meaning of freedom are quite different from Western liberal ideals. Unfortunately, when a discussion of Soviet dissent is involved, many otherwise serious analysts become surprisingly one-sided, if not totally blind.

There are good reasons for the prodissident bias. They include an admirable sympathy for the underdog, deeply rooted in American tradition, and a respect for the courage of individuals who dare to fight an enormous and infamous apparatus of suppression. There is also a natural confusion between enemies of one's enemies and one's friends. During World War II even Stalin was often viewed as a "good guy." Moreover, for many years the outside world perceived the Soviet Union as a tightly controlled monolith; the emergence of visible dissent inevitably fascinates Western observers. Conditions under which foreign reporters function in Moscow also play an important role. Western correspondents are essentially surrounded by two groups of people who for obviously different reasons are not afraid to deal with foreigners—dissidents and KGB informers. The net result is that dissenters become a major source of information about Soviet society and themselves. Their perspective is challenged only by official propaganda, distasteful to anyone with a sense of integrity.

One might suspect that support for Soviet dissidents, in some cases, is primarily a matter of political convenience. Dissidents like Solzhenitsyn and Vladimir E. Maksimov are very useful to those who feel the United States made too many concessions to the Soviet Union, that détente too often has been a one-way street. While the facts about Soviet repression were well known for decades, it required voices from inside the Soviet Union speaking from a position of tremendous moral authority to deliver a message that could arouse the Western public.

Yet disapproval of the oppressive regime should not paralyze one's analytical ability to make an independent, critical judgment about developments within the Soviet system. As Jerry Hough observed, "what is needed is a willingness—indeed, a determination—to subject our assumptions to searching examination

[5] Leonard Shapiro, "Some Afterthoughts on Solzhenitsyn," *The Russian Review* 33 (October 1974): 417.

and to separate our distaste for the Soviet system from our descriptive analysis of it."[6] Otherwise, Americans are bound to become victims of misconceptions.

One such misconception relates to the Public Group to Promote Observance of the Helsinki Agreements in the USSR, chaired by Professor Yuri Orlov. A common view in the American media is that the group was established to monitor Soviet compliance with the Final Act of the Conference on Security and Cooperation in Europe (CSCE) and that its members were unjustly prosecuted for legitimate activity. The facts, however, are slightly different. First, members of the group came almost exclusively from the ranks of the dissident community. Second, the group never had an interest in monitoring the first and second "baskets" dealing with security and economic issues of particular interest to the Soviet government. Quite naturally for political dissenters, they focused on only one basket—"Basket Three"—covering information exchanges and reunification of families. Third, several of the group's statements made it clear that the objective was not just to encourage observance of the Final Act, but also to discredit abroad Soviet repressive practices.

Moreover, the tone of the group's documents was, on a number of occasions, polemical and antagonistic to the regime. In one document the group stated that its main objective was to inform "world public opinion" not only about specific Soviet noncompliance with the Final Act, but also to expose "the real nature of Soviet democracy in general." It was noted with visible satisfaction that "during 1975 at least a part of the Western public apparently gradually rid itself of illusions concerning the Soviet system." Limited steps by the Kremlin to implement "Basket Three" provisions were called "isolated demonstrative concessions" imposed on the Soviet authorities by Western pressure.[7]

Needless to say, this in no way justifies arrests of the group's members. But it does put their activities and the regime's response to them in a different perspective. From the official Soviet standpoint the group represented not a legitimate Helsinki monitoring body, but a group of dissidents using the Final Act to mobilize international opposition to Moscow. The fact that it was using Helsinki as a tool in a political struggle was probably perceived as a matter of tactics. Undoubtedly, Western governments have the right and, indeed, the obligation to point out to the Soviets that police repression of peaceful opposition is incompatible with the spirit of Helsinki. Nevertheless, it is not unreasonable to ask how most Americans would feel about a group of their own dissidents pretending to monitor compliance with the Final Act but limiting its inquiries to human rights violations in the United States and using as its main technique appeals to foreign governments, including unfriendly ones. Members of such a group would certainly not be arrested, but they would likely encounter considerable hostility. Some would probably be subjected to an FBI investigation and would have difficulty obtaining government employment, especially

---

[6] Jerry Hough, "The Soviet System: Petrification or Pluralism?," *Problems of Communism* (March-April 1972), p. 45.

[7] *Reports of Helsinki Accord Monitors in the Soviet Union,* Commission on Security and Cooperation in Europe (February 24, 1977), pp. 6–8.

in sensitive areas. In the Soviet state-controlled society, consequences for challenging the system are traditionally more severe. But while sympathizing with the protesters and deploring the Soviet lack of tolerance and compassion, one should not pretend that the Public Group to Promote Observance of the Helsinki Agreements in the USSR was persecuted purely for its monitoring activities. Evaluation of the group's membership and statements suggests that its purposes were much broader and, in fact, included weakening Soviet international positions.

The group's misconception is just one example of how Western observers confuse their sympathy for dissidents with the description of views and tactics employed by Soviet protesters. It is not the purpose of this essay to provide a detailed analysis of the Soviet opposition movement. However, it seems proper to advance certain basic propositions about the intentions and strategy of dissidents. "Dissidents" as used here does not mean everyone who opposes some particular official policy and is striving for reforms, but only those who are alienated enough from the system to work outside the official framework.

By the very fact of going outside the system, the dissidents challenge the fundamentals of the regime. In the late 1960s, when the dissident movement emerged as a political phenomenon, the situation was quite different. Many protesters felt that their views and those of the regime were not irreconcilable and hoped to find a common language with Soviet officialdom. In most cases, such hopes have ceased to exist, and opposition to particular policies has been replaced by rejection of the regime. Certainly the Soviet authorities, with their constant tendency to overreact and perceive even moderate public criticism channeled through other than officially approved avenues as a threat to the very survival of the system, are the first to blame for the increasing radicalization of dissent. Whatever the reasons, the gap between the Soviet elite and the opposition movement appears at this stage to be unbridgeable.

At the same time, disillusioned about either having a constructive dialogue with the regime or attracting any serious political constituency within the Soviet Union, dissidents adopted appeals to foreign groups and even governments as their main tactic. Leading dissidents admit that without the support of the West their movement could not survive. Soviet officials, in turn, charge that protesters are paid agents of anti-Soviet forces and even intelligence agencies committed to undermining the Soviet system. Undoubtedly, alleged connections between some dissenters and the Central Intelligence Agency are unfounded. Nevertheless, strong links between the Soviet opposition movement and foreign groups hostile to the Kremlin are difficult to deny. The fact that such links are usually based on a similarity of objectives rather than any formal arrangements is an important legal difference. But as far as the regime is concerned, political dissenters represent a Western fifth column in the Soviet Union.

There are Soviet dissident groups whose disagreement with the system is of a less fundamental nature. This is especially true among ethnic movements such as the Jews and the Volga Germans, who are interested primarily in leaving the country, not in changing Soviet society. Significantly, in this field the regime was willing—admittedly under strong international pressure—to grant concessions and allow thousands of applicants the right to move to nations of their choice. Western involvement with emigration movements hardly pleases the Soviet authorities, but it is not necessarily perceived as a threat to the survival of the regime. Prominent activists of the Jewish emigration movement, despite obvious harassment, were still treated more mildly than dissidents striving for domestic change. Typically, the most dramatic recent case of prosecution of a Jewish activist, Anatoli Shcharansky, involved not only participation in the emigration movement, but membership in the Helsinki monitoring group as well.[8]

To sum up, the mainstream of the Soviet dissident movement has gone beyond the advocacy of introducing an element of law and humanity into Soviet official practices. Other than obvious exceptions such as the liberal Marxists like the Medvedev brothers, the dissidents tend to be in opposition to the regime itself, and partial reforms leaving the foundation of the system intact will not satisfy them. The Soviet elite, in turn, feels that the protesters are questioning the legitimacy of its rule, since the political controls they oppose are considered essential for the preservation of the existing order. From this perspective, Western and especially governmental pressure on the dissidents' behalf is viewed by Soviet officialdom as an attempt not merely to protect persecuted individuals but also to support their cause—the abolition of oppressive practices without which the regime does not know how to preserve its political monopoly.

Continuity and Change in Soviet Repression

The Soviet elite is probably particularly bitter about Western involvement with dissidents because it feels that the Soviet Union was slowly, but gradually, moving in a direction of greater respect for human rights. Soviet progress in this field is far from satisfactory. The entire system is based on violence and lack of freedom. Western standards of tolerance and humanity are widely disregarded by the Soviet authorities. Still, one could argue that, relatively speaking, Soviet citizens today enjoy more freedom and more protection under the law than in any other period of Soviet history, including the celebrated Khrushchev thaw. Yet, simultaneously, rights violations are getting more publicity in the West than ever before. As George Kennan observed, "compared with what existed forty years ago, what we have before us today, unjust and uncalled for as it may appear in our eyes, is progress. And yet it is the object of Western press attention and Western protests on a scale far more extensive than were the much greater excesses of the Stalin period."[9]

[8] This is not to suggest that Shcharansky does not deserve strong international support. Not only does all the available evidence indicate that the official charge of treason is without foundation, but refusal to allow Shcharansky to emigrate resulted in his joining the Helsinki Group.

[9] George F. Kennan, *The Cloud of Danger: Current Realities of American Foreign Policy* (Boston: Little, Brown and Company, 1977), p. 214.

Nonetheless, one should not hasten to applaud the Kremlin for ending the mass slaughter of Soviet subjects. The Soviet regime still relies on deceit and coercion. People are still dismissed from their jobs, sent to the Gulag Archipelago, and confined to mental institutions for speaking their minds. And if the number of victims is currently in the thousands rather than in the millions, this is scarcely a reason to praise the Soviet human rights performance. The Soviet Union remains a despotic and closed society.

Encouraging changes have taken place in the Soviet Union, however, and these should be noted. First, unlike in the Stalin era, today almost nobody is arrested under political charges without cause. This is not to say that the persecution of dissidents is in any sense justified, but at least they can feel that they stood for what they believe. Second, real dissident activity, though rarely a violation of the law, is required before the state brings criminal charges, whereas under Stalin and even Khrushchev an innocent political joke was punished with long-term sentences. Contrary to earlier practices, it is enough not to criticize the regime publicly. Third, even public debates on many subjects, except particularly sensitive ones, are allowed in the mass media, especially in professional journals, as long as their participants do not question the foundations of the system and are willing to pay lip service to the official ideology. True, there were debates ranging from genetics to linguistics even in Stalin's time, but they were usually settled by police methods. Today, the authorities rely more on the professional judgment of their experts, avoiding direct interference in their arguments except in extreme circumstances.

Fourth, the growing stratification of Soviet society has made an entire segment of the population (the elite) almost totally immune from political persecution. Under Stalin, political conflicts led to the destruction of numerous officials. Under Khrushchev, executions and imprisonment were replaced with political purges and the public humiliation of opponents. Since his dismissal, however, the price of losing a power struggle is considerably lower. Careers are still destroyed, but this is not unusual in any society. Significantly, top Soviet office holders are now allowed to retire honorably with comfortable pensions. If they have not reached retirement age at the time of their dismissal, they are shifted to minor, but relatively prestigious, positions entitling them to continue receiving the special benefits reserved for the elite. To be stripped of elite status is almost unknown. Even prominent dissenters like Andrei Sakharov and Benjamin Levitch were not expelled from the Soviet Academy of Sciences, and they still maintain their access to special benefits to which their membership in the prestigious Soviet scientific body entitles them. Egalitarian senses may be offended by the privileges enjoyed by important Soviet citizens. Yet it should be remembered that throughout history, rights for all citizens usually emerged initially as privileges for some. In this sense, the fact that at least one Soviet stratum has gained relative security and freedom is not altogether a negative development.

Fifth, the material standards of the masses have been improved considerably. The regime is still unwilling to undertake a major reallocation of resources in favor of the Soviet consumer, and consumer expectations are rising faster than Soviet ability to satisfy them. Yet, Soviet people today have a better diet, are better dressed and housed, and have more consumer durables.

Sixth, the right to privacy has been strengthened. The authorities are much less involved in dictating to the people what clothes they should wear, what hairstyles are appropriate, and what sexual standards should be observed. This is not a minor matter in the everyday life of Soviet citizens who remember the early 1960s when, under Khrushchev, bands of young hoodlums, sporting armbands of the voluntary police, publicly cut citizens' clothing and long hair if they did not correspond to the official standards of good taste and decency. Furthermore, in an important break with previous tradition, party committees are now increasingly reluctant to discuss such private matters as adultery and premarital sex.

Seventh, in the 1970s more than 160,000 Soviet citizens have been allowed to emigrate. Certainly the right to leave the country is still far from being assured. The right to emigrate is essentially limited to minorities, primarily Jews and Germans, who have homelands outside the Soviet Union or to those whose dissident activities have given the authorities reason to be eager to get rid of them. Even representatives of these groups are frequently denied exit visas under the false pretext of having access to state secrets or under objections from parents and other relatives. Nevertheless, for the first time since the 1920s a mass departure from what is supposed to be a socialist paradise has become a reality in Soviet life. True, this has occurred under strong international pressure, but it is probable that in the past no such pressure would have worked. For emigration to be treated as a feasible response to domestic and foreign demands, it required a degree of pragmatism and tolerance that has characterized the Brezhnev era.

If all this is true, why do so many Westerners tend to believe that the Brezhnev era is a step back from the Khrushchev renaissance? One reason is the emergence of dissent highlighting the deficiencies in the Soviet system without placing them in a historical perspective. Also, the Brezhnev regime, having adopted a much more conservative style of leadership, does not inspire the excitement of the Khrushchev era. There is no sense of movement and no promise, even if unjustified, of better days. Brezhnev and his associates do not pay tribute to de-Stalinization, although there is no evidence that they ever seriously intended to return to Stalin's practices. Still the lack of public exposure about Stalin's crimes raises suspicions in the minds of many Soviet intellectuals. Finally, the Brezhnev-dominated leadership is not particularly favorable to the Soviet intelligentsia. The incomes of average intellectuals are rising, but not quite as rapidly as those of workers and collective farmers, on the one hand, and the elite on the other. Furthermore, while there is more freedom of scientific discussion, the creative and artistic processes, ideologically sensitive and considered unessential for production purposes, are still severely limited. It is in these areas that no progress has been made since the Khrushchev era. Before making value judgments, however, one should remember that Khrushchev's de-Stalinization crusade and the accompanying thaw with the intellectual community were a matter of political tactics and, in a way, a tool in the purge of his political opponents, not necessarily any more sympathetic to Stalin than Khrushchev himself.

In approaching the issue of human rights in the Soviet Union it would be wise to evaluate not only its current status, but also the direction in which things are developing. Then it becomes obvious that, on balance, there is some movement, admittedly slow and erratic, to decrease the totality of controls and to rely less on coercion as a way of ruling the country.

American Interests in Relations with the Soviet Union

It is surely in the American interest to accelerate the movement. It is even more important to ensure that it will not be reversed. The evolution of the system toward a more open and tolerant society would not only benefit Soviet citizens, but it could also make Soviet international behavior more predictable and responsible. An opening of Soviet society could result in a reassessment of its economic and social priorities with a diminishing emphasis on defense. The problem is that changes of such magnitude will require considerable time, even according to the most optimistic scenarios of Soviet development. Consequently, Western efforts to encourage the evolution of the Soviet regime can be successful only in the long run. At the same time, the West, particularly the United States, has a number of important interests in its relations with the Soviet Union that demand immediate diplomatic attention.

Among these interests at the top of the United States priority list are prevention of nuclear war without damaging United States security and international standing, genuine arms control, avoidance of Soviet exploitation of international instability, an end to the zero-sum game allowing other countries to take advantage of both superpowers, effective crisis management, and economic and scientific cooperation. Of course, not all these interests are equally pressing. Economic and scientific cooperation with the Soviet Union are clearly not a vital necessity, and their value can be questioned as long as the Soviet Union is unwilling to restrain its military buildup. But these interests all have one element in common: they depend on a constructive, conciliatory attitude of the Soviet elite. It would be difficult to expect such an attitude to develop if the regime receives the impression that the West identifies with its domestic opponents and thereby challenges its legitimacy.

There is a clear conflict between the United States's moral commitment, its long-term interest in Soviet liberalization, and the unpleasant necessity of cooperating with the Kremlin in finding solutions to urgent international problems. To present this conflict in terms of morality versus pragmatism would be an oversimplification. Assuring peace for the world is as moral a commitment as one can imagine, even if the price is dealing with Soviet oligarchs. One may dislike the choice between ideological offensives on the Kremlin and conducting business as usual with it. But the choice does exist, and there is nothing that can be done about it. As George Kennan put it, "in this, Western policy-makers have the heart of the dilemma: for while a little pressure from Western opinion may be useful, too much of it can cause the Kremlin to feel that what is at stake for it is self-preservation; and there will be no question of yielding, for self-preservation is a consideration that would take precedence over any other considerations, all the rest of the Soviet-American relations included, and where there is no question of yielding, there will be no benefit brought to those on whose behalf these protests are being made—only harm to U.S.-Soviet relations."[10]

Obviously, there is no need to overdramatize this dilemma for Western diplomacy. Regardless of how much Americans may identify with the Soviet dissidents, how vocal the criticism of Soviet repression, or how much Moscow resents any Western ideological offensive, nothing short of direct interference in Soviet domestic affairs—which nobody seriously suggests—would override the instinct of survival that the Soviet leaders share with the rest of mankind.

Consequently, what confronts the United States is not an either-or situation. Even if mishandled, human rights diplomacy cannot start a war. And if Moscow likes the terms of American SALT proposals, it will accept them, however harshly the administration may criticize its human rights record. It is in that gray area between entirely acceptable proposals and totally unacceptable ones where conflicts over human rights could have an impact. The task of United States diplomacy is to develop a human rights strategy that would reflect the prevailing attitude of the American public, minimize the damage to other areas of the Soviet-American relationship, benefit those forces and individuals within the Soviet Union that America wishes to support, and, in the long-term perspective, encourage a gradual opening of Soviet society. An all-out ideological offensive on the Kremlin will not accomplish this task. It would lead only to the deterioration of relations between the superpowers, and one result would be a tightening of Soviet domestic controls. In addition to being morally questionable, the other extreme, the total neglect of the Soviet human rights performance, is neither realistic nor politically astute. An optimum strategy should include pressure on behalf of human rights in the Soviet Union. But this pressure should be carefully measured, tactfully applied, and properly directed.

The events surrounding the Jackson amendment indicate that pressure on Moscow to modify some of its less crucial policies can work. But it also demonstrates that embarrassing the Soviets by declaring that they surrendered under foreign pressure does not pay off. Overpressure can be as dangerous as no pressure at all. Liberalization of the Soviet system will only come as a result of a domestic evolutionary process; it cannot be imposed from abroad. Accordingly, it would be a mistake to incorporate the opening of Soviet society as part of American public diplomacy. The United States should encourage conditions for such an opening but not proclaim it as an American objective.

[10] Ibid., p. 215.

The distinction should be made between pressure by public groups and pressure by the United States government. The Soviets are well aware that the views of private organizations do have a bearing on United States official policy. The process of developing an extensive network of contacts between the Soviet and American societies requires the cooperation of American scientists, businessmen, scholars, and so forth. If these groups make it clear that their willingness to participate in exchanges is connected with the Soviet human rights record, Soviet authorities will have to take these feelings into account. Pressure by private groups thus provides the United States government with the teeth for quiet diplomacy. It allows the United States to point out the existence of implicit linkages while avoiding confronting Moscow with humiliating explicit linkages between its human rights performance and other fields of the Soviet-American relationship. For instance, it can be argued that an increase in Soviet oppression against would-be emigrants could create conditions in the United States wherein no administration would be in a position to relax restrictions on trade with the Soviet Union.

Finally, the United States should avoid giving the impression of launching a human rights crusade against the Kremlin in order either to undermine its rule or to embarrass it internationally. It should be made clear from the outset that the United States is seeking a dialogue, not a confrontation, with the Soviet elite. The purpose is not to encourage a siege mentality within the Soviet establishment. On the contrary, it is in the American interest to persuade it that while the United States does not approve of, or sympathize with, the Soviet regime, this country is not in the business of trying to overthrow it. It should be made clear that by articulating differences in Soviet and American values, the United States does not seek to impose its attitudes on Soviet society but means to establish better conditions both for mutual understanding and trust.

In short, if the goal is to speed up the liberalization of the Soviet system, Americans should work with, and not against, those forces in the Soviet Union in a realistic position to initiate reforms. This does not presume surrendering any commitment to the freedom of humanity. Rather, it means that the development of specific policies should be filtered through the prism of American foreign policy interests and the specific Russian traditions and circumstances. Détente should not preclude human rights diplomacy. It is, however, incompatible with political crusades against Moscow under the banner of human rights.

Eurocommunism:
A Threat to Soviet Hegemony?

BOGDAN D. DENITCH

During the first two decades following World War II, most Western analysts assumed that the Communist parties and the organizations under their control in Western Europe and throughout the world were a clear asset to the Soviet Union. The usefulness of this asset obviously varied from country to country and depended on a number of factors, including the proximity of the Soviet army and other institutions that were readily exportable as well as the impact of the foreign Communist party and its institutions on the stability of the society in which they operated. At the very least, Western analysts considered foreign Communist parties as useful propaganda outlets for the Soviet international line of the time—anti-imperialism, peace, friendship, anti-Americanism, disarmament, and so forth. Otherwise, many analysts assumed that the parties whose loyalty to the Soviet Union was unquestioned, both by the hostile foreign observers and the Soviets themselves, were also available for spying, sabotage, resistance to mobilization, and other covert activities. In any case, they were treated as a potential Soviet fifth column. Finally, as parties critical of the existing order and engaged in industrial strife, the Communist parties composed an adversary culture at the very heart of the capitalist world, forming both potential cadres for a future Communist regime and shock troops against the present social order.

Such an idealized and rather fanciful portrait of the roles of the Western European Communist parties nevertheless had a major impact on public opinion in Western Europe and the United States. Although it would accomplish little to reflect on the superficiality of that portrait, a reexamination of the actual role of the Communist parties in the 1940s and 1950s—their most Stalinized period—would help dispel the illusions left by the cold war. To begin with, it is quite clear from its extensive works of espionage and secret agentry that the Soviet Union, like any sensible power, avoided active Communists as much as possible in recruiting their espionage apparatus. Although most Communist party loyalists would probably have considered it their proletarian internationalist duty to help the socialist fartherland, their socialist international patriotism was rarely put to the test. However willing they might have been, the Soviet espionage apparatus found more congenial and reliable recruits, such as former SS men in West Germany's secret service and various tried and trusted military career men like the Swiss and Swedish higher officers uncovered within the last decade.

In the case of the British secret service, the more spectacular Soviet coups ' seemed to have been more sensibly aimed at recruiting decayed, Tory, guilt-ridden homosexuals rather than proletarian activists from the factories. As one of the more spectacular agents of the British Eastern European intelligence operation, Kim Philby was so adequately protected by the establishment after betraying several parties of potential saboteurs and agitators in Albania and Eastern Europe that the Soviets gave him generous severance pay when he was declared a security risk. Compared with such exploits, the Communist parties' own contributions to cold war espionage were at best negligible.

Although the other major contributions made by the Communist parties of Western Europe to Soviet foreign policy breakthroughs are rather more substantial, it is useful to remember that the Stalinized Communist Party of France (PCF), for example, supported the reassertion of French colonial authority in Algeria immediately after World War II, the breaking of the early postwar strikes in France, and the reassertion of the authority of the regular French army's officer cadres against the members of the French Resistance. In short, the PCF behaved as a perfectly respectable government party and only remembered its radical, proletarian mission when it was unceremoniously ejected. Although the Communist parties of Western Europe did their best to block the Marshall Plan and the North Atlantic Treaty Organization (NATO), their best proved to be weak indeed.

One should not ask why the Communist parties were so powerful in a devastated Europe in the late 1940s—particularly in France, Italy, Belgium, and to a lesser extent in the other European countries—but rather why they so easily and quickly surrendered any real prospects of struggling for power. One can place in perspective many of the issues currently under debate about the nature of Eurocommunism only by attempting to understand what politically disabled the large Communist parties of Western Europe in the late 1940s and for the following two decades. A reasonable analysis has to recognize two realities—the acquiescence of the Communist parties in whatever happened to be the international line of the Soviet Union at a given moment, and the strategic and tactical necessities of a mass working class party operating in a hostile milieu. This duality characterized much of the real history of Communist parties outside the geographic limits of the Soviet empire.

The Crack in the Monolith: Polycentrism

By the late 1940s the Italian and French Communist parties, however Stalinized in theory, were much too large and loosely organized to be considered seriously as Leninist parties composed of professional revolutionaries, whatever the claims of the party leadership. More accurately, these parties were analogous in social composition to the traditional mass social democratic parties, but with a Leninist and Stalinist ideology. Each party, therefore, inherently experienced a continual conflict between the ideology and the daily activities of the party and its militants. Whenever the party sought to act more in line with its abstract ideology, the results were organizationally catastrophic. The party grew whenever it subordinated that ideology to its role as a mass party of reform and of trade unionists. This was true of the mass parties as well as the small Communist parties.

The organizational breakthroughs of most Communist parties coincided with politically "broad" periods in their respective countries. The Popular Front and the war against fascism transformed the Communist parties from sectarian split-offs from the Socialist International to mass movements in their own right. Some of the maneuvers, however, by which the parties sought with varying degrees of adroitness to support the Soviet line proved far more costly than others, while some were extremely useful to the parties for practical reasons. Since the leadership suitable to a broad popular front differed from the leadership that could shift toward a revolutionary, isolationist line, the situation exhibited at least latent internal party disputes. Although strict discipline could repress this conflict, the dissolution in 1943 of the Communist International and later of its short-lived successor, the Communist Information Bureau, weakened formal channels for maintaining international cohesion. Consequently, the contact with the Soviet Union of succeeding European Communist party leaders was far more ephemeral than that of their predecessors trained by the Comintern.

Even before the formal splits in the world Communist movement, internal exigencies created latent factions or currents in the Communist parties that identified with the different poles between which the party propaganda necessarily oscillated. A natural "right," popular, mass-oriented wing, stressing an early variant of national Communism, thus opposed a natural internationalist, "left," pro-Soviet wing stressing loyalty to the international movement as such. These contradictions could be contained as long as there was only one ruling Communist party and the unifying factor of a general loyalty to the Soviet Union. However, the heresies of Tito and Mao dealt a fatal blow to the prospects of maintaining a unified Communist movement. Although the Yugoslav line in Eastern and Western Europe had powerful repercussions among Communist cadres, Yugoslavia is a small and relatively insignificant state, and its heresy was perhaps containable. The Chinese break, however, established the reality of a polycentric Communist world, and competing Communist movements made loyalty to world Communism impossible. Only China's relative parochialism and Yugoslavia's weakness postponed this realization.

An apparently endless series of traumas followed the emergence of a polycentric Communist world. Premier Khrushchev's speech at the Twentieth Congress of the Communist Party of the Soviet Union appeared to verify all of the nightmarish claims of ideological enemies about the nature of Soviet society under Stalin. The speech confirmed the barely repressed suspicions that the hated Trotskyists and other socialist opponents were not lying about the purges, forced labor camps, arbitrary police measures, mass executions, one-man rule, and terror directed against the party leadership. Bad as this was, the abortive Hungarian revolution, suppressed with Soviet tanks, worsened the situation and compelled every Communist party to advocate or oppose the Soviet intervention. A party could not defend the ruthless Soviet suppression of a Hungarian revolution legitimized by Imre Nagy, one of the more popular Communist leaders of Eastern Europe, without falsifying in the eyes of its subjects its willingness to defend its national sovereignty.

The suppression of the Hungarian revolution, however, was the last clearly and widely unpopular Soviet action the Communist parties of Western Europe were willing to defend. The events in Hungary traumatized the parties, encouraging a number of militants to leave, and caused even greater harm to sympathetic and allied organizations. The postwar coalition of socialists and Communists in Italy dissolved and increased the possibility of a center-left government. Massive groups of intellectuals and fellow travelers began to defect, and parties began to reassert their native origins and deemphasize their Soviet ties. Finally, the Hungarian experience prepared the parties for the suppression of the Prague experiment by Warsaw Pact troops in 1968. The Communist parties of Western Europe persistently denounced that intervention as incompatible with their view of socialist internationalism, thus announcing what came to be known as Eurocommunism.

The Development of Eurocommunism

A major breaking point in the evolution of Eurocommunism can be located in the period between the Khrushchev revelations and the Hungarian revolution. From that point on, most of the Communist parties began to debate and redefine their policies and roles with respect to the Soviet Union. Of several fortuitous events that helped postpone confrontations and a break with the Soviets, the most important was probably the growing American involvement in an apparently endless war in Indochina that popularized a mass anti-Americanism and shifted attention away from the Soviets. Just at the point when major doubts about the Soviet Union began to surface in the European Communist parties, the American image of the Vietnam war as a struggle for democracy against totalitarianism appeared increasingly tarnished, and anti-Americanism all too easily became the point of agreement between otherwise increasingly antagonistic elements of what had been a world communist movement.

On the basis of the American response to national liberation movements, the sinister omnipresence of the Central Intelligence Agency (CIA), and the increasingly pernicious activities of the United States's allies in the third world, European Communists and other leftists found it reasonable on an international level to view the Soviet Union as at least a lesser danger to world peace than the United States. Individuals outside the traditional Communist movement sympathized with this view, whether or not it was accurate. The New Left, which arose among non-Communist intellectuals and students in the 1960s, and even some of the nonradical currents such as Gaullism shared a fundamental antipathy to the United States independently of their view of Soviet practices. Throughout the 1960s, it was increasingly difficult to find any major force in Europe willing to argue seriously that the Soviets represented an active military threat. Insofar as a threat was perceived at all, it was referred to by such code words as *Finlandization*, or neutralization of Europe, describing a prospect not nearly as unattractive to many Europeans as American policymakers would wish. On the contrary, a whole generation of Western Europeans no doubt secretly cherished their unprecedented exclusion from a major confrontation between the world powers.

As a result, the foreign policy stance of the Western European Communist parties throughout the 1960s no longer jeopardized their domestic influence. American imperialist activities, rather than the Berlin Wall or Soviet intervention in Hungary, began to spark mass demonstrations as the cold war receded. The salient issues of the time increasingly unified rather than divided the forces on the left, attenuating the practical differences between socialists and Communists while seriously weakening the ideological basis of right-wing democratic alliances with the United States. A combination of the Vietnam war, the Bay of Pigs incident, and similar misadventures incalculably harmed the general United States posture in Western Europe in the 1960s. All these issues, however, would not have led to a major redefinition of the role of the Communist parties in Western Europe if certain far more fundamental matters had not begun to change on the European domestic scene.

This period of gestation for the larger Communist parties of Western Europe set the stage for an increasingly dramatic confrontation with the Soviet Union. This confrontation focuses on three fundamental questions—the possibility of a peaceful transition to socialism, the desirability of a pluralist polity following a leftist takeover, and the growing consciousness of human and social rights in the Soviet bloc. Although these issues would increasingly polarize the elements of a formerly unified movement, the renewed prospect of Communist participation in Western European democratic governments lends them greater urgency. Indeed, Eurocommunism could become far more significant than merely an interesting phenomenon comprising politically isolated mass parties if Communist parties join major coalition governments in Western Europe in the near future.

The Diversity of Eurocommunism

Before turning to the specific impact of the Western European Communist parties on the strategic prospects of the Soviet Union and the United States in Europe, one should keep some important distinctions in mind. Eurocommunism itself has been unclearly defined. It has been erroneously treated as a general development affecting most of the Western European parties and requiring a general response. Major distinctions need to be made between the parties large enough to have an impact on their societies—as in Italy, France, Spain, Portugal, Finland, Iceland, Greece, and Cyprus—and lesser parties that exert only a marginal influence, providing a few deputies to help the Socialists attain a left majority, as in the Swedish parliament, or simply operating as a political nuisance, as in West Germany.

Regardless of doctrinal interests, the first group of parties is politically significant. A cursory examination of that group, however, disproves much of the conventional wisdom about Eurocommunism. Not all of the large Eurocommunist parties are in the Mediterranean. The parties of both Iceland and Finland have alternated in and out of government for decades. Not all of them assert their independence from the Soviet Union; substantial Communist parties of Portugal and Cyprus and at least the major Communist party of Greece remain emphatically loyal. Some of the important Western European parties, especially the Communist Party of Portugal, are not evolving in a peaceful, parliamentary direction. Finally, it is entirely possible for a party to be large, committed to the parliamentary road to socialism, independent, and increasingly in conflict with the Soviet Union, and simultaneously sectarian, dogmatic, politically unreasonable, and violently anti-American, like the Communist Party of France (PCF).

One must therefore resist a convenient label for all Western European Communist parties and consider a number of Eurocommunist movements. As the central link that bound the parties—loyalty to the Soviet Union and to the idea of a unified world Communist movement—weakens, the natural differences between the parties will tend to increase and the parties will become more and more fragmented. For practical purposes, one can distinguish between the Italian and Spanish parties on the one hand and the two Scandinavian parties on the other and conveniently group the remainder under a general category of parties that more or less lag behind on some questions in their break from their own pasts and their political isolation.

The two Scandinavian parties of Iceland and Finland are the easiest to dispose of and probably the least well known of the major parties generally described as Eurocommunist. For practical purposes, both are indistinguishable from left-wing social democracy. The Icelandic party has participated in governments with little difficulty and has evolved practically beyond the level of what the world Communist movement tolerates. The party is now rarely invited to consultations with sister parties and has for years coexisted quite comfortably with United States and NATO forces in Iceland. No hint of the party's function as a Soviet asset has even been raised for well over a decade. From the Soviet point of view, the party represents at best a mild neutralism largely indistinguishable from the position of leftist social democracy. Its clear commitment to parliamentary democracy has been repeatedly tested in practice, and in what sense the Icelandic party can be called Communist other than by a vague historical association becomes increasingly difficult to understand.

Although the Finnish party is badly divided between a pro-Soviet and a Eurocommunist wing, the whole matter is more or less irrelevant since the limitations on Finnish foreign policy hinge more on Finland's delicate relations with the Soviet Union and the Soviet Union's veto over foreign policy that affects all Finnish parties. It is not at all clear that the Finnish Communists are in fact an asset to the Soviets. The division of the party is certainly embarrassing, and any attempts by the Finnish party to "destabilize" the democratic parliamentary system would probably be much more of an embarrassment than an asset to the Soviets. After all, if Finlandization is one of the ultimate goals of Soviet policy for Western Europe as a whole, then clearly it must remain attractive to non-Communist political elements that seek to maintain national independence and parliamentary democracy. If anything, the Soviets would therefore have to restrain the more militant and sectarian wing of the Finnish party. Since that wing is also loyal to the Soviet Union, their task is not difficult.

The catchall group contains a variety of Western European parties—including those of France, Portugal, Greece, and Cyprus—that share certain features. They have maintained a more traditional Communist identity than the other large Western European Communist parties. Except for the Communist Party of France (PCF), they have maintained a friendly, loyal relationship with the Soviet Union, and with certain reservations their participation in government would be a Soviet asset. Primarily, the asset is rigidly limited by the tacit agreement of both major powers that no drastic shift in the European balance of power in either direction is acceptable. Although the Soviets would undoubtedly be greatly elated by the participation in power of one of the friendly Communist parties, they would not risk a confrontation with the West in general and the United States in particular. They would not be in a position to supply money, men, arms, and political credit to such a party in that part of the world where NATO has bases and a legitimate presence.

This set of political preconditions severely limits the Soviet Union's ability to exploit its potential assets in Portugal, Greece, or Cyprus. A pro-Soviet Communist party in those countries is in a clearly more advantageous position as an opposition party than it would be as either a minor party in a coalition government or a party trying to take power in its own right. In those cases, the Communist Party of the Soviet Union would take responsibility for the limited set of options of Communist parties in small, relatively isolated countries. Since this prospect is hardly worth the drastic confrontation with the West that would be involved, the Soviets would probably advise caution in those three cases.

In the case of France, the interests of two independent actors genuinely converge in a way that Western observers trained in the cold war mentality find especially difficult to understand. Because its policies coincide with the broad strategic needs of the Soviet Union, particularly on the crucial subject of

Eurosocialism, the PCF may be an "asset" to the Soviet Union for its own organizational and political reasons without losing its independence, taking orders from Moscow, or ceasing to criticize human rights violations in the Soviet Union and Eastern Europe. Having greater insight into the problem of Eurosocialism than their American colleagues, the Soviets wish to avoid the nightmare of a Western Europe dominated by socialist and social democratic parties—sometimes in a coalition with Communists—that aggressively scrutinize human rights and suppression of workers in the Soviet bloc and thus threaten to humanize socialism.

Since anything that would weaken the prospects of a major swing to the left in European politics is presently in the interest of Soviet leaders, the PCF's recent sharp confrontation with the Socialists coincides with the broadest strategic priorities of the Soviet Union. By averting a prospective coalition in France, dominated by the Socialists, the PCF also had to harshen its foreign policy, increasing both its hostility toward the United States and NATO and its convergence with the Gaullist "defense against all points of the compass" policy. Such developments also coincided with the immediate interests of Soviet policy. Faced with a large bloc of deputies opposing, either for Gaullist or Communist reasons, a rapprochement with NATO and its two principal powers (the United States and West Germany), the present French government most nearly approaches an ideal solution for the Soviets of what had begun to resemble a most threatening development.

From the Soviet point of view, however, the freely established convergence of interests of the PCF and the Soviet Union does not necessarily ensure the most stable of long-term relationships. Losing the support of the electorate while numerically and even organizationally losing influence in the trade unions to the socialists, the PCF prevented a coalition not specifically to benefit the Soviet Union but rather to reassert its own organizational priorities. In the future, the same party egoism that compelled the French Communists to accept the possibility of remaining in the opposition rather than serve as a minor party in a left-wing coalition may also compel the PCF to pursue policies that sharply conflict with Soviet aims and needs. In addition, the Soviets do not consider the PCF as Eurocommunist but more dangerously as a classic example of a national Communist party characteristically damaging relations with the Soviet Union. Indeed, the Kremlin must surely feel uneasy about having to depend on an alliance with a sectarian, Jacobin, nationalist, mass workers' party. The fact that the United States will probably continue to blunder by intruding into French politics and publicly lecturing socialist leaders on the dangers of a possible coalition with the Communists is the only prospect at all encouraging to Soviet leaders.

The Communist parties of Italy and Spain epitomize the Eurocommunist movement. Although parties of the Socialist International largely represent the major threat to the Soviets of Eurosocialism, the Communist Party of Italy (CPI) de facto represents that particular current in Italy. As the Italian counterpart to the mass labor and social democratic parties of central and northern Europe, the CPI is by far the largest, most effective, and most intelligent mass workers' party of Western Europe, distinguished from the others by its own independent theoretical roots and a membership larger than all the other Communist parties combined.

Although the Spanish Communist party is smaller than the CPI and therefore competes with the Socialist Workers' Party of Felipe González for hegemony on the left, it is quite similar in other respects to the CPI. Indeed, because the Spanish Communist party is organizationally at least as strong as its socialist rival and superior in regard to committed organizational cadres, its "Italianate" line preserves the prospects of the Spanish left by preventing a traditionally antagonistic and competitive relationship between two large left-wing parties operating in the same area. Having experienced fascism and having learned from Salvador Allende's catastrophic experiment in Chile, the Spanish and Italian Communist parties both assume that the stabilization of democracy and the acceptance by the electorate, specifically the Catholic segment, of the governmental legitimacy of the parties must precede the accession of a Communist party to power.

The necessity of public acceptance represents the CPI's strategy of historical compromise. Precisely the opposite of the confrontationist strategy of the French Communists, this conciliatory approach is even broader than former Chancellor Willy Brandt's grand coalition strategy in Germany. The Italian Communists, aware of other legitimate popular institutions and parties that have their roots in the working class, do not view the coalition of Communists and Catholics as merely a stepping stone to a socialist government; rather, they realize that the Italian polity requires a lasting coalition. Aware of the shallowness of the new democratic order and the reorganization of social forces erasing the traditional divisions between the clerical right and the anticlerical left, Santiago Carillo, the leader of the Spanish Communist party, also repeatedly insists that a leftist government or majority in Spain would be a catastrophe.

Two points need to be made about the domestic prospects of the Spanish and Italian Communist parties. According to Carillo, the Spanish Communist party generally seeks to dissolve the existing Socialist and Communist parties and form a single unitary Spanish labor party analogous, as he puts it, to the Socialist party of Francois Mitterrand in France or to the broadly leftist Labour party of Great Britain. Such an objective means that Carillo's party has reached the logical conclusion of the Eurocommunist movement, that of closing the historical rift between the Socialist and Communist parties and recreating a unitary labor movement. Since a unified labor party of Spain would probably be affiliated with the Socalist International, however, the Spanish Communist party has exceeded the Soviet Union's limits and has excited repeated harsh denunciations in Soviet propaganda.

As the CPI approaches direct government participation, it increasingly clarifies its position on the issue of Europeanism and the need for an economically, politically, and militarily greater integration of Europe. Enrico Berlinguer has stated more than once that the CPI is willing to remain in NATO and that the development of the socialism it favors is today possible only under NATO's aegis. Since the Soviet Union fears any step in the direction of European cohesion and unity and prefers any variant of nationalism opposed to European integration, these positions represent major problems for the Soviets. Indeed, the fundamental antagonism between the Soviet Union and the Spanish and Italian Communist parties lies ultimately in the firm commitment of the Spanish and Italian Communists to a European unification and integration in which they can naturally and easily ally themselves with the socialist and social democratic parties.

The Spanish and Italian Communist parties thus represent not an asset to the Soviet Union but a problem that developments in the Soviet Union and Eastern Europe themselves will naturally exacerbate. As the two parties approach participation in the government, they will have to assert their independence from the Soviet Union, most effectively by continuing to attack violations of human rights and particularly of workers' rights in the Soviet bloc. Since these violations will certainly continue and the Eurocommunists will find it impossible to remain silent about them, the chasm between the Spanish and Italian Communist parties and the Soviet Union will continue to widen. Although independence and even criticism of the Soviet Union will not necessarily mean that a party's self-interests will not occasionally coincide with Soviet strategic needs, the broad general strategies of the Spanish and Italian Communist parties have set them on a collision course with Soviet European strategy. They represent not an asset but ultimately a threat to the Soviet Union's overall interests in Europe.

Détente and Soviet Domestic Politics

PETER H. JUVILER
HANNAH J. ZAWADZKA

Concern over a potential or immediate Soviet military threat has been strongly reasserting itself among United States officials, policymakers, and opinon shapers. It would be a grave error for Soviet observers to dismiss as merely "slander" or "provocations" the genuine Western alarm over newly acquired Soviet global capabilities and military power, over tank armadas that may at any moment "swoop down on Western Europe," or over the possibility that the USSR may wish to cut Western oil lifelines.[1]

With respect to these and other real concerns over the Soviet threat, the significance of Soviet domestic politics should not require elaboration. But there is relatively little consensus on the nature and implications of Soviet internal politics or on their meaning for the Soviet military threat generally or for détente specifically. Is the Soviet home front merely a rear base for Soviet military-political expansion? Or is it, rather, a source of competing influences and possible constraints on Soviet external behavior? While the domestic aspects of Soviet foreign policy cannot be investigated comprehensively here, a preliminary exploration of them may cast some light on the perplexing problems of superpower relations.

For many American analysts, the Soviet leadership has remained monolithic, all-controlling, and motivated by its own versions of Marxist-Leninist ideology. Its shaky legitimacy at home and its fear, if not hatred, of the West provide a stimulus for actively promoting the victory of socialism over capitalist imperialism. Consequently, it is assumed, Soviet leaders are able, willing, and ready to employ their impressive military power, at worst, for a direct military encounter with the West or, at best, for demoralizing and psychologically destroying the Western alliance, as well as for undermining Western interests everywhere in the world. According to informed sources in the Carter administration, its arms control negotiations are running into the objections of those who see a Soviet desire to develop a war-surviving capability. It is feared that this capability would diminish, if not eliminate, the dangers and costs to the Soviets

---

[1] Vitalii Korionov, "Pochemu oni mutiat vodu?" *Pravda*, February 28, 1978.

of a Western retaliatory blow in response to a Soviet nuclear first strike. The development of such capabilities, it is argued, has been greatly assisted by the all-embracing power of the Soviet regime and its all-encompassing control over the home front. These and related arguments stressing the continuity of the totalitarian system of Soviet politics tend to dismiss the major changes that have taken place since Stalin in Soviet leadership and authority and in their social and economic underpinning.

Soviet Leadership and Authority

Major changes in the structure of Soviet authority have occurred since Stalin, the great *vozhd*, or leader. For all his purges and repressions, Stalin was regarded "virtually as a god," according to a recent émigré, who only repeated the recollections that are widespread in the USSR. Stalin dominated Soviet policy-making. To help maintain this domination he placed the secret police above the administrative dyarchy of party and state.

Stalin's paranoiac suspiciousness had a chilling impact on Soviet-American relations after World War II. His suspicions of United States intentions merged with his expectation of future trouble from a resurgent and remilitarized Germany. On the American side, the apparent and real expansions of Soviet control helped to generate an anti-Communist, anti-Soviet hysteria. This, in turn, caused misperceptions of world events ranging from the Stalinization of Eastern Europe to Mao's triumph in China (an event feared by Stalin as well).

Khrushchev tried to continue one-man rule but without Stalinist terror as an instrument of inner-party struggle. In addition, he succeeded in curbing the paralyzing power of the secret police by subordinating it to the Communist party and by fostering limited legal reforms. The change under Khrushchev from purging opponents to their demotion or comfortable retirement is, indeed, "the greatest gain of the post-Stalin era." Because of it, "people in Russia have gained the right to die in their beds."[2] Other gains followed. The relatively relaxed climate of the "thaw" and, then, overt de-Stalinization increased the possibility of debate and factional struggle over alternate courses of both domestic and foreign policy. It promoted a limited freedom of policy-oriented research in the USSR. Moreover, Soviet researchers began to visit their Western counterparts abroad and to receive them in their own research institutes.

Khrushchev was ousted after he antagonized the police, the economic ministers, the military-industrial complex, and, finally, his own party apparatus. His defeat showed his successors the narrow limits of authority without terror. Aware of these limits, Brezhnev initiated a cautious and less "ideological" leadership based on a carefully balanced coalition of representatives of various party, state, and economic interests.

Thus, within the framework of Soviet authoritarianism, the structure of

[2] Alexander Yanov, *Détente after Brezhnev: The Domestic Roots of Soviet Foreign Policy* (Berkeley: Institute of International Studies, University of California, 1977), p. 8.

authority has changed from Stalin's cult of personality to Khrushchev's shaky preeminence and short-lived ideological fervor to Brezhnev's ponderous but durable coalitionism and ideological conservatism. Under Khrushchev, there were some reasons for concluding that the Soviet system was predominantly an "ideological" one, a system "used by political leaders to create a new society along the lines of their own beliefs and aspirations." Today, however, the Soviet system can be more properly described as an increasingly, if not predominantly, "instrumental" system that "merely reflects the established social patterns and is designed to protect the existing character of a society and to promote its growth along established, undisturbed paths."[3] As part of this change in the Soviet political system, domestic policy has come to originate less in blueprints for socioeconomic change from above and more in the needs for reform appearing from below as a consequence of industrial growth and urbanization.

As a second part of this change in the Soviet political system, the structure of authority in the USSR has become decreasingly monolithic. Three very broad groupings have emerged among those sharing and close to top authority in the USSR. For convenience rather than as hard and fast definitions, one may term these groupings "centrist," "conservative," and "liberal." The leaders of these groupings, including Brezhnev, are mostly at or beyond retirement age. As the leader of the centrists, Brezhnev has proved a staunch supporter of détente. At the same time, he has remained susceptible to strong, self-protective pressures from the conservatives, a powerful grouping headed by influential Politburo members with a strong following among the provincial party secretaries, the military, the leaders of defense industries, Stalinists among various occupational elites, economic ministers, and segments of the police and judiciary.

An incident still talked about by some Moscovites may serve to illustrate the ongoing tension between Brezhnev and the conservatives. In 1974 an article by Vladimir Yagodkin, secretary for ideological matters in the Moscow City Party Committee, appeared in *Kommunist*, the theoretical journal of the Communist Party Central Committee. Yagodkin, a well-known conservative and anti-Semite, warned that the increased international contacts accompanying détente "increase the possibility for the penetration into our midst of alien ideas, views, national prejudices, etc." This statement did not go unnoticed by high-level proponents of détente. They managed to interrupt distribution of that issue of *Kommunist*, destroying hundreds of thousands of copies not sent to subscribers and replacing them with copies that carried an extra phrase before the warnings about ideological subversion. The added phrase put détente in a better light by asserting that it "favors the peaceful advance of world socialism and the wider dissemination of communist ideas in the whole world."[4] Yagodkin's protectors

---

[3] Zbigniew K. Brzezinski and Samuel P. Huntington, *Political Power: USA/USSR* (New York: The Viking Press, 1964), p. 71.

[4] V. Yagodkin, "Nekotorye voprosy ideologicheskoi raboty v sovremennykh usloviiakh," *Kommunist*, no. 3 (1974), p. 39.

kept him on in the Moscow Party Committee for a while. Eventually, though, he was removed and demoted.

There is little question that both the centrists and the conservatives remain wary about the possibilities of Western ideological and cultural subversion. In the tradition of modernizing czars, Soviet leaders have tried to borrow Western technology without allowing in Western ideas that might subvert their authority. The main difference between the two groupings seems to be that for the sake of other benefits of détente the centrists are willing to run greater risks of subversion than are the conservatives. The conservatives, on the other hand, seem willing to run greater risks of isolation, confrontation, and economic deprivation for the sake of limiting détente and its unwanted cultural inflows. The main concern of the conservatives is to preserve the highest growth rates and the present priorities of resource allocation for defense-oriented industries and at least current growth rates of military budgets. They have had a vested interest in East-West tension as a pretext both for sealing off Soviet society from the West and for increased claims on positions of power and on resource allocations to their sectors. They strongly support the suppression of dissidents of the so-called democratic movement in the USSR. But according to Alexander Yanov, the former leading Soviet political and sociological writer, some conservatives retain sympathy for right nationalist Russian extremists now underground and for their program of revived Great Russian pan-Slavism, anti-Westernism, and anti-Semitism.

The conservatives have been most influential during interregnums. New leaders may tend to adopt rightist, promilitary stances in order to win power, as Khrushchev did. Yet in the long run they find that the conservative program simply does conform with Soviet needs. This is not a guaranteed pattern of conflict, but it serves to convey something of the nature of the succession struggle in the USSR.

At the other extreme of the Soviet policymaking elite are the liberals, the most weakly represented grouping of the three in the party Secretariat and Politburo, yet an indispensable source of expertise on the economy, law, social processes, demography, foreign policy, and the arts. The liberals' concern is with economic, administrative, political, and social reforms, not with subversion. If they have any links with the dissidents, it is quite likely to be with Roy Medvedev, the historian and anti-Stalinist author of *On Socialist Democracy* and a neo-Leninist leading a semilegal existence as an exponent of democratization within the Soviet system. At one time the liberals regarded Alexander Dubcek's "socialism with a human face" as a hopeful model for Soviet democratization. After Dubcek fell and as Soviet dissidents became more repressed and isolated by the KGB, many liberals, frightened or disheartened, turned inward to a preoccupation with personal well-being and advancement. In the perceptions of many liberals today, Eurocommunism is the new hope for a democratic model and a new source of worry for the Soviet leadership.

A misplaced concreteness is to be avoided in analyzing the three major policy groupings. Overlapping group memberships and crosscutting interests must be expected within each grouping. The boundaries of the groupings are not well defined. They have no overall internal organizations. And one must expect persons who are simply opportunists to flit from grouping to grouping on various issues as the times and the opportunists' personal interests dictate.

The positions of centrists like Brezhnev, moreover, must necessarily remain ill defined or even contradictory on certain controversial issues. But centrists manifest some important changes in outlook, as compared with the outlooks tolerated in Stalin's day. Centrists like Brezhnev long ago abandoned the idea that all leaders in any Western country are uniformly anti-Soviet "imperialists." Even in moments of exasperation at the United States, Brezhnev distinguished between what he called "forces that are interested neither in good relations between the U.S. and the U.S.S.R. nor in the relaxation of tensions in general," on the one hand, and "responsible figures in the U.S." on the other.[5] Brezhnev also dropped the old Khrushchevian rhetoric about the "inevitability" of the triumph of socialism over "the world capitalist system as a whole" that, according to the 1961 Party Program, "has become ripe for the social revolution of the proletariat." The omissions of such rhetoric are noteworthy both in major speeches and statements[6] and in a more permanent document, the USSR Constitution of 1977. Meant as a description of things as they have become in the USSR, the new constitution is the fruit of fifteen years of discussion and political bargaining. It is, therefore, as close as any Soviet document can come to being a consensual statement of basic principles of Soviet policy and governmental expectations.

The constitution contains an unusual feature, a chapter 4 on "Foreign Policy." Article 29 of that chapter, on relations with other states, lists conventional principles such as sovereign equality and noninterference in other states' internal affairs, respect for principles of international law, and "respect for human rights and basic freedoms." The last is an internationally desirable phrase but in some ways still an empty one. Article 30 enunciates a policy of friendship and cooperation with "the socialist countries on the basis of the principles of socialist internationalism." This last expression has in the past served as a code expression for Soviet intentions under the so-called Brezhnev doctrine of justified intervention in other socialist states in order to preserve their socialist regimes, as when the USSR led the Warsaw Pact invasion of Czechoslovakia in 1968. Article 28 of chapter 4 appears to state the priorities of foreign policy. It says that the foreign policy of the USSR "aims at securing favorable international conditions for building communism in the USSR." The second aim is also Soviet-centered: "the defense of the state interests of the Soviet Union." The third stated aim is "the strengthening of the position of world socialism" but not its triumph or final victory. The fourth stated aim is "the support of people's struggle for national liberation and social progress," an active part of Soviet policy. The fifth stated aim is a propeace "basket" of "averting aggressive wars,

---

[5] *New York Times*, Feb. 25, 1978.

[6] *Pravda*, June 5, Oct. 5, Oct. 8, Nov. 8, Dec. 24, 1977, Feb. 10 and Feb. 24, 1978.

achieving general and complete disarmament and the consistent realization of the principle of peaceful coexistence of states with different social systems."

Behind formal documents such as this constitution lie the spoken and unspoken attitudes of the Soviet elites and populace toward the outside world. If there is a hostility permeating Soviet public opinion from top to bottom, it is not directed toward the West but rather toward China, the erstwhile Communist ally. On the level of public discourse, the Soviet press has been attacking China for its alleged militarism and Maoist extremism, for its hostility toward the socialist Soviet Union, and, presently, for the "strange unity between" China and "the imperialist military bloc" with which it is seeking closer economic ties, and for telling the West that the USSR is the main enemy of both China and the West, a "socialist imperialist" country with whom détente is dangerous.[7] When and if this official antagonism wanes, there will remain the deep-rooted hostility toward China among Soviet people, a distrust and fear that is racialist rather than philosophical. The bitter and bloody battle between Chinese and Soviet troops over several Amur River islands in 1969 has only served to confirm this racial distrust of the Chinese among Russians.

During the early 1960s some American opponents of détente dismissed the Sino-Soviet conflict as a sham. Now that it is clearly not a sham, some opponents of détente tend to dismiss the dispute as insignificant. It is hard to agree with this view. The strength and continuity of the mutual antagonism of the USSR and China suggest that China remains a large factor in the international balance of power and a constraint on whatever Soviet hostility may exist in some quarters toward the West. Apprehension about China is perhaps the one sentiment uniting centrists, liberals, and conservatives as well as dissidents.

Some Social Underpinnings of Authority

One argument heard against the possibility of an extensive détente with the USSR is that it is futile because the Soviet leadership is alienated from its people and seeks legitimacy in a policy of expansionism or world mission. Social evidence to support this assumption is as dubious as the evidence of ideology appeared to be. That the Soviet people think of their government as "they" should be interpreted not from the standpoint of American participatory political culture but from the standpoint of Russian and Soviet subject political culture, wherein government is legitimized not by consent but by the grace of tradition and the justification of special insight, special excellence, and service to the people.

Marxism has little to do with the case one way or the other. Most Soviet people were never and are not now Marxists in any doctrinal sense. One encounters many intellectuals, moreover, who accept the Soviet system as legitimate not because they are Marxists and not because they believe that the party has special doctrinal insights or virtues, but because they believe that the present author-

[7] *Pravda*, Dec. 2, 1977.

itarian system is the only viable alternative permitted by the long course of Russian autocracy. The other alternative, they think, is anarchy. For Russians, the legitimacy of their regime comes from custom and a historical determinism that is more Tolstoyan in its fatalism and Dostoyevskian in its Russian nationalism than it is Marxist. Liberals, for example, do not like their regime in its present repressive form. But they think it can be democratized only gradually. Moreover, the regime's successful organization of the defense of the motherland against the Germans and its apparent role as a bulwark against possible future threats from either the West or China augment its legitimacy for many Soviet citizens. Many exceptions to this popular support are to be found, however, among non-Russian nationalities, especially in the Western Ukraine, in the border republics, and among uprooted groups like the Volga Germans and Crimean Tatars. Current demographic trends indicate that Russians will soon be a minority of the Soviet population. The largely Russian leadership is unlikely to find in the nationality picture a source of encouragement to risk a major war. They must remember the unrest and breakaways among border nationalities during World War I, the civil war, and World War II.

East-West rapprochement has produced its own privileged partisans in Soviet society with a large material or occupational stake in détente. This "new 'new class' " is an ideologically and socially diverse segment of society with protectors at the party summit. "The Western-oriented group at the very top, in the Politburo (the Centrist group), has become the political representative of a large, privileged and Western-oriented stratum below that runs through the entire Soviet hierarchy of Soviet society—from the middle ranking conformist scholar who for the first time has gained the opportunity to openly acquire antiques . . . to the hairdresser who wins prizes at a competition in Brussels," from diplomats and tourist guides to sailors.[8] Their stake in détente is shared by Soviet participants in scholarly and scientific exchanges and by managerial experts and technicians seeking transfusions for their ailing economy.

The Economic Underpinnings of Authority

The Soviet economy resembles a massive building with its right side, defense industry, resting on strong pillars and its left side—consumer industry, distribution, and agriculture—resting on weak posts. The operators of this building, the party leaders, contemplated three structural changes to prevent its collapse: large subsidies to farming, which helped but not enough; priority of growth rates for consumer goods rather than heavy industry, which happened only briefly in the late 1960s; and decentralizing industrial management in the reforms of 1965, which failed in the face of bureaucratic opposition and habits of centralized control. Also, the party has promoted trade and technical borrowing from the West.

The economic edifice still faces possible collapse. Growth rates are slowly

[8] Yanov, pp. 4–5.

dropping toward zero. For example, the percentage increase in national income used for consumption and investment dropped from 5.4 in 1976 to 3.5 in 1977 and reached the lowest point recorded in handbook statistics, which go back to 1951. The percentage increase in industrial production was 4.8 in 1976, the lowest, again, on record. It rose in 1977 to 5.7 but is planned at only 4.5 for 1978.[9] The Soviet leaders may soon face some difficult choices if they are not to have a populace as disaffected as it was becoming under Khrushchev as he vainly struggled to break through bureaucratic barriers to greater economic efficiency. These policy choices could be pressing during the power struggles accompanying future changes of leadership. The outcome both of these choices and of the succession struggles could well depend on how actively and broadly Western trading partners of the USSR press economic détente, particularly their policies on credits, tariffs, pricing, licensing, and possible joint ventures. Western responses to Soviet difficulties may well influence the balance of power among conservatives, centrists, and liberals in the USSR and, therefore, the Soviet stance toward arms control, détente, and foreign policy generally.

Soviet attitudes toward war are no less difficult to analyze than the Soviet economy. The attitudes are ambivalent. Older Soviet generations now moving to the peaks of their careers or toward retirement carry vivid memories of wartime devastation, the austere sacrifices, and even the famine during the early postwar period of reconstruction and rearming. Occasionally, such grim memories come to life for youths, too, as when recently a young Komsomol was blown up by a World War II shell he was carrying away from his friends in a potato field.[10] Not for a long time will either leaders or people in the USSR regard large-scale war as only a gaming abstraction, or as something one can safely conduct somewhere overseas. In all these senses, wartime memories may act as constraints on Soviet expansionism and risk-taking. On the other hand, there is the Soviet belief that the wartime experience of the USSR and its civil defense program make it better able than is the Western world to sustain wartime damage and destruction. Also, as one decorated veteran Soviet army officer and war hero commented during a visit to the Sevastopol war memorial, "they now glorify war, but we veterans know what a horror it was."

Conclusion

These reflections about the home front have presented several hypotheses about recent trends there. They call into question many assumptions that underlie criticisms of détente with the USSR.

First, the Soviet leadership can no longer be described as a monolith (if it ever was). De-Stalinization, even if incomplete, has ended terror within the party and has encouraged debate, rule by coalition, wide consultation of experts,

---

[9] *Narodnoe khoziaistvo SSSR za 60 let* (Moscow: Statistika, 1977), pp. 77–79; *Pravda*, Jan. 28, 1978.

[10] *Komsomolskaia pravda*, Jan. 22, 1978, p. 4.

and a sensitivity among top leaders to the political importance of diverse interests and outlooks in the governing bureaucracies.

Second, the Soviet political elite forms three loose, shifting groupings. It is the conservatives who most dwell on both a military and a subversive Western threat. On the other hand, major segments of Soviet society oriented to centrist or liberal positions, or simply to opportunism, have been developing a growing stake in East-West contacts and East-West trade. Centrists like Brezhnev must balance policy between conflicting Soviet needs that are voiced by liberals on the one hand and conservatives on the other. They must defend the resulting limited détente from conservative attack.

Third, as to assumptions about ideology, there is no doubt that central Soviet authority remains powerful and far-reaching within the USSR. But the doctrines and policies it propagates have moved far from both the hostile Stalinist imperial isolationism and from the driven revolutionary fanaticism that is still associated in some quarters with all Communist regimes. Soviet speeches and documents are important both for how they say what they say and for what they omit. Recently a major omission from these Soviet documents has been the time honored universalist goal of the world victory of socialism to which successive Soviet leaderships paid lip service—and at times more than lip service. None of the major groupings apparent in Soviet politics appears to pursue a goal of world revolution or world conquest. Each has other, more immediate priorities.

Fourth, the all-encompassing Soviet social controls work imperfectly. More-over, strong social and economic constraints exist on Soviet external behavior. Among such constraints are tensions between nationalities, especially between the Russians and certain other national minorities; material and career interests in détente; in one sense, the memories of World War II; and the growing problems of sustaining economic growth.

The interaction between domestic and external aspects of Soviet policy is too complex to permit unqualified conclusions and precise prediction. At best, one can suggest probabilities or discount patently unfounded assumptions, as was attempted here. The debate over détente involves perceptions of a Soviet threat that one can only tentatively appraise and about whose domestic aspects one can draw only cautious conclusions.

The first of these conclusions returns one to the question of the nature of the Soviet home front. In some respects, it is the headquarters and material base for a far-flung and probing Soviet military presence. But that is only one side of the picture. Even this brief review of politics, society, and economics on the home front shows it to be also a source of competing and conflicting influences and restraints on Soviet external behavior.

Disparities between economic needs and current forms of economic controls in the USSR raise the possibility of domestic tensions, even of a crisis over policy, bound up with the post-Brezhnev succession struggle. Should such a crisis occur, the West may have to deal with the Soviet version of the tendency of a weakened or internally divided regime to seek to evade the crisis by turning to expansion or war abroad, or by creating an external crisis to distract attention from the internal one. But that is only one of several policy alternatives: international confrontationism, isolationism, and domestic repression, or an active policy of greater collaboration with the West. None of these policies is preordained. But an active Western policy of détente is most likely to bring about the outcome of the Soviet succession struggle that favors a policy of greater collaboration with the West.

More than ever, the regulation of Soviet-American military competition will depend on "the whole array of U.S.–Soviet relationships." The arms race and the Soviet threat will be checked only if "there is in operation a whole range of constraints and incentives which give each side a stake in restraint."[11]

Soon a new generation of Soviet rulers will replace the present Soviet gerontocracy. This shift of rule will occur in many posts at roughly the same time, as the present leaders die or retire in quick succession. An active and carefully balanced long-range policy of détente holds out hope of demonstrating to the upcoming Soviet leaders that they may safely and usefully deal with their American and other Western opposites in an atmosphere of growing interdependence. This treatment of ideological factors in Soviet external behavior supports the opinion of John Lewis Gaddis, who discerned the passing of the era of intolerant universalisms, that is, of aspirations to shape the whole world in the image of one's own society and of outlooks that "equate security with homogeneity."[12] Instead, the era of universal problems is arriving—the problems of nuclear weapons, energy, hunger, and the despoiling of the planet. The world faces the old question posed by Bertrand Russell: "Will the human race survive or will it not?" Soviet-American relations and the development of a fuller, secure détente remain central to that question.

---

[11] Helmut Sonnenfeldt, "Russia, America and Détente," *Foreign Affairs* 56 (January 1978): 293.

[12] John Lewis Gaddis, *Russia, The Soviet Union, and the United States: An Interpretive History* (New York: John Wiley and Sons, 1978), p. 277.

The Reality of the Soviet Threat *

MAXWELL D. TAYLOR

From the beginning of the cold war until comparatively recent times, there has been little tendency to question the reality of the threat to American purposes and interests posed by the prolonged hostility of the Soviet Union. Even before its transformation into a Communist state, de Tocqueville had warned that the United States and imperial Russia were "two great nations which, starting from different points, seem to be advancing toward the same goal." In due course, that goal has become the global triumph of one of the two rival politicoeconomic systems each represents, a goal that over recent decades has provided a central theme for international politics.

From the outset, the United States has been reluctant to accept the fundamental nature of a confrontation that seemed forced upon it by circumstance rather than the result of choice. Left to its own devices, the United States would have much preferred a relationship of peaceful coexistence. Hence, Americans' sense of the reality of this adversary relation has varied with the intensity of the frictions and collisions of interest during the postwar period. Recognition of danger peaked at such times as the Berlin airlift, the Greek civil war, the launching of Sputnik, and the Cuban missile crisis. It ebbed following the death of Stalin, the Sino-Soviet rift, and the relatively restrained Soviet conduct during the Vietnam war. More recently, encouraged by the slogans of peaceful coexistence and détente of the Brezhnev period, many Americans came to hope for an era of normal relations with their rival.

Even at the height of détente, however, there were skeptics who warned of euphoria and pointed to evidence that détente meant little more to Moscow than a continuation of the cold war conducted in less strident terms and with greater care to avoid a direct military confrontation of the principals. To prove this point, they cited continued Soviet provocation in the Middle East, interventionist activities in Africa, and, above all, the steady expansion of the Soviet armed forces over more than a decade as the United States military establishment declined in size. Without perceptible defensive requirements to justify

* An address delivered at a conference sponsored by the Academy of Political Science and the Program of Continuing Education, Columbia University, in New York City on October 17, 1977.

it, hawkish Americans have viewed this expansion as a direct threat, raising doubt as to the nation's ability to support national policy in overseas areas where clashes of interest may occur.

Such a thesis brings forth as its antithesis an apologia for Soviet conduct from another segment of American opinion. The Soviet Union's urge to rearm, it has been said, arose from its humiliation in the Cuban missile crisis, a reversal that it attributed to American superiority in strategic weapons and military technology. The Soviet Union's large conventional forces are required to offset NATO strength in Europe and the Chinese threat on their eastern frontiers. It has the problem of keeping order in the satellite countries and within their non-Russian minorities at home. Its naval expansion is merely a renewed expression of a traditional yearning for access to warm salt water coupled with a recent need to keep American nuclear submarines at a distance from its borders. The Soviets are in Africa not to compete with the United States but to restrain Chinese influence and to discourage the West from intervening to preserve the racist states of Rhodesia and South Africa. Whatever the extent of its activities, its long list of reversals in countries like Egypt, the Sudan, Ghana, Zaire, and now Somalia would not suggest a serious threat to the United States or its allies.

With such divergent views of Soviet power and purposes, it is timely to review the evidence as to whether a Soviet threat truly exists and warrants the heavy expenditures of national resources that appear necessary to forestall it. To reach an affirmative conclusion as to its reality, it would be necessary to agree on the likelihood of continued Soviet hostility expressed in policies and courses of action conflicting with American interests, the adequacy of Soviet power to inflict serious damage on the United States and its interests, and the strong probability that the Soviet leaders will perceive opportunities to use this power against the United States under conditions promising remunerative rewards. These points provide the framework for a more thorough analysis.

Continuing Soviet Hostility

Past and current Soviet behavior gives no indication that Moscow has any intention of renouncing its pursuit of hegemony over a world eventually to consist of Communist states erected on the ruins of capitalism. As long as this commitment persists, there can be little hope of permanently reconciling policies or normalizing relations between the United States and the Soviet Union.

Even if this doctrinal conflict did not exist, any nation with the manifold strength of the Soviet Union, derived from a base of power embracing one-sixth of the earth's surface astride Europe and Asia, would by its mere existence pose a formidable threat to the United States. Even a non-Communist Russia that still pursued the objectives of its czarist past—the subjugation of weak neighbors, access to warm oceans, and world recognition of its great-power status—would necessarily be a major adversary and as much the focal point of American foreign policy as the Soviet Union is in the 1970s.

Obviously, its adherence to Marxist-Leninist beliefs adds to the difficulties of relations, the more so since Moscow must constantly compete with Peking and other possible rivals for acceptance as the sole, legitimate standard-bearer of world Communism. The Soviet Union must repeatedly assert its dedication to Marxism-Leninism and its hostility to all opponents and hence must systematically treat the United States as the most dangerous leader of global anti-Communist forces. For these reasons, the Kremlin could never feel fully at ease without the United States as the rival justifying the sacrifices demanded of the Soviet people to pay the heavy costs of the military programs.

Because of expansionist national goals and the imperatives of Communist dogma, one must expect continuing conflicts to disturb American relations with the Soviet Union. As in the past, each rival will be concerned over possible shifts to its disadvantage in the world balance of power and will do its utmost to prevent them. To compensate for the defection of China and Yugoslavia from the true faith, Moscow will seek to weaken or seduce the United States's friends and allies, while recruiting new supporters in the third world. As viewed by Moscow, a pound lost from the United States side of the power scale is as good as one gained by the Soviets—hence its efforts to reduce United States power and influence.

In considering where conflicts with the Soviets may occur, one finds that the area includes large parts of Europe, the Mediterranean, the Middle East, Africa, northeast Asia, and Latin America. Except for the Western Hemisphere, the Soviet Union enjoys the advantages of proximity or prior presence in all these regions. Collisions in Europe, the Mediterranean, and the Middle East would be the most dangerous because the importance of the issues involved could justify to one side or the other the risk of resorting to arms. Although the stakes elsewhere are important, they are likely to be measured in gains or losses of regionally significant political or economic advantages. But everywhere the probability of conflict in some form is high, with the danger to the United States depending on the available Soviet power for use against us in the particular locality and the Soviet evaluation of the likely outcome of such action.

By this line of reasoning, one is led to consider the nature and extent of the power that the Soviets might employ to inflict damage on important American interests. Past experience indicates that the predominant danger would stem from Soviet use of political and military power in various forms and combinations. Although Soviet leaders, as good disciples of Clausewitz, would not be inclined to draw sharp distinctions between these categories, American practice normally treats them separately. Hence, in the present context, Soviet political power will be regarded as the aggregate of effectual means that the leaders derive from control of the government and the economy. Similarly, military power is that derived from the armed forces whereby Moscow may threaten or use armed force to advance national purposes.

In employing political means against the United States, Soviet leaders enjoy the advantage of having at their disposal essentially all the human and material resources of the nation that they can exploit without the many restraints imposed on a president by the American constitutional system. To a degree, however, they operate under handicaps which hinder the efficient use of these resources, most of them a result of inadequate leadership and defects in the Communist system itself. The latter include an aging oligarchy superimposed on a ponderous, centralized bureaucracy, coupled with the inherent weaknesses of a Communist economic system deficient in capital, technology, and the production incentives arising from a free market system.

Regardless of these defects, the Soviets have many political assets that make them a formidable adversary. Soviet diplomats are experts in the use of propaganda, bribes, threats, subversion, and intimidation to gain their ends. As negotiators, they are tough bargainers adept at wearing down opponents to obtain unrequited concessions or ambiguously phrased agreements permitting subsequent interpretation to their advantage. They are trained for diplomacy as diligently as Soviet generals are prepared for war, and they are expected to display at the conference table the same meticulous preparation and ruthless determination as the military on the battlefield.

Although it is alleged that the Soviet Union has no allies, only subjects, surrogates, and clients, it derives many of the advantages of an alliance from overseas Communist parties and subversive indigenous elements which perform valuable services in stirring up trouble in Western and nonaligned countries. In addition, the Soviets enlist mercenaries to fight their battles in distant places like Greece, Korea, Indochina, and Africa and thereby avoid exposing Soviet troops to hostile bullets. They have often been successful in employing subversive, terrorist, and guerrilla operations, sometimes combined in a so-called War of National Liberation, a technique still favored for the expansion of Communism.

In their unending campaign to extend political and ideological influence, the Soviet leaders are encouraged by an impressive record of past successes, which includes the addition of some fifteen nations to the Communist community since 1948. Although in the meantime the Soviets have suffered occasional reverses, they expect eventually to recoup their losses as they progress to ultimate victory. In the course of overcoming their adversaries, the Soviet Union has acquired a well-earned reputation for cold-blooded effectiveness in suppressing opposition at home and in its satellites. The Soviets obviously admire strength, openly seek to acquire more, and are always ready to use what they have to intimidate or coerce. Such qualities, added to a singleness of national purpose, make the Soviet Union a dangerous political opponent of the West.

Soviet Military Power

Despite the effectiveness of their political tools, Soviet leaders have always given highest importance to military power. They believe that the maintenance of an adequate military force is the primary duty of a socialist state and expend ever-increasing efforts and resources to ensure a military establishment commensurate with an expansive foreign policy. Although virtually ignored for more than a decade, the Soviet arms buildup is now so well documented that only a few significant aspects require comment. The dominant fact is that the Soviets have achieved a numerical superiority over the United States in virtually all principal categories of major units, weapons, and equipment—the notable exceptions being missile warheads, long-range bombers, and aircraft carriers. They are decisively ahead in military personnel (4.4 million to 2.1 million), army divisions (168 to 16), tanks (42,000 to 10,000), surface combatant ships (226 to 182), and sea-control submarines (253 to 73). Although both sides presently have enough strategic weapons to wreak reciprocal disaster, the United States lags in strategic missiles (1,710 to 2,378) and by a one-to-three ratio in missile throw-weight (i.e., useful missile payload).

The present situation will worsen, however, if the current Soviet arms build-up increases. The Soviets continue to develop new and larger ICBMs which will increase their throw-weight superiority to a five-to-one ratio, an advantage that may be used to obtain a parallel increase in the number of deliverable warheads. They will also have two new submarine-launched ballistic missiles as well as many of the controversial Backfire bombers, which are believed capable of reaching targets in the United States. Meanwhile, the modernization of their conventional forces continues unabated, but at a price. In the aggregate their current and projected military programs constitute a heavy fiscal burden for the Soviet economy and require the allocation of at least 11 to 13 percent of the gross national product to military purposes.

These impressive statistics, however, are inadequate as a definitive measure of the true military strength of the Soviet Union. In the first place, they are the product of United States intelligence agencies, since the Soviet authorities never submit their own figures, even in the course of strategic arms limitation negotiations, but merely accept American estimates without comment. While our intelligence experts have displayed great skill and ingenuity in penetrating Soviet military secrecy, there are bound to be substantial inaccuracies in their computations. But even if accurate, numbers are inherently incapable of measuring the quality of the personnel and materiel tabulated—such matters as the combat and logistic readiness of troops or the accuracy, reliability, and overall effectiveness of weapons and equipment—and fundamental determinants of true military strength like enemy intentions, motives, morale, or determination.

As a final objection, figures convey a deceptive impression of reliability and foster the feeling that since "figures don't lie" their testimony must have substance. By overemphasizing the factor of numerical superiority, statistics encourage the conclusion—not always accurate—that two missiles or two battalions are better than one. In this way, the mystique of numbers can create a distorted impression of Soviet military strength that, if accepted without question, may lead to a serious misappraisal of relative military power. Department of Defense officials in recent years have given a certain authenticity to this mystique by adopting essential numerical equivalence with Soviet forces as the measure of adequacy of American strategic forces. It would be far preferable to dispel the illusion by exposing its fallacies rather than appear to equate the threat of apparent strength based largely upon numbers to real strength, which depends upon many other factors.

Despite the imperfections of numerical comparisons, it must be added that the available data give adequate evidence of a formidable Soviet military threat. Soviet strategic forces are capable of carrying out a destructive surprise attack on United States ICBM and bomber forces and seriously depleting American retaliatory power. Soviet land forces have sufficient superiority to place the defense of NATO against a major conventional attack in doubt. The growing naval forces of the Soviet Union, particularly its submarine fleet, are capable of challenging American control of the seas in many quarters and could thus endanger this country's trade with essential overseas markets, upon which we are increasingly dependent for oil and minerals.

This imposing posture of military strength offers the Soviets the possibility of intimidating opponents, attracting new clients, and extending Soviet influence into new areas overseas, often to the detriment of American interests. The Soviets have the option of exploiting this potential if they become convinced that the probable gains from agressive action would substantially exceed the possible costs and risks. The problem for us is to determine the probable conclusion the Soviets would draw from such an evaluation. Without privileged access to the collective thinking of the Politburo, the best one can do is to examine a few plausible contingencies in which the Soviets might be tempted to use military force against the United States and then try to appraise the profit-loss factors from the Soviet point of view.

A major American concern of long standing is the possibility of a surprise nuclear attack on targets in the United States. Since the late 1950s, a primary objective of our military policy has been to maintain enough strategic forces to deter such an attack, an objective most Americans felt satisfactorily achieved before realizing the magnitude of the new Soviet missile programs. The fear is now expressed that the Soviets are striving for a clearly perceived superiority in order to intimidate this country or, if intimidation fails, to enable the Soviet Union to fight, survive, and win an unlimited nuclear war. Advocates of this hypothesis argue that Moscow rejects our view that such a war is unthinkable and unwinnable and that this attitude accounts for the profusion of land, air, and naval weapons systems presently in Soviet hands, presumably to ensure a residual war-winning strength after absorbing enemy-inflicted losses.

Personally I find little reason to believe that the Soviets would ever initiate such an attack unless they had reliable assurance that the United States would never retaliate in response. For one thing, the Soviets can never be sure of the accuracy or reliability of their own missiles since none has ever been completely tested from launch to detonation at a distant target. They would encounter formidable problems in effecting the synchronized arrival of missiles and bombs on American strategic targets, which is essential for a successful surprise. Even if the attack destroyed most American ICBMs and bombers on the ground, the

Soviets would still suffer devastating losses from submarine-launched missiles and those bombers escaping the first strike.

It is sometimes said that, having survived and won World War II despite suffering over 20 million dead, the Soviets would not flinch from accepting similar losses in a general nuclear war. A contrary reaction would appear more likely on the part of a leadership that not only recalls the consequences of that disaster but must realize that the Soviet Union would suffer as many casualties in a few hours of strategic war as it did in four years of World War II. A further cause for restraint would be the likely reaction of local enemies to the prostration of the Soviet Union in the immediate aftermath of a nuclear exchange. The stricken superpower would be at the mercy of suppressed minorities, rebellious satellites, and Chinese armies bent on recovering the lost territories of the Central Kingdom. Communist oligarchs responsible for such a disaster might well fear retributive justice at the hands of their own people.

If Soviet leaders of the 1970s reach approximately similar conclusions about the outcome of a surprise nuclear attack on the United States, it is hard to believe that they would choose it as a deliberate action. It would seem far more plausible that, while continuing to expand strategic systems and maneuvering for advantage in arms negotiations, they would exploit to a maximum their awesome image of power to impress bystanders, frighten enemies, and exact tribute. Nevertheless, the first-strike option, however improbable it appears, cannot be ignored as a threat because of the dire consequences to the United States if it were carried out.

A second form of Soviet military threat warranting evaluation is a major nonnuclear attack on the NATO alliance. The Soviet Union and its Warsaw Pact allies not only have ample conventional means to overcome NATO defenses but also cogent reasons to consider the option because of important possible gains offered by success. The latter include the elimination of a hostile military coalition, the ejection of the American military presence from Europe, and the economic advantages anticipated from gaining control of European industries. Finally, such a victory would bring enormous prestige to the Soviet Union and the Communist cause.

Given the many visible weaknesses of NATO nations, the Soviets might consider the timing propitious for decisive action against the alliance. In most cases, unimpressive leaders govern by the grace of precariously thin majorities in countries plagued with economic stagnation and threatened by further recession. Italy and France have strong Communist parties asserting their right to participate in government. Germany and the Netherlands have been deeply shaken by terrorist atrocities, while Greece and Turkey show more interest in fighting each other than the Warsaw Pact countries.

Even without such internal problems, the alliance would be incapable of a prolonged defense against a major attack. There are many defects in its military posture arising from the exposed disposition of its forces beyond the Rhine, uneven standards of combat readiness in national contingents, and the absence of a logistic structure capable of supporting extended combat or of accommodating reinforcements from the United States after the outbreak of conflict. This logistic inadequacy has existed since the action of President Charles de Gaulle in 1966 requiring NATO forces to leave France and the United States to roll up the supply line connecting its force in Germany with French Atlantic ports. Since then, logistic problems have increased with the vulnerability of North Atlantic shipping to Soviet submarines and the exposure of European ports, airfields, and oil reserves to Soviet bomber and missile attack.

While such conditions might encourage the Soviets to take aggressive action at an early date, other considerations should give them pause. Even if they overcame the NATO forward defenses quickly, alliance leaders might reply with tactical nuclear weapons that would greatly increase Soviet losses while destroying much of the German industrial plant that the Soviets would hope to acquire intact. Also, there would be the ever-present danger of further escalation to general strategic war with the dire consequences foreseen above. Even in the favorable circumstance of a quick victory by conventional means, the Soviets would be left with a prolonged occupation of hostile, hungry, war-damaged countries that would require the indefinite presence in Western Europe of a large part of the Soviet army. Even if the Soviets succeeded in restoring comparative normalcy, they might justifiably doubt their ability to absorb European industry productively into the Communist system. On this point, their record in managing their own national economy would tend to discourage optimism.

On balance it would seem likely that the Soviets would limit immediate pressure on NATO to threatening postures, followed by tests of strength in peripheral areas like Berlin, selective support for Eurocommunist movements, and any other measures that might contribute to European economic or spiritual depression. They could continue present efforts to divide the alliance and particularly to entice Turkey to turn from the West, while keeping Aegean and Mediterranean waters roiled by riparian quarrels. After evaluating the effectiveness of such actions, they would then have ample time to determine the need for more drastic and dangerous courses. After all, a devout Communist ideologue convinced of the historical inevitability of the collapse of capitalism is not justified in taking undue risks.

Although the occurrence of either of the foregoing military threats has a low order of probability, both have such a serious damage potential if carried out that they cannot be ignored. The only legitimate question is the priority to give them in the use of resources allocated to national security.

The Nonmilitary Soviet Threat

Quite different issues arise when one considers the possibilities of primarily nonmilitary attack upon the United States economy. America's growing dependence on imports of foreign oil and important minerals leaves it increasingly vulnerable to any action limiting access to markets in four key regions—the

Middle East, sub-Saharan Africa, Latin America, and the southwest Pacific. Soviet naval leaders are well aware of this vulnerability and often use it to justify the expansion of their fleet.

In designing a program for undermining the American economy, the Soviets will be inclined to give top priority to efforts impeding or interrupting the flow of Middle East oil to the United States and other Western markets. In wartime, this could be readily accomplished by submarine attacks on tankers en route from the Persian Gulf, supplemented if necessary by air or missile attacks on oil fields and associated facilities in producer countries. In time of peace, the Soviets could accomplish their purpose at least in part by resort to political, covert, and terrorist measures. From the Soviet viewpoint, the most useful effect would be a renewal of the Arab-Israeli war, preferably accompanied by another OPEC oil embargo as a reprisal for American aid to Israel. Other events—such as the assassination or overthrow of moderate Arab leaders like Sadat and Hussein, sabotage actions against oil and pipeline facilities, or terrorist attacks upon governmental or religious centers—could contribute to this outcome.

Trouble of any sort arising anywhere in this region could serve the Soviet purpose—conflicts involving Iran, Iraq, or Saudi Arabia, irrational outbreaks by Colonel Qadhafi of Libya, or actions designed to frighten shipowners from the Persian Gulf; e.g., a tanker bombed in port or a few mines laid in the Strait of Hormuz. All such measures would have degrees of feasibility, depending on time, place, and circumstance. Many would appeal to the Soviet leaders because of the threat posed to the capitalist jugular vein—the oil stream to the West from the Persian Gulf.

Although it is the predominant present concern of the American economy, Middle East oil is not the only important market with access exposed to Soviet inspired threats. The United States obtains increasing amounts of oil and scarce minerals from Africa and Latin America, regions where the Soviets could employ many of the same destabilizing techniques as in the Middle East. Unfortunately, in combatting such measures in the third world, the United States will be handicapped by past blunders and insensitivity in its relations with many of the nations that it will need as trade partners. American support of Israel has aroused the enmity of many Arab countries. Despite recent changes in its policy, we continue to be charged by much of black Africa with partiality toward Rhodesia and South Africa. In Latin America, anti-Americanism is always rife, arising from our apparent indifference to regional problems, allegedly unfair trade practices, and past interventions in the internal affairs of small nations. Current measures under consideration in Washington for the control of illegal immigration from Mexico promise to become an additional contentious issue in hemispheric relations.

In all quarters, the United States suffers from its image as the archetype of selfish affluent capitalism, one that makes it a natural target for the resentment of the underprivileged world. As these disadvantaged nations feel more keenly the consequences of excessive population growth—mounting poverty, hunger, misery, and despair—the United States will be held increasingly responsible for their troubles, particularly as food shortages become more critical and hungry masses look to America for relief that can never be sufficient. Such conditions offer the Soviets the opportunity to support loudly the demand of the have-nots for a new international economic order based upon a more equitable distribution of wealth between the rich and the poor. Thus, in a sense, world environmental conditions collaborate in supporting the Soviet objective of overturning the present world order to make way for the predestined Communist succession.

It is hardly necessary to enumerate the potential advantages to the Soviets from these nonmilitary measures aimed at interrupting trade and damaging United States relations with producer countries. Their gains could include the total or partial exclusion of the United States from important markets, a consequent depression in American economic growth and productivity, and mounting difficulties with inflation and unemployment that other industrial countries would share. Such conditions would seriously reduce the vast influence the United States has exercised in the past as the result of its economic preeminence.

In achieving such gains, the Soviets would run few risks at little cost. Since these measures could be carried out without overt Soviet involvement, they would not have to fear the consequences of armed conflict with the possibility of nuclear escalation. American reprisals in kind would be unlikely since the Soviets have limited dependence on overseas trade. Most of these activities would entail few additional costs since they are already in progress as a routine aspect of Soviet trouble-making. Their success would be facilitated by powerful environmental forces which make for turbulence and disorder in the third world. Of these forces, population growth with its dismal consequences would be the most valuable ally in creating conditions preparing the way to world revolution. Finally, these nonmilitary threats satisfy all the criteria of reality—feasibility, probability, and damage-potential—and thus warrant particularly strong preventive measures on the part of the United States.

In conclusion, one should recall the basic argument on which the case for the reality of the Soviet threat rests. The Soviet leaders have at their disposal multiform power capable of inflicting damage on the United States ranging from moderate to fatal. They have ample reason to use this power arising from the natural rivalry between the two superpowers which often pursue conflicting policies, from the doctrinal animosity resulting from Soviet commitment to the Marxist-Leninist dogma of inevitable class conflict leading to the downfall of capitalism, and from nationalist ambitions inherited from czarist times for universal acceptance of the Soviet Union as a great power. An added incentive is the possibility of important gains resulting from some of the courses of action discussed, particularly those directed at the vulnerable economic underbelly of the United States and its industrial partners. A weakness in the case presented in this essay may be the temerity displayed in deciding the Soviet interest in various critical situations and a readiness to assume a necessary coincidence between Soviet and American conclusions on such matters. The possibility of error in such a procedure is indeed present, but the margin of effectual Soviet power and the strength of the incentive to use it against the United States are sufficient to establish the reality of the aggregate threat and thus to justify on the part of the United States the expenditure of whatever resources are necessary to forestall or defeat it.

Index